The Voice of Love

Hope Breaking Out of Shattered Places

Sandy Phillipps

Copyright

ISBN: 978-1-7773868-2-5 Paperback
ISBN: 978- 1-7773868-0-1 Electronic
ISBN: 978-1-7773868-3-2 Audio

Photography credits

Nightshift photo courtesy of Ingrid Roeske Good (Part Two photos)

Sandy Phillipps photo courtesy of Jocelyn Isaak Photography

Bible Translations

Endorsements

What an amazing story by a gifted writer! It kept me captivated from cover to cover. You have come through so much in your life. Your life is a testimony of perseverance, tenacity, courage, honesty, and transparency. Your scars are truly your testimony.

Psalm 30:5, "Weeping may endure for a night, but joy cometh in the morning," reminds me of your life. May your joy spill out to the hearts that read your amazing story of trials and triumph.

God's not finished with you my dear friend. May He continue to use and guide you to minister and touch the lives of those He places in your path.

MaryAnne Conner "Mac" (Rev, RPC)
Author of *The Shift*
Founder of Nightshift Street Ministries, Surrey B.C.

I have known Sandy for over thirty years. She is my dear friend and soul sister. I have seen her when she is full of joy and have also been with her during times of dark despair. I have always been amazed at how she is able to rise above her angst with love, patience, caring and without malice. I have watched her journey to seek wholeness, always turning to the Lord for guidance. She is truly a unique individual! While I knew much of her story, to see it in print is both powerful and compelling. This is an incredible journey and a beacon of hope for any reader. I am so proud that she has chosen to share her life story in this book.

Catheryne (Cathie) Meehan, MD

Extraordinary memoir by a fresh author, an ordinary person with an extraordinary life story. Sandy shares her story with complete transparency and transformative insight—something she describes as "what happens when you let food colouring drop into a glass of water." Her word—images convey encouraging truths hidden in the complexities of life. Beyond the wisdom, her grace and compassion are so evident that by the end of the book you will feel you have a new friend.

Kathy Doyle, LL.B

Famed China pioneer missionary Hudson Taylor called his two-volume autobiography The Growth of a Soul, and The Growth of a Work of God—titles which aptly describe the life-trajectory Sandy Phillipps outlines with transparent yet appropriate details in her own memoir, entitled The Voice of Love. In a beautiful tribute to Jesus' ability to transform anyone with the mindset of a helpless victim to become an active agent of change, Sandy describes her experience of attaining a renewed mind and its practical overflow into her life: "I truly found that the well of joy inside me was much deeper than the depth of suffering I had endured." (ch. 11)

In her honest, vulnerable account, Sandy traces how the inviting voice of Love was present all along, even during some of the rougher times, and how the volume of that voice increased as she chose to pay closer attention to it, and drowned out those negative voices, whether of the inner critic or the enemy of our faith.

Although parts of her story might be difficult for some to digest, her focus remains firmly fixed on the goodness, kindness, and faithfulness of God as a loving Father towards her. This redemption continues to flow through her in bringing dignity and value to other people, especially those on the margins.

I recommend this engaging story of a lost child who felt unwanted and unloved; who heard a gentle, caring voice, the Voice of Love, which then changed everything.

Paul Hughes, PhD
Senior Leader,
The River Fellowship
Langley, BC
(theriverfellowship.com)

This book is dedicated to YOU, my reader.

My hope is that you, too,
will have that graffiti on your heart washed away.

That the knife that has carved your soul,
falls to the ground.

That you pick up God's pen,
His quill, which writes your purpose,
your destiny, and the longings of your heart.

May something in this book
challenge your courage and tenacity
to burst through to
freedom and joy.

I am honoured you have chosen
to open this story of my journey with
the Voice of Love.

JESUS talking …

"Are you tired? Worn out? Burned out on religion? Come to me. Get away with me and you'll recover your life. I'll show you how to take a real rest. Walk with me and work with me—watch how I do it. Learn the unforced rhythms of grace. I won't lay anything heavy or ill-fitting on you. Keep company with me and you'll learn to live freely and lightly." (Matthew 11:28-30 MSG)

Table of Contents

Acknowledgments

First, thank you God. This whole project has felt so blessed, even anointed. I have watched in amazement as person after person was sent in my direction to assist in every way.

Dan. What a solid rock and sounding board you have been as I've spent months pouring over my journals of pain and heartache. You are my beloved husband, best friend, and confidant. You have been there every step of the way as we journeyed together to write this book. Looking through those hard years to revisit the deep heartache. This has not been easy, but you, my beloved Dan, have made it so much more bearable and even delightful as we have reminisced the good times, too.

Thank you to my dear children, David & Jocelyn, Andrew & Shaniah, and Kimber, who have patiently listened as I have needed to talk non-stop about this book every time we have met.

Judy Sluys, where would this book be without you?! You have been a gift that fell out of heaven. I dumped my whole manuscript in your lap and sat in amazement as you laboured long and hard. You became a true surrogate mother to this endeavour, bringing order, clarity, and endless hours of hard work in editing. So much of this book holds parts of you, too.

My editor, Lindsay Morton, what a gift you have been as your patience and skill brought this work to a whole new level of excellence.

Dr. Paul Hughes what a delight and honour to have you do the final edit. Thank you.

To the artistic ones, who drew the designs: Thank you, Kimber, and thank you, Sheznay!

My former prayer team who have become lifelong friends. My cheering squad. Thank you! Karen C, Denise N, Julie B, Lois W,

Erika K, Elaine M, Verona J, Janet L, Carla S, Yvonne B, Carolyn C.

A huge shoutout to all those who encouraged me to take that leap that felt utterly impossible. Shaniah, you gave me the courage to take that plunge. Those of you who have supported me and given me your feedback have blessed me in immense ways. This book has felt like a community effort as so many have rallied to cheer me on. I am so grateful for the tremendous support and encouragement by too many people to name. I pray you know who you are.

Serenity at Dometree Publishing, you have become my friend as you have guided me through a process that I knew nothing about. Your patience and skills are amazing. Thank you!

Note to the Reader

This book is about the redemptive power of God. It begins with an overview of what appeared to be a carefree happy childhood before a downward spin into troubling and tumultuous teen years. It was not the intent of the author to go into great depths of those years, but rather to set the stage of how her life unfolded from her perspective at the time. She was oblivious to the unspeakable purpose of the encroaching evil, and found herself dragged into a dark abyss.

But God.

Protecting her from further evil, God's staying power held back the tsunami that threatened to destroy her, allowing her to experience healing in stages. While the journey included many years of pain and confusion, each step was a new opportunity to embrace courage, freedom and joy. And this is the heart of the book—to show how God's love working through His Word and His people brought her to peace and victory.

Foreward

You are invited to enter into the adventure of healing and hope alongside an incredible woman. You will find her to be endearing as you walk through her look at the life she lived. You will cry with her as she faces the losses and the scars that marred her life. You will be aghast with her as she re-lives abuse, including ritualistic abuse and comes out not only alive, but more alive in Christ than ever before. This is a woman who faces life with a bravery and courage that is rare. She is a precious jewel who shines. The more she searches out God and healing from His Holy throne and His River of Life that flows from God's throne; the more of Jesus that she invites in; the more she purposefully walks into surgery with the Holy Spirit, the stronger she becomes.

This woman is a warrior princess whom I am privileged to know. Enter into these pages of a life well lived and fought for through the power of Christ. Meet Sandra, as I have met her, as she tells stories of her childhood in Kenya, her strange downfall onto the streets of Vancouver while being a teenager, her foray into drugs and alcohol. Sandra went through severe trauma in her early years. The memories were so shattering and painful, so cruel in the making that they were buried deep within her—held by dissociated parts that were formed to hold the trauma. The birth and subsequent early passing of their precious daughter Amber rushed the memories to the surface in a tsunami of grief. Bit by bit the memories of the years of satanic ritual abuse where she suffered from emotional manipulation and satanic programming along with severe sexual abuse in Kenya as part of the horrific rituals surfaced and threatened to overwhelm her.

The beauty of Sandra's story is Christ within. He claimed her as His own as we went through one imprint after another of bits of memories. God put it together enough for His healing hand to shine through and His love and wisdom to pour into me for Sandra's healing. From that endurance training of healing emerged Sandy ... the beautiful, healed woman and daughter of God that always was there beneath the pain. Shed was the cocoon of old habits, old thoughts and old ways. Now she flies like a butterfly in freedom with Christ with wings of beauty that are powered by our miraculous healing Heavenly Father.

You will now meet Sandy, the woman who has overcome by the precious Blood of the Lamb of God! Sandy, the woman who walked into my office for the sake of her kids to heal even more. Sandy, the woman who loves the Lord and hears from Him daily as she enters into prayer and worship. Sandy, the lover of Christ, overcomer, and now made new through her courage to walk through healing with Christ as her guide.

You will be glad you met her. I know I am. Be brave and enter in. Be brave and take courage as you also search out your healing in Christ.

May blessings of our Lord and Savior Jesus Christ fall on all who read these words. May the words within bring you closer to the One who made you and loves you extravagantly! May the Lord lead you ever closer to Him as you enter the pages of this book—this life. Welcome to the gift and the privilege of sharing in Sandy's life.

Laurel Hildebrandt MTSC, CCC
Counsellor, Author, Speaker
Wellspring Christian Counselling

Prologue

As our baby grew in my womb, so did the pressure and pain in my chest. It was so debilitating that I really thought it could be the end. Then the pain would shift to crazy thoughts and I would be absolutely tormented in my mind. I couldn't decide which was worse, the physical pressure and pain or the tormenting thoughts. I asked my doctor for a certain medication that had helped me in my teen years. I tried everything I could think of to find some relief. Day and night the pain and torment would build and build until I thought I would either explode or die.

I became aware that there was something else wrong with me, something other than the death of my child. This was more than just grief.

PART ONE

BEGINNINGS

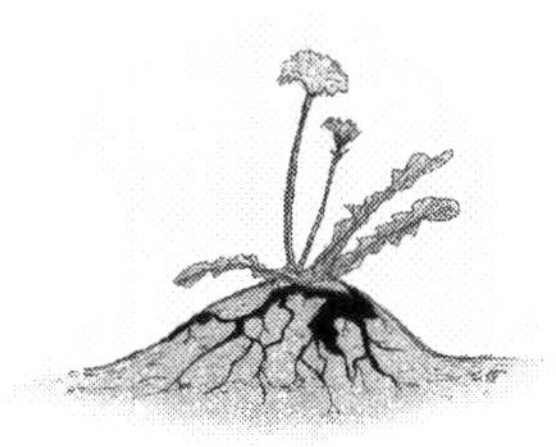

Chapter One

The Beginning

Once upon a time there was a little girl named Sandra, born into a missionary family in Kenya. That is how I would like to start my story, like a fairy tale. Even though much of my life has felt as unreal as a fairy tale gone bad, it's a true story, and this is how it began.

I was born in Kenya; the fourth child, the second daughter, in what would be a family of five children. My parents boarded a ship after marrying hurriedly during World War II so they could start their life calling—to be missionaries to Kenya. They didn't realize as they boarded the ship what a danger it was to be at sea during wartime. This was the last passenger ship for a long time and in fact, passengers had only been let on by mistake. The frightening journey took several months. My mother clung onto scripture to help combat her fears when their boat was targeted by submarines and bombers.

My parents' missionary pattern was to work in Kenya for five years and then go home to Canada for a one-year furlough. While back in Canada, they would travel across the country, stopping at various churches to report on their work in Africa. My parents continued this all their married life. Well past retirement, they would still go back to fill in for other missionaries wanting a short leave or a furlough of their own. They loved Africa dearly.

People tend to say to me, "Oh! What was it like growing up in Africa?" as if it were a strange place to be raised. To me, Africa was normal, and Canada was strange.

My earliest memories of our house had a guesthouse and a dwelling for the houseboy (not actually a boy but a grown man; typically an African servant who would perform general duties in the home and yard). I have few specific memories of my early childhood, except for fleeting pictures of sharing a bed with my sister and hiding behind the door to suck my thumb. My parents offered me great bribes to stop the habit, figuring I was too old for it. The only other memory I have under five years of age is walking with Middle Brother when a mean dog bit him. The dog then tried to bite me, but his teeth went only as deep as my thick plaid skirt and did not really hurt me.

When I was five years old we moved to another house, with an acre of land. Again, there was a dwelling for a houseboy. There were many disadvantaged people around us, so giving a man the opportunity to work for us was mutually beneficial. This houseboy would live on our property and go home to his village occasionally to see his wife and his family.

Younger Sister joined our family soon after the move. I was an enormously proud sister when I was given the privilege of holding her in the car on the way home from the hospital.

I adored Middle Brother and followed him around everywhere. We loved to build forts and wander the neighbourhood. We were outside much of the time as the weather was favourable for outdoor play with temperatures that averaged 70°F. There were only two seasons—the rainy season and the dry season. When it rained, it poured! Huge forceful drops would hit the ground and bounce back up. I had a raincoat for such days, but only needed a sweater the rest of the year. There was no heat in our home as it was never cold enough to need added heat.

Oldest Brother, ten years older than me, always felt more like an uncle than a brother. He left home at the age of 15. In actuality, he ran away. I never heard what happened between him and my parents; in our home we didn't talk about such things—anything serious or personal or painful. All I knew was that he had become "a bad boy." One day he suddenly showed up in our yard and asked me to go into my Dad's closet and bring him Dad's suit. He offered me five shillings. I was happy to help him and did so eagerly. I never heard my parents say anything about the missing suit.

I loved to give, and Valentine's Day was always special to me. I would place a small gift of my artwork on each plate at our family dinner table. One year I had enough allowance money to buy donuts to share with everyone!

Our family always went to the coastal city of Mombasa in December for our holidays. Since it was a dangerous and long ride, we needed to leave early in the morning to ensure that we would reach our destination before nightfall. We would not want to have to change a flat tire in the dark! It was there in the Indian Ocean that I learned to swim. With all that African sunshine and me having red hair and fair skin, I remember having sunstroke at least twice. Every year it would be fun to peel off my skin as it tried to heal from the sunburn. The coral reef, the shells, the sounds and feel of Africa; the lizards climbing the walls in our rented house; the many palm trees and monkeys climbing them were all part of our family's typical vacation. I loved the coconuts, straight from the trees! We would drink the milk fresh, right out of the shell. Our family ate chocolate bars only at this holiday time at the coast. Each bar would be cut and shared. And this was also the only time of the year we would have pop. A large bomb of Coca-Cola (a two-liter bottle) was such a delight to share!

Christmas was the highlight of our year. What great excitement when a parcel arrived from Canada! Churches would send us clothes and gifts for Christmas. One year my family gave me a bicycle. Thrilled, I took off riding down the hill with Big Sister. However, I was not familiar with this strange bike that had brakes on the handlebars. To brake on my earlier bike, I'd pedal backwards. My Sister, thinking I was going too fast, called to me to slow down. As I braked, I took a tumble head over heels, and fell on the road, hitting my head on the sidewalk. A kind passerby drove me home. When I later awoke in the hospital, such a white and sterile place, I thought for a moment that I was in heaven. Back in those days the nurses' clothing was all starched, and so white!

Schooling in Africa

Because we lived in the city, I was able to attend a school close by. In later years, Younger Sister was sent away to boarding school. The school year started in January and ended in December, which gave us a long break at Christmas. There was no kindergarten, so I started Standard 1 (Grade 1) at age five. I was always a very compliant, quiet child and loved my teachers. I was also a sensitive child and would be deeply hurt if I perceived ridicule or rejection. My sensitive spirit gave me great compassion for a girl in my class who had thalidomide syndrome. She only had short "flippers" for arms, and I competed with other classmates to help her.

It was not until high school that I had fellow students that were African or East Indian. The education system in Kenya was British, and all the white people in my school, other than us, were British. In the lower grades, I remember only white kids being in my school. I had a classmate invite me to her house one day. It was one of the few times I remember going to a friend's house. She convinced me she had a crocodile living in the pond behind her house. We were good friends all the way through school.

One day, early on in Standard 1, I asked if I could go to the bathroom. The teacher told me, "No, you have to wait," but I could not wait, and to my horror watched a puddle form on the floor at my feet. The teacher gave me fresh underwear and told me to have my mother wash it and return it to school. I felt so humiliated telling my mom what had happened. Another time I took my lunch bag into the bathroom with me at recess. A teacher soundly scolded me for taking food into such an unclean place. Such scolding had a deep impact on me. I worked hard to be an easy, pleasant, co-operative child.

I liked many things about school, such as roller-skating during my lunch hour. My favourite class was Latin, taught by the headmaster. In my last year I also took Swahili. It wasn't necessary for me to learn Swahili since church services were in English and our houseboys spoke English. Learning a foreign language came easily for me, unlike many of my other classes.

Every year, at the beginning of each grade, I would determine in my heart to try really hard to do better. But no matter how hard I tried; I was still only an average student. Sometimes, if a student misbehaved, they were sent to the headmaster's office to get the strap. The only time I was reprimanded, I was sent outside to sit under a tree because I had been talking in class. I was immensely embarrassed when the headmaster walked by and noticed me.

One day, in Standard 5, the kids were all talking about a prostitute and they wondered what it was. I plucked up my courage and offered to go ask the teacher what that word meant. I still can see the embarrassment on her face as she fumbled with how to answer me. She crossly sent me back to my seat. All I understood was that I must have said a bad word.

The bus rides and riding my bicycle to school were not always pleasant. One day I witnessed a man fall off his bike. To my horror I saw his face so severely injured, it looked like there was no skin left on it! Feeling alone and so frightened, I continued on my way to school.

My parents strongly believed all movies, as well as dancing, were bad and sinful. They believed that World War III was about to break out and that JESUS could come back at any time. Therefore, we needed to always be aware of what we were doing in case He came at that specific moment. In Standard 7, all the other students were listening to music from *The Sound of Music*. I was so confused both in my body and my heart when I would hear it. They were dancing and singing along, simply enjoying the songs and the music. My body wanted to move in response, but I had been told it was wrong. I couldn't understand why my body wanted to dance with joy if this was wicked. We were, however, the first missionaries to get a TV. It was a small box, black and white, and we loved to watch it. Lassie was our favourite but, as I was enrolled in Brownies, I had to often miss this beloved show.

My overarching memory of my school all the way up to Standard 7 was that of kids cooperating and being respectful. I never heard anyone swear or be bullied. There certainly were some kids who were more popular than others, and not everyone was friends with everybody, but it felt like a good environment. Nobody was picked on.

Standard 7 itself was a stressful year. In order to graduate and be allowed to enter high school, each student had to pass an exam covering all seven years of schooling. My father helped me prepare, and the dreaded day arrived when my entire class went to write the exam. I passed, and was greatly relieved when that was over, and I could enter Form 1 (the first year of high school).

Animal Friends

My parents allowed us to have many animals, on one condition: We had to look after them ourselves. We bought a Bush Baby; a small, saucer-eyed primate, and he lived with us in our house. A Golden Crested Crane, a 3-foot-tall bird, came home with us after a trip to a village. Our dog was my best friend, and I was ecstatic whenever she had puppies. I dressed them in doll clothes and pushed them in a pram. We never had a problem selling the puppies. Since we didn't have many toys, and friends didn't come over, my pets were my world. Trips to the escarpment usually resulted in our parents allowing us to bring home a rabbit or guinea pig, purchased from an African selling them on the side of the road. We would keep them in a pen we built in our yard, but sometimes wandering dogs would kill them in the night. This broke my heart every time.

The game reserves were wonderful places to visit. We were thrilled when elephants and giraffes crossed the road in front of us. The crocodiles were amazing, as were the hippos. What joy! I developed a very keen eye for spotting animals. Sometimes a guide would get in our car and take us to where they knew the elephants were. They did the same for the giraffes and multitudes of antelope as well. One time a guide took us to where lions had made a fresh kill. To our surprise, he asked my father if he wanted a leg from the zebra that the lions had killed! The guide explained that because the lions were full, sleepy, and lazy, he could safely take a leg. My father took that zebra leg home and made a lamp out of it.

We had wonderful animals around our home, too. An anteater lived down the hill from our house. We had cobra babies living under the floorboards of our bedroom, and I loved to put them in a wooden matchbox and scare people with them. It never occurred to me to wonder where the mama snake was! I dearly loved the many hedgehogs that ran free in our yard. One year a smart mother hedgehog realized she could cry at my bedroom window at night and I would fetch milk and bread to feed her and her babies. I learned to pet their soft underbelly until they relaxed their prickles enough for me to stroke them. Frogs lived in one short palm tree in our yard. I considered them my personal pets even though they never came in the house.

Animals were not only my friends but also my toys. I had many chameleons that I would parade around on my shoulder or arm. I had so much fun intimidating visitors from America who came to see "wild Africa." They expected Africa to be wild and scary, and I wanted to affirm their belief. Because the chameleon would change its colour to match the colour of my clothes, visitors didn't always notice it a first. When they finally did see it, I secretly enjoyed watching their reaction. I had to be careful, though, when I returned the chameleon to a tree. If I put it on a branch with another chameleon that had a different number of horns on its head, the two chameleons would start fighting.

I spent countless hours in the dirt on top of our garage roof playing with my friends—the grubs! I played and played with them and would be delighted when they would have babies. Sometimes Middle Brother and I would pour water down a tarantula's hole in our yard, forcing it to run out the other hole so we could see it. I interacted with all these creatures as if they were my friends, because they were!

On Furlough

Our family went back to Canada on furlough during my Grade 3 year. The voyage by ship took about three months, and my father, a former teacher, spent a significant amount of time being my temporary teacher. As we crossed the equator, the crew on this Norwegian ship entertained the passengers with various celebrations. One such celebration was a ritual or "rite of passage" where they invited passengers to take part in the ceremony. After a Norwegian custom of eating raw fish (yuck!), I was dedicated to a god as part of the ceremony. My parents believed this was done "all in fun" and kept a picture of the event, although I look back on it with great confusion.

While in Canada, we stayed on my uncle and aunt's farm in Ontario. They lived in a great farmhouse with a fancy parlour that we hardly ever entered. I learned that my dad and sisters had been born in that house. My uncle made me feel important, showing great interest in whatever I had to say. My aunt was so special to me, too. I don't remember why she was the one to give me my allowance, but on allowance day she would pull the money out of her storage place, her bra! The thrill of getting this token amount of money matched the delight of raiding her pantry containing tin after tin of delicious cookies.

While on furlough, my father travelled across Canada to speak in different churches, often leaving the rest of us behind on the farm to attend school. Sometimes we would travel with him, attending the services where he spoke about the work in Africa. During those church services our family was expected to sit on the platform, and I learned to "sit like a lady" and present well. I understood what it was like to be a pastor's kid that was in view and on parade. I preferred staying home while he traveled, enjoying the freedom of the farm and going to school.

That year of Grade 3 was the best year of my childhood. Middle Brother and I would walk to the school—one room for all seven grades. All our desks were lined up in rows, each grade in its own row, with one teacher for all. I was so proud when I mastered the times-tables and worked hard on memorizing "arithmetic" as it was called. I was also immensely proud of my brother. Having a popular, well-liked brother in Grade 7 made me feel important! One day the teacher took all the students into the woods. The vegetation, trees, flowers, and birds of Ontario were so foreign to me!

I loved the cows and the farm life. I worked in the field gathering hay and scooping the cow dung. I loved every minute of every chore and I loved every animal. Learning to milk cows and listening to country music was my new delight! Once, Middle Brother and I built the most amazing tree house, and then we slept in it all night. In winter we built an igloo. I loved the snow and did not feel the cold. I considered my brother to be my best friend.

I don't remember which year it was that tragedy struck, and my uncle and aunt's lives were changed forever. We were back in Kenya at the time. My aunt had placed a paint can on top of the wood stove to warm it up a little so she could paint. The stove was the only source of heat for the house, and early every morning my uncle would light it. Somehow, as my aunt reached for the paint, the top of the can opened and paint spilled over her, igniting her clothing on fire. She ran outside screaming in pain as the flames burned her body. My uncle ran to her and rolled her on the ground to extinguish the flames. Thankfully she recovered, but her vocal cords were permanently damaged and she lost her voice. When I saw them again it took me a long time to be able to decipher her mumbles and garbled speech, but amazingly, my uncle could understand her.

There was even more to this terrible time in my uncle and aunt's lives. Her and my dad's mother died of cancer. Then word came to us that their sister had died. My parents never spoke to us about any of it, but years later, talk amongst us kids helped me realize it was probably a suicide. She was found on a train track under mysterious circumstances. As time went by, there were rumours regarding her husband's involvement, but as he was the Chief of Police, the family was unable to get any answers. She apparently could not see without her glasses, and yet, when they found her body, her glasses were still safely at home. The only other thing I knew about her is that she suffered terribly from migraine headaches, and would typically get one on Sunday mornings so she couldn't go to church. Suicide was not a word ever mentioned.

Furthering the heartache, my uncle and aunt's daughter, their only child, was diagnosed with multiple sclerosis the year she graduated from teachers' college. She never left home and never worked. But love her I did! In my childish mind I always imagined that Oldest Brother would marry her so she could be happy. I loved them all dearly!

Back in Africa

When we returned to Kenya, we lived in a different house. Middle brother had a bedroom to himself while we three girls shared a room. Again, there was a dwelling on our property for the houseboy. My father was now pastoring the English-speaking church in our city, so our house was the next-door parsonage. He would sometimes go to the African church and I would visit with him. I would marvel at the dirt floor of the church and the babies with no pants that would be placed on the floor to pee.

Middle Brother and I spent endless hours building forts and wandering the neighbourhood, cutting through backyards of homes with large properties. We spent a lot of energy trying to capture a monkey that swung through the trees. During all my childhood I felt free to wander.

Friends had been looking after our dog while we were in Canada that year, and we happily took her back on our return. We were also delighted when a nearby hotel let us swim in their pool, but every time we went swimming, I had to lock up my dog. She must have thought I was drowning, because every time I went in the pool she wanted to jump in, too, as if to rescue me! We collected more puppies, guinea pigs, budgies, and a cat. My father's rule, that we could have any animal we wanted on the condition we cared for them properly, was enforced one night when our rabbit was served for dinner! I was so grateful when my mother allowed me to leave the table and go to my room.

Middle Brother liked to shoot birds and we cooked and ate some pigeons that he shot. He kept some of the carcasses in his room and used formaldehyde to preserve them. His hunting days ended abruptly after he shot a bat and found a wee baby tucked under her wing. Even though he tried to save the bat pup, he was unsuccessful, and I don't think he shot a gun again after that. I was immensely proud of his tender heart and loved him for it.

My father had a study behind the house. My memories of him are of someone very austere. When he preached, I sat so still and quiet, sometimes writing in the hymn books to pass the time. If I needed correction, my father only needed to glance at me, and I'd sit up straighter. I was afraid to displease him. To me, my father acted the same at home as when he was in the pulpit. He never softened or changed roles to be a dad at home. Comfortable in his role as teacher, he taught me how to play piano. He said I could make a mistake but if I made the same mistake twice, I would receive a smack across my knuckles with a ruler.

I know it happened, but I don't remember ever being spanked or punished by my parents. I do, however, remember hearing that my father broke our huge ruler over Oldest Brother's back before he ran away from home. My mother would use the spatula to spank, usually telling us to hold out an open hand. One day, one of us kids wrote on the spatula the verse from Ephesians 6:4 (NKJV), "Do not provoke your children to wrath." We feared greatly the day our parents would find it. I don't know why I can't recall getting spanked myself.

I also don't remember much about my mother those years, except that I would play with her fingers during church services when she wasn't playing the piano. Sometimes Big Sister filled the role of pianist. When I was around 12, my mother needed surgery that required her to be in the hospital for a few days. We were left without her for the very first time. I felt so incredibly grown up when my father allowed me to walk all the way to the hospital by myself to visit with her. I was even allowed to miss church!

We had church services each Sunday morning and evening as well as a mid-week evening. My weekly bath time was on Saturday evening and included my mother curling my hair with rollers. We had to look our best for Sunday services! After morning church, we always had a nap. I loved avoiding mine by rubbing my mother's back while she slept. After nap time, we would have tea and go back for evening service. I don't remember an exact moment of trusting JESUS. I just accepted everything I was taught about God, the same way I learned to read, write, and talk: with a child-like faith. (Since JESUS has done such incredible healing in my life, I always capitalize His whole name).

One Sunday afternoon I asked for more cookies and was told "no". I was so indignant that my request was refused, I considered it reason enough to run away from home. Looking back, I can hardly believe I did that—it seemed so contrary to my nature. Yet not only did I run away–I took my five-year-old sister with me. We ran away from home, in Africa! However, as it got dark, which I had not anticipated, we tried to sneak home. The evening service was already underway in the church, so we began to quietly go through the backyard into the garage, where we kept my dog and her puppies. My plan was to stay there all night and sleep with them. However, the geese proved themselves to be better guards than any watch dog, and announced our arrival by honking loudly. My mother heard them from the church and came home as soon as she was done playing the piano. She came out into the dark garage, feeling her way around the walls until she found us both. She told us to go in the house, go to bed and await our father's return. That was one of the scariest moments of my life—waiting to find out what my punishment would be! My parents must have been just so relieved to have us home safely, because nothing more came of it other than a brief conversation with my father.

My dog Lassie never came in the house, she always stayed outside. One terrible night we heard the screech of brakes and a crash. My family jumped out of bed and ran to see what had happened on our busy street. As we ran outside, someone carried my dog home and laid her on our front porch. Lassie was bleeding from her rectum and her mouth and her condition seemed hopeless. After awhile my mother sent us all back to bed. When no one was looking I grabbed my blanket, quietly slipped back outside, and slept the rest of the night with my beloved dog. She lived, and I took some of the credit for staying with her and being there for her, even when it meant disobeying my mother.

During the mid-week Bible study time, we children stayed at home since our house was right next door. This was a prime opportunity for us siblings to fight. It was horrible, but when my parents came home, we wouldn't say a word about it. I was very mean to Little Sister. Being older than her, I knew how to hurt her without making a mark. She would respond by digging her fingernails into my skin. I would then have some evidence to show to my mother, so my sister would get into trouble, not me. I think each of us took our frustrations out on a younger child. The secretive domination was a hurtful thing amongst us kids. On one of those nights, when my parents came home, Middle Brother was in such distress that the doctor was called. The doctor found nothing wrong physically, but told my mother that my brother was emotionally stressed about something.

One year my grandparents came for a visit. What a thrilling time for me as I loved showing them around. It made me feel so proud when one day they stood up for me and defended me in front of my siblings. A strange and wonderful feeling came over me as I realized that I, too, could stand up for myself.

I didn't have much of a relationship with Big Sister who was five years older than me. The time came for her to graduate from high school and she chose to attend university in Canada. She travelled there alone—all by herself! I could hardly imagine the courage that it would take to get on a plane all by yourself and be gone from everyone you knew! The days after she left were strange for me. My mother mourned Big Sister's leaving and would say, "We were like two peas in a pod." My mother explained that because she had lost a baby boy at birth, and the doctor told her she could never have another child, she felt much closer to my older sister as she was afraid she would have no more children. I started to wonder what that meant to me.

Life began to change for me, too. I was growing up, approaching adolescence. I started high school: my school uniform included wearing a necktie and a hat called a boater. I made new friends, and my best friend was from India. Because of this bi-racial friendship, I no longer fit in well with the mostly British, white students. Segregation was a whole new experience for me. I had somehow grown up in an atmosphere where I simply had not perceived prejudice. And now, my accepting attitude of some classmates resulted in me being alienated from others.

I rode a double decker bus to high school. One day an African man befriended me, and from then on, we frequently rode together. I told my parents of this friendship, and when I invited him to church, he came! Soon after that, when I saw him on the bus again, it seemed he had been drinking. He tried to convince me to go off to live in his village with him. After that I was afraid of him, but I never saw him again.

At the same time, my parents were preparing to leave for the next furlough. Everyday there was more and more talk of us returning to Canada. One day, after school, I found to my dismay that Lassie was missing. When I asked my mother where Lassie was, she angrily told me I should have known we would have to "put her down" before we left for Canada. "She was too old for us to re-home while we were away," my mother scowled. I was absolutely devastated. I felt so disrespected. I wanted to have been able to say goodbye to her, to have been told what they were planning so that I could prepare myself, but there was no going back. This was the first big divide that started between my parents and me. I felt damaged as a result of Lassie being ripped away from me, and not being given the chance to deal with the loss. Crazy how even today as I write these words, I still feel that pain in my heart.

My father did not particularly like pets, yet shortly before we left on furlough, he decided to buy two Pekingese dogs. He thought he could make some good money on selling the puppies, so we brought the dogs with us to Vancouver. I always made sure my heart never got attached to those dogs.

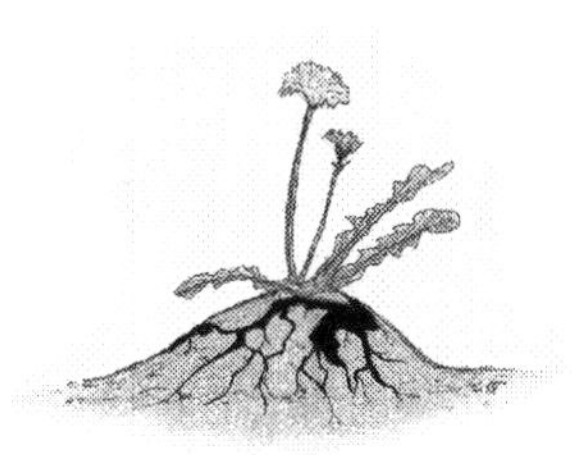

Chapter Two

The Beginning of the End

Every time my family went back to Canada, we would visit various places along the way. This trip included stopping in Israel. Little Sister and I were treated to a ride on a tall camel. We also visited pyramids in Egypt before travelling to London, England.

On an earlier furlough we had lived with my grandparents in their amazing log house on Vancouver Island. This time, however, my family chose Vancouver itself, maybe because Big Sister was attending University of British Columbia (UBC) there and Oldest Brother, now married, lived there, too. We were about to meet his wife! Our arrival, and being reunited with family, was an extremely exciting time for us. There was a lot of fear and laughter as my father tried to navigate the car. The British system in Kenya meant driving on the opposite side of the road and, in his excitement, he would forget which was the correct side.

My parents bought a house in Vancouver and made the downstairs suitable to rent out to UBC students. Oldest Brother and his wife were living nearby. Big Sister moved back home and worked part time in a clothing shop. She had become so independent and knew so much! She appeared thrilled to be back with Little Sister, and established herself once again in our family. Middle Brother and I became involved in our church. I loved youth group; I had never experienced anything like that before. My parents instructed me to make friends at church, not at school.

School was daunting. My high school was the largest building I had ever been in. It was very frightening learning how to navigate the halls and find where I should be. But that wasn't the biggest challenge. Since the school year in Africa was January to December, every time we came back to Canada the school had to figure out which grade to put me in. I had started Form 1 in Kenya, or Grade 8. The school in Vancouver chose to place me in Grade 9, even though I had spent only a brief time in Grade 8. That meant I was just 13 years old entering Grade 9 in a system I knew nothing about. The other students were already familiar with New Math; I had never heard of it before. I also had to learn about the Canadian parliament system and other new subjects. I soon became overwhelmed with all the new courses, as well as being in a foreign learning environment, and fell behind in my studies.

The school seemed so foreign to me. I had never heard of recreational drugs and had never known anyone who smoked cigarettes. Now my classmates were slipping out for a smoke at recess. I had been taught that women could not wear pants, and that even wearing lipstick was questionable. I was so terribly naïve, and confused, and now I was in an environment where all these things were common and accepted. I felt like such a freak with my red hair (cut by my mother), bright freckles all over my face and body, and my distinctly British accent. I stood out like a sore thumb.

My father was gone much of that year, visiting churches across the country. Then, for some reason unknown to me, my father took a pastorate position. We were going to stay in Canada. Middle Brother and I had already settled into a large church and chose to keep going there. This furthered my disconnect with my family as we now attended different churches. Brother and I thrived in our church and were voted youth leaders of our youth group. I loved the Lord and loved church. My parents were pleased that I had made friends there and were more than happy for me to be attending the youth group and youth functions. They even let me go on a weekend retreat with my new friends. I had my first boyfriend, and he would frequently drive me home after church.

Big Sister, because of her job at the clothing store, had such nice clothes compared to my wardrobe. I started to secretly borrow her clothes and change into them at school. I also started to smoke cigarettes with a friend at school. It was my attempt to appear to "fit in." I wanted to look more normal, more Canadian. I started hitchhiking so that I could use the bus money my parents gave me to buy cigarettes.

Somebody must have seen me hitchhiking, although I never knew for sure because no one in my family was ever up front about anything. From that point on though, my relationship with my parents began a downward spiral. When I came home at night, my mother would be waiting for me, smelling my fingers as I came through the door to check if I smelled like smoke.

As the friction grew, I fell into increasingly riskier behaviour. I tried hashish and marijuana. Big Sister and her boyfriend wanted to try it, too, so I tried to buy it from a girl at school. Her father found out and came knocking on our door. My father answered the door and I slunk away in fear and trembling, as this man told my father that I was buying drugs from his daughter. My parents were devastated and demanded I tell them who I was buying the marijuana for. I refused to tell them it was for my sister. They kept me up late into the night, trying to force me into telling. Eventually, as we were all falling asleep while waiting for me to cooperate, they gave up and sent me to bed. I was proud of myself for keeping trust with Big Sister; I was strong. But my parents viewed me as rebellious and stubborn. I found it confusing, to have what I thought was me maturing be described as wilful stubbornness.

A fellow around my age at church had access to heroin and I asked him to get me some. The day he came to my house, he stood out in the front yard and held out his hand to give me the small bag. But then, he looked in my eyes and said, "I can't do this to you," and he opened the bag and blew the stuff into the air. I never tried to get heroin again.

By then I was in Grade 11, and my favourite classes were band and typing. Every other subject was dismal. My typing teacher cared about me and encouraged me so much. I made friends with one of the band teachers, and she would invite me to her house. That was where I had my first beer. She offered it to me like I was an adult, as an adult thing to do.

I never felt like I was being rebellious; I was trying desperately to navigate in such unfamiliar circumstances. The band class planned a trip to Japan and I wanted to go, too. My parents did not seem happy about this and expressed difficulty in paying my way. This made me feel unworthy and I felt badly that it would take so much of their money. Once they started putting pressure on me, I decided not to go. When my band class left and the school thought I had gone, too, I skipped classes. I didn't feel accountable to anyone and had plenty of free time.

But as the friction grew between me and my parents, I made darker choices. I do not remember the first time I took LSD, but I do remember that it was the first time I did self-harm. My parents saw marks on my arms and assumed I was now a heroin addict, and things only got worse in our relationship.

One evening, as my parents were about to leave for their weekly prayer meeting, they called me into the living room to talk. My father read me some Scripture verses from the book of Timothy, stating that in order for a man to be in leadership, he must have his own house in order. My father told me that I was not behaving like the daughter they needed me to be. Therefore, I had to either change or leave. He told me that they wanted me gone before they got back from the prayer meeting that night.

I do not have a word in my vocabulary to describe what I felt that night. Devastated does not begin to be adequate. I had never thought about leaving home. I was 15 years old. After they left, I called Oldest Brother and sobbed into the phone, "They told me to leave!" He told me, "Pack your things and come right over." I went to stay with Oldest Brother and his wife. I continued going to school and tried to keep going on with my life, but I was in utter shock. Oldest Brother and his wife were kind, and gave me a nice room to stay in. One day, to pass the time, I started going through things in the room. I found some special coins and laid them out with my belongings.

I felt angry with my parents. They should not have rejected me, and I couldn't understand it. They should have helped me—I was just a child! I needed money and things to survive. In my anger I went back into my parents' house, now no longer my home. I chose a time when I knew my mother would be out, and took her grocery money for the week. It was $50. I told Little Sister, who was home at the time, that she was not to tell, and I left. The next day, when I was at school, my mother went into my room at my brother's house and went through all my belongings, looking for her money. When I got back from school, my sister-in-law confronted me. They had found her coins sitting out with my things and she thought I had also stolen her money. I was crushed beyond description, humiliated, and hurt that my mother would come after her money but not come after me. I didn't know that they knew where I was. There was no attempt to talk to me. She only came for her money.

On the Streets

That was the day I went to live on the streets. I walked out of that house, and truly became homeless. No turning back. I would ride the busses all night until they quit running. Sometimes I would sleep on the school steps and then go to class. I still went to church and tried to keep my life going.

I was not aware of my parents ever coming to look for me or doing anything to try to help me. Then one day the school principal called me into his office to talk about my situation. He asked me if I would be willing to have tea with my mother. I said sure! He phoned her right then and arranged for me to go see her. We sat and drank our tea and had a very strained conversation. There was no offer of … anything. We looked at each other, politely spoke a few words and then I left. Nothing happened, nothing changed.

I went back out onto the streets, specifically 4th Ave., which back in 1970 was the "place to be" if you wanted to be a hippie. Some nights I sat up all night talking to other homeless people. One friendly fellow whom I sat next to for warmth told me how he and his father had literally frozen up north. Only he got to live; his father had not survived.

I discovered I could easily break into my church at night. I had developed a special relationship with the church custodian; I loved him, and I thought he loved me. But I didn't want him to unexpectedly come across me sleeping, so I would sleep on the floor behind the piano with my coat as a pillow. That way, I hoped, I would have time to get up and at least be awake if he or someone else walked in. I also remembered my parents had an empty room downstairs that they had not rented out. I would sneak in after everyone was asleep and sleep in a bed. I don't remember how I got drugs during that period, but I do remember breaking a mirror and causing myself harm in their downstairs room while high on LSD. My mother found out I was there and the next morning informed me I had to leave. I was not welcome to sleep in their room downstairs or any other part of their house. If I wanted to be in their house, I had to be the daughter they wanted me to be. She wouldn't explain more. I had no idea what she meant, no idea what they wanted from me. I could hardly process the fact that my mother would rather have me sleeping out on the streets than under her own roof.

The senior pastor of my church invited me home with them after church one Sunday. I ate a nice lunch and slept in a bed. What bliss to have a nap in a real bed. Softer than floating on clouds! After a few hours, I left their house. They never said a word to me about my situation. No questions, no suggestions. They acted like they did not even know the crisis I was in.

I found out that my school guidance counsellor told my parents that she had seen me on 4th Ave., high on something and leaning up against a lamppost. I couldn't understand why, if my parents knew where I was, they did not come after me or at least talk to me. Having grown up in Africa, I wasn't familiar with social workers or any available resources. I had no idea how to get any help.

Soon after this, the church secretary came to find me one morning before church started. This is a memory that is seared into my mind and heart. She walked down that long staircase, came to me and informed me that it was against fire regulations for anyone to sleep in the church; I was not to do it again. She seemed to me to be such an ancient woman, with no connection or relationship with me whatsoever. Why did the church choose to have her come and tell me not to sleep there again? I was friends with the pastor, why didn't he tell me? My family had been the adopted missionary family this church had lifted up in prayer for many years. How could this be happening?

Soon after, the pastor called me into his office. He talked with me, but I can only remember one thing he said. It upset me to my very core. He said, "You are just trying to get attention and I want you to stop. It's time to grow up." I left feeling absolutely devastated.

By now I had stopped going to school and started waitressing at a local restaurant. I lied to them in the interview and said I was 21, and had a couple of years' experience waitressing in Kenya. This backfired on me, as it meant they did not train me the way that they would have if they knew I had no experience in

… anything! The houseboy had done all the work in our house growing up; I hadn't done any housework or cooking.

When I left my pastor's office that day, reeling in shock from his words, I went to my job at the restaurant. The boss called me into his office, telling me that he didn't think I really wanted to be a waitress. He fired me, moments after the devastating appointment with my pastor.

The Hospital

As I got on the bus that fateful day, I decided to end my life. My entire world had been my family and my church family. Now I was thoroughly rejected by both.

I have no idea why I went back into my parent's house to die. As I laid myself down, I thought, "God, I know You know why I have done this, and I know You understand." I fully expected that the next thing I would experience would be me waking up before God.

My mother came home sooner than I had anticipated, and because of the trail of blood was able to find me quickly. As the paramedic wheeled my stretcher to the ambulance, I heard my mother's voice. Even in my unconscious state I heard love in her voice. I was shocked to my core. I didn't know she loved me. I truly did not know she loved me. Something in my heart awakened. This, I believe, is the reason I survived. I heard her love. The love in her voice stirred within me the desire to live.

Even though this desire was short lived, it made the difference between life and death that day. The next memory I have of her voice is later in the hospital, where I was recovering. As I was awakening, I heard her complaining how the blood had ruined the mattress. She would have to throw it out. What hope I had allowed to arise in my heart, I let die once again.

I now know that the love I heard in her voice was actually God. His Voice of Love has proven to be a thread woven throughout my entire life. Every time I came to the end of myself, God, in His great love and mercy, awakened in me the desire and ability to hear His love. There is nothing better in this life on earth than to hear that love.

So much of this time is lost to memory. I stayed in the hospital as long as I was allowed. I was then transferred to the UBC hospital where I stayed for three months. I felt like everyone had abandoned me. My friends who were teenagers themselves had no idea what to do with me. It seemed as though everyone stayed away; scattered. Big Sister bought me corduroy pants, the most beautiful pants I had ever owned, and my now thinner body slipped so easily into them. Occasionally my mother came to visit me; another time the psychiatrist arranged a meeting with me and my parents. I can remember him explaining to us that all we do is react to each other. Two women from my Dad's church who I had never met before, took it upon themselves to visit me once a week. I really liked that.

The pastor finally came to see me. I was so happy that he had come. I was lying in bed when he entered the room, and as he placed flowers on the nightstand, he said he was sorry, and quickly left. I called after him, "Wait! Please stay!" but he hurried off, saying his wife was waiting in the car. I could see that he was so distraught that he was not able to speak to me or look at me. I tried to imagine in my teenage brain what that visit must have been like for him.

I made friends in the hospital. A woman I befriended had jumped off the Oak Street bridge in a suicide attempt. Her two young children and beloved husband would come in to visit her. She was in a complete body cast, hardly able to respond to anyone, not even with a smile. One man had lost his wife and children on a visit to England, when a car accident took all their lives in one fell swoop. It had happened a few years earlier and he had been frozen in time ever since, not capable of moving out of his despair. Bones would regularly break in his body, maybe indicating his broken heart. We became good friends, and sometime later, after we were both discharged, he asked me to marry him. He told me that if I said no, he would take his life. A year later he died in his cabin, after he had set fire to it.

Another friend that became very dear to me, Marianne, told me that she heard me say once that I wanted to run away to New York and become a hippie. I had no memory of ever saying such a thing. Regardless, Marianne figured I was much too nice a kid to do that, so she invited me home with her to look after her kids. Her husband was a doctor in Penticton. She suffered from alcoholism and needed help with childcare. It was a miracle when her husband said yes! Can you imagine your wife in a psychiatric hospital telling you she's met a teenager she wants to bring home to look after your kids? And you say sure?! Yet Dr. T did, and this got me off the streets and started on a brand-new life.

Penticton

Now that I had been discharged from the hospital, a social worker became involved. We had a visit in my parents' house where the social worker asked them if they would be alright with me moving to live with this family in Penticton. It was such a serious, somber time, but while we were all sitting around feeling awkward, in walked Middle Brother's pet skunk. The social worker screeched and climbed up on the couch, shouting. It certainly lightened up a difficult moment! My brother would walk his skunk on a leash near our house. One of our neighbours was a reporter with the Vancouver Sun and had sent a picture of my brother's skunk to the newspaper, but the social worker didn't know that!

It took a lot of courage for me to get in that big car and ride off to Penticton. I still felt pangs of sorrow that my parents had no problem with me moving four and a half hours away to live with strangers. I will never forget rounding that corner and seeing Skaha Lake, and then discovering that I would be living right beside the lake! I met the children and settled in.

Dr. T was the nicest man I had ever met. He absolutely delighted in his three children and made them the center of attention at every dinner time. I thought I had just agreed to looking after the children, and had no idea I was also expected to cook. I felt very intimidated. Somehow, I had never learned to cook anything. I had not done anything more than bake a cake out of a box! My mother had always enjoyed cooking and had been happy to do it for us. The first big meal I prepared was pork chops and mashed potatoes. I did not know how to make mashed potatoes, and I couldn't find a cookbook with a recipe on how to mash potatoes. I knew Dr. T liked his meat rare, so I made sure to cook the pork chops rare. After he got home from work, we all sat around the table and began eating. Dr. T then graciously got up from the table and stated that he'd like to cook his meat a little longer. Then he asked, "Would anybody else like theirs cooked a little longer?" taking each piece of meat back to the pan. It was the most gracious thing anybody had ever done for me. He helped me without embarrassing me. I loved him for that.

Dr. T offered to pay for me to take any course that I wanted. I chose driving school. Up to that point I had been comfortable with hitchhiking and did that to get wherever I wanted to go. Not only did he pay for driving school, but Dr. T even allowed me to learn on his car!

My mother, at one point, drove five hours to Penticton to visit me. I was so impressed. I knew it would have been a very intimidating thing for her to drive alone all that way. It made me feel important.

The oldest daughter and I shared a room, and after about a year, things started to become tense between us. This meant I had to leave, so I got a job as a cook at A&W and moved into a motel. The boss, an usher at my church, invited me to live with his family. However, he began to be sexually inappropriate with me. His wife found out, and I came home one day to find my bags all packed up and placed outside the house. There was no opportunity for me to explain my innocence.

Life continued to be an awfully hard struggle for me. I felt so lost inside, wondering how to help myself. I remember sitting on the white line in the middle of the road one night, waiting and wanting the police to pick me up. I thought that a night in jail would be better than having nowhere to sleep. No one noticed what I was doing. I had some more hospital admissions. After being in and out of the hospital a few times, the psychiatrist told me about someone interested in helping me. Although only 26 years old, she was the Director of Nursing in that hospital. She had previously expressed to the doctor a desire to help someone in need. She told him that if he ever happened to come across someone special that could benefit from a helping hand, she was interested.

We met, and I went home to live in her house with her. I wanted to try and finish high school, so she encouraged me to apply for welfare. While at the welfare office, I was told that my parents would need to sign a form saying they would not support me. Although grateful for this resource, another knife cut deep into my heart. I wanted my parents to want me, not sign a form saying they would not help me.

High school was again very overwhelming for me, and I soon dropped out. At times I felt a great urgency to visit my parents. One time I called them, collect. My father answered. When asked by the telephone operator if he would accept the charges, I heard him say, "Just a minute," and he went to call my mother. My heart grieved. Why couldn't he say, "Yes?" He did not want to talk to me, not even to say hello.

I would hitchhike all the way to Vancouver to visit my parents. Those visits seemed all right, and they would give me money for bus fare home. I was happy to pocket the money and hitchhike back to Penticton. I learned to take care of myself and figured that, if I checked for a door handle as I entered a stranger's car, I would be all right. A few times I jumped out at a traffic light to get away from someone sketchy, but I never met anything I could not handle. Except for the speeders on that Hope-Princeton highway. They really scared me.

Looking back, I now realize that I had faced death when I first chose to die. From then on, death didn't frighten me. I was able to face frightening circumstances without pulling away, such as riding a greyhound bus that looked like it would crash over the edge of a sharp drop off. Instead of being afraid, I realized that I would be okay with that if it really did happen. I became very reckless with my life.

Fresh Start

At 17, I moved back to Vancouver and found a place to rent. Shortly after that, my parents decided to return to Kenya. During our childhood, my parents never informed us or involved us in any decisions. We would find out what was happening only after the plan was already in motion. Things hadn't changed. The day quickly came to say goodbye, and I found my emotions out of control. I cried loud sobs watching them leave.

I got a job and began to establish myself. I found a church that I loved and made what I considered "an adult decision"—to go all the way with God. I had been a Christian all along but felt the need to make a bigger statement. I chose to be water baptized Easter Sunday. I had already been baptized at age 12, but felt that, even though I had been sincere, it had been to please my parents. Now I wanted to own it for myself.

My heart was filled with joy and I felt the desire to quit smoking. It was an extremely difficult thing for me to do. I would hitchhike to and from church with my Bible clutched under one arm and a cigarette in my other hand. That meant I had no hand to use to hitchhike! It bothered me immensely to be conflicted about holding a Bible and a cigarette at the same time.

At bedtime one night I felt this struggle in an extreme way. Usually the last thing I would do before going to sleep was smoke a cigarette, but I wanted reading my Bible to be the last thing I did. This particular night, I realized I was not comfortable doing those two things at the same time. No way should I smoke while reading God's Word. So, I put down my cigarettes and said aloud, "This time, God, I choose You." As I read, I found myself repeating my words over and over in my spirit. *"This time, God, I choose You."* Then, I thought, does that mean that if I smoke, I am not choosing God but a cigarette? This troubled me to such an extent that I quit smoking. The next day, as I went to work and every day after, every time I wanted a cigarette I would say, "This time, God, I choose You." It was so liberating.

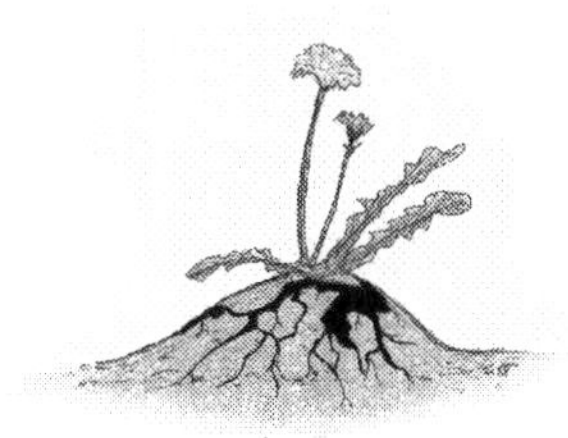

Chapter Three

A New Beginning

A short time later, a group from Australia, travelling around the world, came to our church. They were so "on fire" for God, believing the Bible should be taken literally and performing visible healing miracles. I wanted to be part of that! I could not pack my bags fast enough to join them. My love for God was reinforced, and I prepared to leave immediately. I tried to re-home my beloved cat, and was devastated when my only option seemed to be to take him to the animal shelter. While on the bus to the shelter, I broke down in tears. A kind couple on the bus asked me, "Why the tears?" As I told them my need to find a new home for my cat, they happily agreed to take him home with them. I was thrilled. God also cared about my cat!

At 17, I was on the road again. The group's next stop was Virginia. I instantly fell in love with the people there and their communal lifestyle. They tried to live as they imagined the first New Testament church lived. My new Australian friends went on to finish their world trip, but I chose to stay in Virginia. I ended up being there for four years. It was like Bible school for me; I finally had a place to finish growing up. I felt like I had died and gone to heaven. The sky was the limit for me in potential for my life, and I was so happy. The community believed that the gifts of the Spirit taught in the Bible were like a toolbox and we could use whatever one we wanted, whenever we wanted. Angels were seen in the trees, and miracles happened all the time. Camp in the summer brought hundreds of people for special meetings. People would line up for hours to receive a personal prophetic word from God. I felt so fulfilled and received much inner healing for my broken heart.

Being in Virginia, far from friends and family, was an incredible opportunity for me to start over afresh. Nobody knew me; I could tell people as much or as little as I wanted to tell them. I could have given a different name if I wanted. I could leave my depression behind and live anew. Yet to my surprise, I discovered I could not leave myself behind. In time I realized that I had brought *me* with me, into my new life. Moving far away did not leave *me* behind. However, to my joy, I had found a place of acceptance and potential growth. It was here the Lord gave me my first life verse:

"Trust in the LORD with all your heart, and do not lean on your own understanding. In all your ways acknowledge Him, and he will make straight your paths." (Proverbs 3:5–6)

I became the camp cook, year-round. I learned to preach, prophesy, lead worship, cut up a tree with a chain saw, build buildings, and install toilets. I was also the camp driver, driving twenty miles with a group of people sitting on folding metal chairs in the back of a bread van. I learned to drive very delicately! It was such a wonderful time. I felt incredibly fulfilled, and I committed my life to this group.

When I was around 19, we went on a mission trip to Mexico, Russia and Israel. One of the most profound times in my life was in Russia, lining up for blocks to see Lenin's mausoleum, his body surrounded by all the stark black marble. Such a somber environment. Because we were tourists, we were sent to the front of the line. I had never experienced such spiritual darkness and such coldness as I did in Russia. Nobody smiled. Someone watched us all the time. The man that followed us all the time was the same man that served us communion in the church!

From there we travelled directly to the empty tomb in Jerusalem. What contrast! So much joy surrounding the place of Christ, once in death, now an empty tomb. What a difference between remembering a death in one place and a resurrected life in another! I was baptized in the Jordan River—what joy. Yes, baptized for the third time! First at age 12, then at age 17 when I made a more adult decision to go all the way in my faith, and now with a group of believers in Israel. I could hardly pass up the opportunity, could I?

Our group had the opportunity to speak in a church in Egypt. The women were seated up in a balcony, men on the main floor. It was a daunting but thrilling experience for me to take my turn on the platform and give my few words in an atmosphere that appeared to not typically give women a place on stage. As I quoted a Scripture, "I would rather be a doorkeeper in the house of my God than dwell in the tents of wickedness (Psalm 84:10b)," the crowd erupted in applause.

When we were back in Virginia again, we frequently travelled across the state with a huge gospel tent. I would knock on doors to invite people, preach on street corners, and swing a sledgehammer to help erect the tent. I seemed to have been made for this.

We believed hearing God's voice should be a daily occurrence, and it was. I would sometimes know that there would be money in the mail on a certain day. God was providing and teaching me to hear His voice at the same time! The freedom of dancing in the Spirit captured my heart, especially with the innocent carefree children, but also with the adults. Fasting was never a requirement and was taught in a healthy atmosphere that did not contribute to things such as eating disorders. I learned the benefits of the practice of fasting, and for a period of a year I would fast three days a week, eventually doing a 40-day fast once a year.

In the community, people believed that living by faith meant you did not work for an income, but trusted God to bring in the money. They did not believe in doctors or medicine. One year I had an oozing sore on my leg that lasted for months. It bothered me as it would seep through my pantyhose. Years later I saw pictures on the Internet of what cancer looks like, and it looked just the same. I never went to a doctor. After many months it disappeared. I lived a "holiness lifestyle," wearing my uncut hair up in a bun and my dresses long enough to cover my wrists and knees.

At one point I took care of five children in their home while their mother was away on a mission trip. One day while the kids were at school, for some reason, I had concerns for our safety and did a fair amount of praying. I asked God to place a hedge of angels around the property to keep us safe. One of the children was exceptionally aware of spiritual things, and when she came home from school, she said she could see angels all around the property making what looked like a fence. This was such evidence of my prayers in such a dramatic way!

I learned the discipline of memorizing sacred, beloved scriptures. The church would have competitions, especially for the young people, to see who could read the Bible cover to cover the most times in a specific period. I read the Bible through many times. My plan was to eventually go to Israel as a missionary.

Here I had found something to which I could commit all of myself. Although the atmosphere seemed motivated more by obedience and sacrifice than love, I thrived in this atmosphere. Having received my license to preach from this church, I was soon to be ordained.

It was around this time in 1978 that disaster happened in Jonestown, with all those poor people drinking poisoned Kool-Aid. More than 900 members of an American cult, Peoples Temple, died in that mass suicide-murder under the direction of their leader. I could totally understand how that could happen. I was that committed to this group of people, although I knew they would not ask something like that of us.

I was so "sold out for God" that I wanted to publicly make a commitment to never marry. My wholehearted devotion to God would include singleness, too, if that was what He wanted. That was how much I loved JESUS. I planned to announce this from the platform. Shortly before I did, however, the Holy Spirit grabbed my heart and told me, "No, I have someone for you." I immediately had a vision of a pair of men's shoes: an old-fashioned kind of dress shoe. I also heard a verse from Isaiah 58:12 about building up the ancient ruins and restoring old paths, repairing the breach and broken walls. I knew this man would be old-fashioned. After that I backtracked in my plans of declaring I would not marry!

Soon after this, one of the leaders began to go 'off track' with very wrong and dangerous teachings, saying there needed to be some sort of sexual union with God in order to bring the kingdom to earth. Eventually I plucked up my courage, went to a member of the family that ran the camp, and told them what was happening. Unfortunately, I was rejected. I was told if I ever told anybody of these things, something would happen to me that I would never be able to get over. As this leader spoke, I became aware of a dark cloud wanting to come over my body to cloak me. The next few months were difficult for me; my glorious time there was ending. Feeling increasingly out of place and awkward, I started to sleep outside in a field, on the ground. One morning I woke up to a herd of cows surrounding me. Their look of great surprise to find someone sleeping in their field matched mine at finding them staring at me!

Back to Canada

Around 22 years of age, I boarded a bus and returned to British Columbia, once again feeling devastated. How could I have trusted God with all my heart, given everything I had, and still have everything go so wrong? How could people preaching such faith and miracles go so wrong? I promised in my heart that I would never again involve myself with an independent group like that, one that wasn't part of a larger denomination. That experience furthered my understanding of human frailty. I learned to accept that all people, no matter what position they hold, make mistakes and fail others. It does not change or affect who God is. It was a hard lesson for me to learn.

My parents had finished their time in Kenya and were back on furlough. I joined them in their home in Abbotsford. Re-adjusting to life back in Canada was difficult; I felt like I didn't really know my parents, and they didn't know who I had become. I had done a lot of growing up.

Feeling shattered and full of doubt, I began to see a psychologist, who went into detail explaining to me the part of my brain that believed in God. On a large diagram, he pointed to the place, so small in the picture. If I would adjust that part of my brain and stop believing in God, I could be better.

This only added to the confusion of that time. I had heard so clearly from God all those years living in Virginia. Now I could only talk to God if I walked or kept busy. If I tried to quiet myself to concentrate or pray, I would have such torment in my thoughts and vision. Some sessions with a deliverance ministry helped, but also cast big questions on why there was such a deep fracture in my life and family.

At the end of their furlough year, my parents' plan was for Little Sister to stay in Canada and live in their duplex. I asked if I could live there, too. Their response was that they would have to think about it for a while. This hurt me so deeply. How could I be that bad of a person that they would have to "think about" letting me live with my sister in their house?

We did end up sharing a suite and establishing our own lives. I studied and wrote my GED, (high school equivalence exam) to receive a B.C. high school diploma. Even though I achieved this certificate, I still feel like I did not have schooling beyond Grade 7. The change from life in Africa to life in Canada had been so traumatic for me that I had stopped learning years earlier. And now, Little Sister attended university while I worked. She made a trip to Kenya to visit our parents, and came home with an African grey parrot that some children had sold at their door for 10 shillings. The kids had rescued it from some crows that were trying to kill it, and then realized they could make a little money from it. The bird smelled like curry and we taught him to speak English.

Two Became One

Not long after this, a mutual friend wanting to do some match making, set up a dinner invitation and I met Dan. My friend was right, we hit it off! We immediately fell in love. It was a fast engagement and we moved quickly to marriage. I had never been in love before and we figured at the age of 25 we knew what we were doing! We chose a small church for the wedding, with cows in a field and mountains for a backdrop. Dan already owned a mobile home in Surrey, and after a two-week honeymoon in California and Mexico, he carried me over the threshold to begin life as a married couple. We entered the front door where he kept the very same shoes I had seen in that vision in Virginia. And yes, he is a very old-fashioned, sentimental man, just like the Lord had described to me years earlier.

On our honeymoon I absentmindedly placed the hot toaster-oven on one of the motel chairs, and to my horror, it burned a hole in the fabric! Dan quickly assured me all was well and hurried off to speak to the manager and fix the problem. I could hardly believe I had married such an incredible prince who would take the blame for me and make things right.

We had a good start to married life, enjoying a simple life as a couple. We had a lot in common… except for my smoking habit. Because my last days in Virginia had been so stressful, and I returned to Canada feeling shunned and very confused, I started smoking again. This quickly became a big problem in our marriage, and I found it extremely difficult to quit this time. It was a huge adjustment for me to give up working outside the home, give up all my independence, and start a new life as a wife. I did start classes to learn oil painting and needlework (which I hated), while trying desperately to quit smoking. Thankfully, I succeeded in a short while.

I had been so "on fire" for God in my time in Virginia, yet felt so defeated and spiritually lost after returning to Canada. I puzzled as to how I had heard so clearly from God in that atmosphere and why all of that ended when I moved back. Dan and I faithfully attended church every Sunday but did not become involved. Dan had his own wounds and disappointments after going to the mission field himself. He had previously gone to Aruba as a missionary and had come home early, feeling disillusioned with missions. My plans to be a missionary in Israel had come crashing down. I certainly wanted nothing to do with missions anymore. I had strong feelings about missionaries who sacrificed their children. That is how I interpreted anyone putting their child in boarding school. I found a lot of resentment in my heart, so we 'laid low' with our involvement in a church community. We had trusted and we had been hurt, disappointed. Dan and I made a great pair!

Our mobile home park did not allow dogs or cats and I soon set out to find what animal I could have without breaking the rules. I didn't think I would like birds for pets but realized it was something we could have, so I bought cockatiels. Then my wonderful husband agreed that I could buy a pet skunk, but none were to be found. However, the pet store did have a ferret. I had never seen one before but came home that day with a new pet. Initially Dan had a huge struggle accepting the ferret as he *hates* mice and rats, and the ferret's face was too similar. We named him Musky and, once we were able to coax him out from hiding behind our fridge, Dan began to see a personality behind those ferret eyes. Dan's tender heart fell in love with all of our pets.

I soon realized that if I had two birds and two ferrets, they could have babies! This was the start of a home business. I learned to breed both birds and ferrets, selling many of them to people living in apartments and other places where larger pets were not allowed. The ferrets used a litter box like a cat, and when de-scented and kept clean, made excellent pets in a restricted place. We made many trips on our motorcycle with the ferrets tied to a harness and leash, hidden inside my coat, and poking out their noses whenever we stopped at red lights. I had plenty of time to invest in training them and eventually we could even sneak them into a restaurant hidden in my coat. We also made many trips to Vancouver Island where we stayed in my grandparents' cabin. These became regular trips as we combined Dan's work on the Island with a holiday.

Time to Grow Up

In the early days of our marriage, I had a distinct feeling that God was calling me to be like the bow of a ship. I said to Dan, "There is something terribly wrong in my family of origin, and I have no idea what it is. Something, maybe, like witchcraft. I am going to be like the bow of a ship and break through whatever is wrong in my family. Then, after me, anyone else in my family who wants freedom will find it more easily, as I will make the way first."

It seemed such an odd thing to say but I clearly remember it to this day. It was like God's call on my life.

Dan knew about my struggle with my parents but believed that, since there are two sides to every story, he could mediate and help our relationship to be healed. I had been so surprised with his comments when I explained to him the Scripture my father read to me at age 15, while telling me to leave their home. Dan explained that the Scripture in 1 Timothy 3:4 should apply to my father, not to me. I had always accepted all the blame as if I was a bad person. Somehow, all of life's problems seemed to be my fault, as if I always did the wrong thing. When I thought of myself as a child, if I spilled my milk, it was because I was a bad girl. I had believed that, if I were a good girl, my milk would not be spilled. As I was growing in this new understanding, I wanted to talk with my parents.

A few years into our marriage, my parents came back to Canada to retire. I wanted to build a relationship with them, so we would invite them over and we would attend family dinners. One day I decided that I wanted to have a conversation with both of my parents about everything that had transpired with my leaving home. We had never discussed this heart-wrenching time in our history. I wanted an apology.

I invited them over and plucked up all my courage. I figured the best way to open the door to receiving an apology from them would be for me to first offer mine. So, I told my mother and father that I was sorry for the pain I had caused in their life around that time I left home as a teenager. I watched as my father sat back. He looked so comfortable and confident as he stretched one arm over the back of the couch. Then he said, "I have lived my life and I have no regrets." End of subject. I was so shocked I did not know how to continue the conversation. Another memory seared into my heart and mind.

My mother commented that what I had said of the circumstances around that time was untrue, that I had been a rebellious teenager and run away from home. That was it. They soon left, and once again I was shocked to the core of my being. They appeared to be in complete denial of what had happened in our lives and unwilling to even discuss it.

As I watched them walking out of my home, I allowed something significant to happen in my heart. I made an adult decision. I realized I would *never* get the love from my parents that I so desperately wanted. I made a conscious decision that day to give up striving to get their approval, give up waiting for them to voice their love for me. No more trying. That is the day I grew up. I was 28 years old and from then on, I was much happier and felt more freedom in my life. I did not need anything from them. This relieved the pressure between my parents and me, and we went on to try to at least have a surface relationship.

When Dan and I decided to buy a home of our own, we rented half of my parents' duplex so we could have time to look around before deciding what to buy. Any hopes and aspirations Dan had of being a peacemaker in my relationship with my parents ended abruptly when we both concluded that we did not know how to move forward in knowing them. The disquiet that kept arising between us is too difficult to even describe.

New Home

We bought our dream house with a spectacular view of mountains, overlooking the city and Pattullo Bridge. Our house became a home as we made it our own. I built an aviary downstairs for all my birds. I had learned that if I took away the baby cockatiels two weeks after hatching and hand-raised them myself, they became great pets. I sometimes had a waiting list of buyers for my babies. Canaries were so much fun to raise and sell, as was my attempt to raise Pekin robins. Once I realized how hard it was to go away on any holiday when you have a large bird, I started my own small business of boarding birds while owners were away. We enjoyed a macaw, Amazon parrots, and an African grey that boarded with us off and on for 15 years. It was so nice to bird-sit for pay and then send them home when they got too noisy!

One evening a customer came late, and I had to awaken the birds so he could choose a baby. After he left, one of my birds cried loudly and relentlessly. I finally went to the aviary to figure out what was wrong. I realized, to my horror, I had mistakenly sold the mother, not the baby! Her mate was crying his heart out, as these birds mate for life. My genius husband just so happened to have noticed the customer's license plate number and the make of his car. After a couple of phone calls to the police, he found a compassionate police officer. The officer told Dan he could not give out confidential information, but he would call the man himself and ask him to call us. The next day he did, and we managed to swap the birds and fix my mistake. What a man I married! And what a kind police officer!

A stressful part of this endeavour was when small birds would come to board and my cat wanted to eat them. I went to great lengths to help my cat become acquainted with the cockatiels, allowing him to smell and touch a bird, under my supervision. This proved more successful than I could have imagined. One day, after I had forgotten yet again to repair a hole in the top of the bird aviary, I came downstairs in time to see the cat all sprawled out on top of the cage, with one of the loose cockatiels preening the cat's whiskers! The cat was totally relaxed, and the birds were not afraid of him. One day he brought me a newborn baby pet rat that had fallen out of the nest, laying it carefully at my feet. Having no hair yet, the rat would have certainly died if the cat hadn't saved its life. This same patience also proved effective with our dog and the rabbits I boarded. The Bible says that one day the lion will lay down with a lamb and there will be much peace. We could already see a glimpse of that in our home!

A Growing Family

Our house seemed so big for only two people, but for both Dan and me, buying the house had been an astounding time in hearing and responding to God's leading. We both knew beyond any doubt that God wanted us to buy that house. It was His gift and His choice for us. After a few years we wondered why we had such a big house for just the two of us. Early in our marriage we had talked about children. I did not seem to have that deep desire for children that most people I knew had. I didn't feel I needed a child to find completeness in my life and felt I would have been okay if we never had a child. Dan felt the same way. But a couple of years into our marriage I had a change of heart.

I very nervously approached the subject with my man. I can still remember the spot we were driving on King George Highway when I dared to tell him I was having a change of heart about children. To my delight, he said he was feeling the same way!

Six years into our marriage, we wondered if we should foster children. We were not getting pregnant and seemed to have so much room to spare and so much love to give. While we were attending orientations to learn how to become foster parents, I found out I was pregnant. Wow! Our son was just 6 months old when we had our first foster child, aged 4 months. Two babies at once to manage with grocery shopping and taking them and the groceries in and out of the car—my goodness!

I was concerned that I would not be able to separate well when the foster children had to leave, so I requested only short-term placements. One baby placed with us was the child of a teen mom. The social worker did not think the mom would be able to give up her baby, so they placed the baby in care to see if the mom could let go. The child was then adopted out from our home. A couple of older girls were with us over Mother's Day. Their mother was in hospital and they had nowhere else to go. Dan did incredibly well with these girls, and a lot of healing and growth happened in their lives to the point where their doctor asked what we had done with them. They seemed no longer afraid to see him alone.

I had many fears about becoming a mother, not knowing how to take care of a little one. All my concerns disappeared the moment we brought David home from the hospital. This was a life-altering moment. I had been quite self-focused, enjoying our own little world. I had my sisters and brothers nearby. My life was simple, quiet. I did not read a newspaper, nor did I care much about what was going on around us. On that drive home from the hospital, we heard on the radio that an important newspaper editor had just been shot. In our neighbourhood! I was so upset! I realized I was bringing my brand-new son home to live in Whalley, the worst area to live in Surrey. Suddenly I cared about my community, my world! My heart cried, *What have I done in choosing to bring a child into this world? This now wicked world!*

I had felt such a disconnect from God those first years back in Canada, but I had experienced a wonderful connection with Him when we clearly heard the Lord about the house we bought. I was also confident that God had sent me my husband, and now I was about to hear from Him again.

As I tried to settle in with my new son, the Lord spoke profoundly to my heart. The story in the Bible about Eli, in 1 Samuel 2, tells of how badly Eli messed up as a dad. God judged him for failing his sons, for not being responsible enough. Yet God chose to place Samuel, as a young boy, under the care of Eli. A new confidence flooded my heart as I realized how God took good care of Samuel. This little boy was raised without his mother, under the care of Eli who had already made mistakes. Would God not also care for my son even though he was going to grow up in Whalley? I knew I could trust God with my boy and the neighbourhood in which he lived.

Being a mother came naturally to me. It was as if I was born for the role. I loved every single minute of motherhood and didn't ever wish to take a break from it. I never left David with anyone until I was about to give birth to our daughter. I would just take him anywhere I wanted to go, and he was happy to cooperate!

After David was born, my heart changed towards my parents. I felt very protective of our son. While I wanted to withdraw from them, I was still trying to reach out to find a connecting point. As Mother's Day approached, I went to my mother and asked if I could take her out for lunch. She agreed, but just then one of my sisters-in-law came through the door and invited her to a fancy restaurant in White Rock for Mother's Day. My mother squealed in delight at the offer. After a while I quietly left the house, with no one even noticing. There was never another word said of my invitation. My value, or lack thereof, was once again made clear. I could not understand my parents and wanted to protect my son from the confusion I felt around them. When family invitations came, I found myself wanting to decline. Dan commented that a family invitation felt like a summons. To my surprise, when we politely declined one of these invitations, huge displeasure erupted from my parents. The more I tried to put up a boundary defining my home and life from my parents' life, the more the friction grew. I realized that, in their eyes, I was not supposed to say no. My parents informed me that we "owed them" because they had been away for so many years. But it was their choice to be away in Africa all those years. That didn't mean I owed them to make up for their losses.

Defining Moments

The day came when my parents made an unexpected visit to our home. While growing up, I had never heard them disagree or argue. Ever! This day, as they walked in, their anger was palpable. We had declined their offer to an upcoming family dinner. Dan picked up David and held him on his hip as my mother and father both vented their rage. I was truly afraid for their health. I thought someone would have a heart attack right then and there! I had never seen this before, my parents so visibly worked up. My offense, as far as I could tell, was that I wanted to step back and withdraw a little. I wanted to have my own home with walls that were not seen over or crossed over at someone else's whim or will. In my entire life, I had never stood up in anger or been mean to my parents. As I stood up to them this day, I watched in shock. Their visit ended abruptly when my father, voice raised and shaking in anger, told Dan that he did not have authority over me. That my father had authority over me, not Dan. My mother said she could not wait for my child to rebel against me so I would know what it was like to be rebelled against. Then they left. That was the last time they were in our house.

To my surprise, as I tried to pick up the pieces, my siblings were noticeably absent. I did not realize that my drawing a defined line with my parents would result in all my siblings also taking a step back from me. As the years went by, I concluded that they could not handle the courage I had mustered to stand up to my parents. My parents wanted me under their control. Even though my siblings would complain about our parents, they still did whatever our parents wanted them to do. My own courage is what separated me from the rest of my family. The choices I made to protect and build my own family cost me my family of origin. I did not want my child to grow up with the confusion I had experienced, confusion around how to be and function as a Christian and how to interpret the Bible.

We now had a more defined boundary between us, yet my parents tried repeatedly to meet, talk, visit, or phone us. Suddenly strange things started to happen. A gift given to David as a wee boy caused him to cry as if in pain when he would get near it. I took him to the doctor to get his ears checked to see if there was something wrong with his hearing. We would experience oppression in our home if my parents would leave flowers on our doorstep while we were out. If I did talk with them, Dan would have unexplainable complications where he worked. The connection became clear enough that Dan would sometimes come home from work and say, "You had contact with your parents today, didn't you?" Special ornaments would fall off a shelf and shatter on the floor, or a baby bird would suddenly die, or the toilet would overflow. Necropsy results on the deaths of my birds showed many different causes. When nothing made sense after much testing, the vet advised that I cull all the birds and build a new aviary.

To my surprise, the Lord was opening my eyes to see that there was something very wrong, and that it was best for us to step away from my family of origin. Every time I allowed my brain to override this thinking and "test the waters" and try again, something would happen that made us regret it. It was as though God wanted us to establish our family away from my parents. So, we did. As for our birds, they were first pets and then a business, so we kept them. They went on to flourish and do well, no longer sickly. Finally, we were able to develop a peace in our home that was no longer shattered.

I agonized over whether I was honouring God by drawing these lines with my parents. As I took it to God in prayer, I finally camped on this thought. The Bible says to honour your parents. The way I was choosing to live my life *was* bringing honour to them. I was living my life as a good citizen, a respectful, loving and kind person. I loved my husband and was a good mother. That would honour them and that was all I could do. I allowed myself to accept it was enough.

A boyhood dream of Dan's had been to find the first car his father ever owned and then sold in 1951, a blue 1939 Chevy 2 door Sedan. His sister helped in the search and they finally found that very car, abandoned for over 20 years in a farmer's field. Being frozen in Alberta winters had helped keep the car free from rust. The bullet hole and mice nests did not deter us from bringing it home and parking it in our driveway. This neighborhood eye-sore became a labour of love as Dan spent countless hours restoring the car to a far greater vehicle than originally imagined. It soon became an object lesson for his Sunday school classes. He used that car to illustrate the pounding and grinding work necessary in restoring something that appeared so broken and useless. This brought back the words the Lord had spoken to me as a young woman. He said that He had someone for me to marry, someone who would respect and love old things. Dan is very sentimental and poured his heart into this special car, a car that his dad had owned, that his great-grandfather had ridden in, a car that held so many family memories.

We had many picnics with our son, many trips to California, and frequent visits with Dan's parents and Grandma who lived close by. We enjoyed a good life, and yet I was very lonely and felt a deep sadness and depression. With few friends and no real connection at church, the animals, birds, my son, and husband were my world. When David was old enough to go to children's church, I started to want to be involved in church. We had been attending a new church and I decided to put in the effort. Dan taught the preteen Sunday School class, and I taught the Grade 5 girls. It was a happy time in our lives. Then, with immense joy, I found out that I was pregnant again.

I made a good friend at our new church, and one day over tea I said to her, "I am so committed to God; I can't imagine anything happening that would cause me to not be totally 'sold out' for God." I was so happy and felt such fulfillment. But as I voiced those words, I had the strangest chill come over me. I felt as though I had challenged unseen forces that were now called to attention. It was very foreboding. Soon after, while I was watching TV, a commercial came on in which a large tiger attacks, and it looked like the animal was going to pounce right through the screen. As I watched this, which I had done countless times before, it turned into a strange experience. I felt as if the animal leapt out of the TV and sunk its teeth into my heart. I had never experienced anything like that.

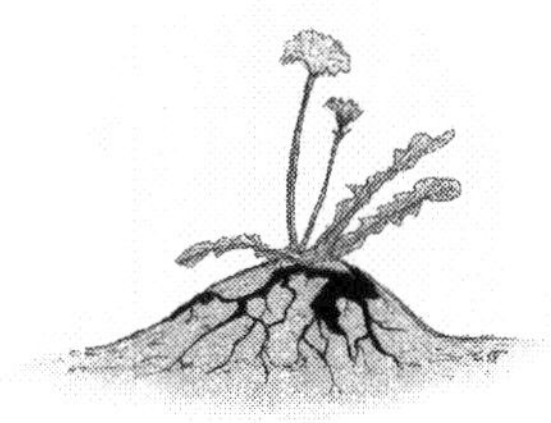

Chapter Four

A Gift for God

During this period in my life, I felt overwhelmed by God's endless love for me. Frequently, I would stop dead in my tracks as I would sense God's love flood over my body. One time, in an audience of hundreds of people, my name was drawn to win a prize. I had taken off my shoes, as I was so sure I wouldn't be called up front since I had never won anything in my life. I quickly put my shoes back on and ran up to the stage to receive my prize, acutely aware that God had singled me out to show me He loves me. He was highlighting me. My whole pregnancy was filled with confirmation of God's great love for me as an individual.

When I was in labour with David, my doctor was unavailable, so a different physician delivered him. I instantly fell in love with her; she was so compassionate, caring, and humble. I had not known a humble doctor before. She had even grabbed a mop to clean up the spilled garbage bag full of birthing debris! There were no airs about this wonderful woman.

I was so grateful when Dr. Cathie agreed to take me on as her patient for my second pregnancy. Over the years, I had prayed for her from time to time. Now she was here to deliver our beautiful daughter, Amber. My labour with David had been long and difficult: 27 hours of work. Amber was so cooperative! She came during the doctor's lunch hour, allowing the doctor to go right back to work. Her Apgar score was a perfect 10 and she weighed close to 9 lbs. So pink and beautiful! The whole pregnancy and birth were delightful. I lay back in my bed with such a deep satisfaction. Our family felt complete. A son and now a daughter.

Sometime in the night I got up to nurse my new baby. I was surprised to find her in an incubator. The nurse quickly assured me not to worry; Amber was just cold, and they wanted to warm her. I did, however, notice the nurse's sharp eye on me, as she watched me feed Amber. Once Amber finished nursing, I went back to bed.

Early the next morning, a doctor woke me up, saying they found something seriously wrong with Amber. He did not know what this issue was but was concerned about a hole in her heart. They had already called Children's Hospital to arrange for a transfer. I frantically leapt out of bed to call Dan to come as quickly as possible. He arrived just as Amber was being transported to the ambulance. As I hurried after the attendants, I wanted to ask them to please slow down as I had trouble walking so fast. I had just given birth! I sat in front of Amber during the trip while the kind ambulance attendant tried to keep me talking the entire time. The ambulance driver commented on what a great driver my husband was, as he kept close behind us through all that busy traffic.

At the hospital I was grateful to find a phone I could use to call my church's prayer chain. I had never realized how immensely valuable a church prayer chain could be. A kind voice answered, and I blurted out my horrifying news. Within moments I knew that many people from our church would be praying for us all. That brought me great comfort.

It didn't take long at all before several hospital staff members called Dan and me into a room. They delivered us news that was a blow like no other. Half of Amber's heart was missing, had never been formed. The diagnosis was Hypoplastic Left Heart

Syndrome. We were told that there was presently a moratorium on heart transplants and there was nothing that could be done for Amber. Then they left the room. Once alone, I turned to Dan and we embraced each other for a long hug. I told him, "We will not allow this to come between us."

I could not wait to get Amber into our car and go home. A nurse came out to our car, concerned that we wanted to leave so fast. I wanted to get Amber home, put her in her own clothes and nurse her without anyone watching me. Dan wanted to go home to switch cars so that Amber could ride in his precious old Chevy to pick up her brother from their grandparents' house.

As soon as we left the hospital parking lot, I asked Dan to pull over. I took Amber out of the car seat and held her in my lap. Thinking irrationally, I figured that since she was going to die anyways, if we happened to crash on the way home, then why not have her die in my arms instead of in a cold car seat? We went home, changed her clothes into a pink outfit I had bought for her, and hurried out to pick up her big brother. I could not wait for David to meet his sister. It was his fourth birthday that day. He was born August 20; Amber was born August 19.

Once we got back with the children, we put on music, wanting to make Amber feel at home. She had heard that music all the nine months I had carried her. I pulled David close to me as I told him his new sister was not going to live. He pulled her close to his chest and said in his soft 4-year-old voice, "But I don't want her to die!"

Dr. Cathie came to our house to explain what to expect and how to give Amber morphine. She made me promise not to call 911 as they would only try to resuscitate Amber, and that would be of no benefit. She held her finger up in front of my face and told me several times the importance of taking pictures. That was the last thing in the world I had on my mind. Taking pictures at a time like this seemed so futile, but she was adamant that we would value them down the road. She then instructed us that, when Amber did leave us, we were to call her, not 911.

After Dr. Cathie left, we attempted to make a fun evening for David as he had been away staying with his grandparents. We laughed and listened to music. Dan made a long nose out of masking tape and I took pictures as they played and laughed. I thought how Amber must really know she is home, with this atmosphere of laughter and play. I had a sense of deep satisfaction that we could create an environment like this, at a time like this.

Our pastor came over to pray. I felt resentment toward his wife for wanting to hold Amber, as I wanted every second with her. The same went for the visitor that showed up on our doorstep, just wanting to have a look but with absolutely nothing to say. One lady insisted that I had misunderstood the doctor with, "No, she is not going to die!" Sometimes people confuse faith with denial. I was deeply grateful for our pastor's knowledge of decisions such as burial versus cremation. I had never had a reason to think these things through before. He helped me see the value in having a physical place to go to grieve. My grandmother was the only one I knew who had died, but she was old. You were supposed to die when you were old. As he prayed for our wee girl, we asked God in heaven to heal her little body. I believed with all my heart that God could heal her. I also accepted His decision if He were to take her. I gave Him my child. "If you want her, you can have her."

It was the first time of my life that I felt like I had something to give God, the God of the universe, heaven itself. How could I ever give God something? Now I had something so precious and valued. I finally had something to give Him. So, we prayed for healing, YES … believing for it, but also accepting whatever His decision would be.

Once David was in bed for the night, Dan and I went to our bed, with Amber laying between us or on my chest. We talked and talked and finally, out of exhaustion, fell asleep. The doctors told us we would have her up to three weeks. I could not wait to dress her in the clothes I had chosen for her before she was born. I had no idea I would get to put only one outfit on her. Her breathing was so laboured, heavy, and loud. It sounded like a machine.

At midnight, as my precious daughter slept on my chest, I looked up in the corner of my bedroom, close to the ceiling, and I saw JESUS's great, big, open arms, and I saw Amber's spirit go with Him. We dozed and slept in our sorrow. Suddenly, at 3 a.m., both of us awakened with a jolt. The rhythmic, loud breathing had stopped, Amber had left her little body. We jumped out of bed. Dan went to the phone to call Dr. Cathie. I placed Amber in her bassinet and walked out of the room. Our doctor immediately climbed in her car, at 3 a.m., and came all the way from White Rock to sit with me until it was time for her to go to work. We had no idea what to do and were so grateful that she knew to call a funeral home to get Amber's body. With dismay, I saw what I perceived to be a horrible man who wreaked of smoke take my little baby away. Dr. Cathie hung on to me tightly to keep me from going after him. She stayed all those hours, sitting on the couch with me. I happened to mention that I believed God had made Amber the way He wanted her to be. As if with immense relief, my doctor let out a big sigh and asked, "You're a Christian?" Then she told me that she was a new believer herself. As we sat and talked, a miracle happened. God told me, "Even though you're losing a daughter, I'm giving you a solid friend, someone you can love the rest of your life." In that moment we became sisters. Dan also felt he gained a sister.

Frozen in Time

The morning after Amber left us, I was sitting on the couch with the door open. A large blue jay flew down and perched right at the door, looked inside, and loudly squawked. It was shockingly loud and unusual. But to my surprise, it felt like Amber's spirit had come to say goodbye! Then the bird quickly flew away.

David went outside to play on the swing. He stayed for such a long time; I became concerned. Once back in the house, I asked him what he was doing so long on that swing. He said, "I tried to swing higher and higher, as high as I could, so that I could maybe reach the sky and go to JESUS like Amber." My heart broke.

Those first days were like being frozen in time. I walked around like a zombie, unable to think about what I was doing. I would find the oven mitts in the fridge and other odd things in odd places. Eating, sleeping, normal routines were suspended as if I had no needs. No feelings, no responses, not even any need to eat. Just suspended in nothingness. Except for when it was time to throw away Amber's dirty diaper, the only one I had. I had feelings for that! It was so hard to part with that dirty diaper—it was all I had left of her. I learned that there were pills that could make my milk dry up. My milk that my body made for Amber.

Funeral plans required my attention and I found the courage and ability to write a tribute for a bulletin. Our church was gracious, kind, and supportive. The day of the funeral for my precious daughter, I delighted to see the sign in front of our church changed to say, "Thank you, Lord, for Amber 1 p.m."

Another one of those moments seared into my memory, like a tattoo branded on my soul, was walking to the front of the church and being shown where to sit. It was an extremely long bench with no one there but Dan, me, his mom, and wee David. Dan's father was not well enough to attend, and his sister lived too far away. I had never felt so alone in all my life. I had a beautiful picture of Amber (thanks to Dr. Cathie) blown up large and propped up at the front of the church. A tiny coffin lay closed, never to open again.

I had no other family. None at all. My parents lived around the corner from us and they had not even known I was pregnant. It was my choice to be so separated from my family. My choice that my siblings did not even know I was pregnant. Now I was at my daughter's funeral. It had been my choice but that did not make it any easier to sit there alone, with none of my family present. I felt as if I were totally naked at the front of the church.

Dr. Cathie had said she would come. We waited and waited, and then the pastor finally said that we couldn't wait any longer, we needed to go ahead. At that moment, she arrived. My doctor slipped in beside me and gave me a huge warm hug. I was instantly all right. Feeling suddenly clothed, I could manage anything. I held my head high and knew I could face the day. The worship leader's daughter, only a child herself, sang a song. She was in my Sunday School class. "JESUS loves me, this I know…" Her voice cracked as she nervously struggled, but I chose to believe it was her tears. She was crying for me, too. We also sang one of my favorite hymns: "It will be worth it all when we see JESUS…"

While planning this service I had been offended when asked about food, sandwiches, and sweets. I could hardly process that people would want to mingle and eat and drink. How could you be so insensitive at a time like this?! Obviously, I had no experience with funerals. I had been known to be different my whole life, never fitting into the norm of cultural expectations, and now I said "no" to refreshments. We did, however, invite people to come and talk with us, to read the tribute I had written. Then we all climbed into our cars to go to the cemetery. I had really wanted David with us, but my mother-in-law had strongly discouraged it, saying that she felt it would be inappropriate for a boy as young as 4 to go to a cemetery. We left him with someone living next to the church. At the gravesite, a few words were spoken, and as her coffin was lowered into the ground, I could no longer watch. We got in the car and left. Gone … home, home without our baby. She was left in the ground.

The first few weeks I felt held up in a cloud and sustained. This was the result of people's prayers. I felt a close connection with the Lord and could think of ways to be grateful. That very first Sunday we went back to church. A lady asked me how I could possibly still have faith in God after what had just happened, saying she certainly would not keep her faith if that happened to her. It felt oddly like a rebuke from her of my attitude.

Starting to Journal

I had never kept a journal before. A diary yes, as a kid. But I started to write a journal after Amber left us. These are some of my journal entries:

> **September 8, 1992.**
> I sat in the Sunday morning service August 16th wondering where and what I would be doing the next Sunday. Surely I could not still be so big and uncomfortable with my baby about to be born. Would I be in the hospital? Could I be home again? I wondered how long it would be before I would be back in church again. Little did I know, the next time would be for my daughter's funeral. How little we know of what our future holds. I've been told, "Oh, if only I could have faith like yours, it would be so marvelous." What we've experienced from the Lord has not much to do with the amount of faith we've attained.
>
> Although scriptures hidden in our heart have been of great comfort, the truth is, it is not what we know but who we know. If all we had was faith in what amount of faith we have, we would have been swept away with grief, anguish, and anger. The Person of JESUS Christ and knowing His sweet gentleness and Presence is all you need. People have wondered whether to stay away from me or what could they do to reach out to us? I have longed for and been so satisfied just by a warm comforting hug. I have not needed people to understand at all—just hug me with warmth. This

has been done through even just a little message left on our door, cards, listening to me or just a few kind words. I'll never again think I have to understand a person's pain before I can reach out and hug them (literally or figuratively). What I'm going through is like Job sitting out openly scrapping his sores and so abased and pitiful.

I have had the most overwhelming confidence of God's Spirit making me a strong and mighty tower. I have received amazing strength from the Lord, from people praying and from talking to people and telling them what I am experiencing has given great strength. In the first 2 or 3 days I envisioned JESUS as He was beaten with stripes and every lash, I felt a blow across my heart of agony, yet there was a satisfying and good feeling about it. The verse "That I many know him, and the power of his resurrection, and the fellowship of his sufferings, being made conformable unto His death." Many times, I caught myself thinking of my womb and the tomb and the words "it is empty, come and see" and it was good.

David's first response when we told him Amber had a bad heart and was going to die, his face clouded, and you could see him trying to control himself. He said "but I don't want JESUS to take Amber. I don't want her to die." And he grabbed her, pulled her to himself, and hugged her. I have seen glimpses of David's maturing amazingly fast since I took him out to Abbotsford 7 days ago.

August 27, 1992
David's prayer at bedtime "Dear JESUS, why did you take the baby, we are all very sad but every day, every day we'll be happier and happier."

August 28, 1992

David: "Do you think I could shoot JESUS? Could JESUS die if I shot Him?" I told David when JESUS comes, He will have Amber with Him. He asked excitedly, "will they come here?" I said no, we will go with them to heaven. The boy's face shone with excitement and pleasure. He had a "quickening of his spirit" of revelation and Hope.

Sunday September 6th, 1992
This past week has been exceedingly difficult. Last Sunday I realized I had been sustained the whole time as if up on a cloud. None of it of unreality at all—just pure comfort and protection from God's Spirit as well as people's prayers and kindness. Well last Sunday I came crashing down from the cloud so hard and hit the ground in a broken, aching mess. My whole body ached. The problem was I allowed people's comments to get the better of me. It started with the question, "Would I rather Amber had been a miscarriage?"

October 6, 1992
David said on the way for his doctor appointment, "Maybe Amber died because we didn't love her enough. Babies die because no one loves them."

After four weeks, I was still consumed with the memories of my pregnancy with Amber and her birth. I had three ultrasounds; every one of them could have shown half her heart was missing. Only on the last one, the technician noted a "shadow." The doctor decided that since it was so close to my due date it would be better to just wait. I was so glad I had not known! I was deeply grateful that I had nine months of sheer pleasure and anticipation of our new child's arrival. Even the birth seemed perfect! Amber was so beautiful, pink, and healthy when she was born. Nothing amiss to cause anyone a second look. Over and over I would re-live that fabulous birth. All of that counted now in immense ways in my memory bank. It was all good. If I had known I was going to give birth to a baby that had no chance at life … I do not know how I could have borne it.

After a month, I started to take sleeping pills. I listened over and over to the cassette tape from the funeral. Again, here are some words from my journal:

> It was four weeks yesterday since Amber was born and it has been the birth I go back to over and over—not the Thursday of her death. We have finally listened to the tape of the funeral. But I felt so different yesterday. Before, grief came in waves and would leave. Dr. Cathie explained it at first as contractions. But yesterday a blanket of grief settled on my heart and it aches! And it does not seem to leave. Is this where they talk about the first month being in shock and then the reality sets in?
>
> This is harder than I thought it would be. I thought I could manage it ok. Although I have gone to the brink and wondered about insanity and found I can bring myself back. This pain, and grief is not as bad as the two times before that I have hit bottom. I understand why I hurt now. I did not understand before or know what to do about it. Twice before my life ended. Amber was not the end of my life. It hurts, but not as bad.

My church gave me the opportunity to continue with my volunteering, but there was no way I could resume my life as if nothing had happened. We had borrowed a crib from someone at church so took it back to church. They left it up against the wall for weeks. Every time we went to church, I would see the crib. The one that was supposed to be in my house, with my baby in it. David started to question if we loved him and acted insecure. His headaches and tummy aches resulted in many doctor visits.

A kind woman in our church gave us a huge gift by often taking David to her house to play with her boys. What a treasure!

When a child is born the time comes to call and register the birth. It was so ridiculously hard to pick up that phone and tell the man on the other end, "I am calling to report that the child I gave birth to is no longer alive." To my immense relief, the voice on the other end of the line was one of the most compassionate, caring men I have encountered. He was so kind. He was so sorry. With great difficulty he explained to me that he would need to send me a birth certificate stamped DECEASED. Not long after the call an envelope arrived in the mail. It was an act of God. We received a birth certificate for Amber Lynne Phillipps. Nothing stamped on it! This brought me so much joy in such a tough time. Was this a mistake or was it the kindness of a compassionate man?

> **November 12, 1992**
> It has been so long since I wrote because I have been in such a deep pit, I could not write. I would never want anyone to see the words I would have written. I thought my two earlier depressions were bad, but they were nothing in comparison. I had debilitating pain in my chest. Deep dark pit. No reason to get out of bed. Literally lived from phone call to phone call from Dr. Cathie. Seeing her once a week. An eternity between visits. I have kept going for her. I have felt like the children of Israel crossing the Red Sea and the waters closing in on me halfway across. Also, I have felt very much like I was drowning, allowed up at moments to gasp for air and pushed down again. Have not "felt" God—only that Dr Cathie has been there every time I have reached out and lots of other people keep phoning me and being kind. It is like God sustained me by His Spirit for four weeks and then let me experience His love through other people.

After twelve weeks I started to write about wanting to shake off the deep grief. "*Will it take me longer?*" I asked myself, after reading a book about someone else's grief. Mine felt so much worse than her written words. Mine I described as the three D's–Devastation, Despair, Destroyed. I started to record the number of good days I had in a row. They grew from four consecutive days to six! I finally felt I could climb up and out of the pit. Although my heart was aching and burning like fire, I was climbing out. I discovered what it meant that my heart could bleed. I would bleed drops of pain. I would shock myself with the ferocity of my feelings and reactions. I wondered about the casket lowered in the ground. I did not watch. What if they never put her in there? When I went to the cemetery my body reacted violently towards the caretakers of the grounds. I shouted inside my head; *How could you be such horrible men as to want to work the grounds of this awful place*?! I wanted to pound them with my fists.

Then I would spiral downward, wondering if it was my fault. Were my baths too hot while I was carrying Amber? Did God put His finger on her heart to stop it from growing? Was it our waterbed? A trip to the pediatrician for David made me wonder even more about Amber's condition. The doctor said there had been a high number of births with the same condition as Amber. The doctor said if he were us, he would have that investigated. Why so many in our area? Check the water we were drinking or…? But I had no energy to pursue something like this.

When I talked about Amber in front of David and said the words "*had* a baby," he corrected me and said, 'No, Mama, you *have* her." He went on to describe a vivid dream he had where God showed him that we would also have another baby girl. I attended the funeral of a friend's mother and, as I observed the casket, had another violently strong reaction. My internal being cried that I wanted to be the one to crawl right into that casket. Let me be the one! I felt that God had destroyed me in every area of my life, and I wanted to be the one in there. Then the gentle words of my Saviour spoke so clearly right to my heart, "Because He lives, you will live also."

I wrote;

> I wish I could love Amber in proportion to how long I had her. Such a brief time. But no, I love her just as much as I love David; it hurts that much.

A cousin of Dan's sent a Scripture that really surprised me. The Lord said to Moses in Exodus 4:11,

"Who has made man's mouth? Who makes him mute, or deaf, or seeing, or blind? Is it not I, the Lord?"

I now had scripture confirming the thoughts that had already been planted in my heart. I could willingly release Amber to the Lord. When Dan and I called a wonderful helpline, they told us we were exceptional as we were miles ahead in our healing than most couples at that stage.

"It is of the Lord's mercies that we are not consumed, because his compassions fail not. They are new every morning: great is thy faithfulness. But though he cause grief, yet will he have compassion according to the multitude of his mercies." (Lamentations 3:22–23, 32 KJV)

David

One November day that year, close to Remembrance Day, when I picked up David from preschool, he asked me if I knew what happened to dead people's bodies. Flooded with remorse that we had kept David from attending the graveside with Amber, I pulled the car to the side of the road. As I explained to my little son about the casket and the graveside, I asked him if I had made a mistake in keeping him from being there with us. He immediately said, "Yes!" I pulled him close and he burst into tears. His whole body shook with sobs. He cried, "But I wanted just a wee peek of Amber when she was dead." I told him how we took him to play with children at the church while we went to the cemetery. His face looked so troubled. I asked if he would like to go right then to see where she was buried. When we arrived at the cemetery, he climbed out of our car and asked, "Exactly where is she so I can put my finger on it?" Once standing by the grave, he asked, "Can we dig the dirt up so I can see her?"

I regretted not including David at the graveside service, so we made many decisions to specifically include him. I had heard about studies with children in similar circumstances. The ones who were sent away to stay somewhere else until their families were over the worst of their grieving did not fare as well as children who stayed with their parents. I was so grateful that the three of us pulled together when we could have been pushed apart.

That first Easter after Amber died, I was in a grocery store with David when I spotted a beautiful stuffy: a white Easter bunny. Tears pooled around my heart. I wished I could buy it for Amber, but I had no Amber to give it to. I tried to pull myself together for David's sake, and then thought, *No! I will include him.* Pointing to the rabbit, I said to him, "If we had Amber, I would buy that rabbit for her." David reached for the bunny and exclaimed, "Let's buy it anyway!" So, we did. We named her Amber-Bunny and she still sits on my bed to this day. God showed us grace and mercy, but I was not able to see it well at the time.

Pregnant!

To our utter surprise, three months after Amber was born, we were pregnant again. Having had so much trouble in the past with becoming pregnant, combined with our shattered hearts in grief, we had not yet entertained the thought of another baby. We were thrilled! Everywhere I went, I saw someone pregnant or with a new baby. Now, finding myself pregnant again suddenly opened opportunities for me to look at life through fresh eyes. I could look at baby items in hopes of my new child, instead of only through heartache and loss.

Sadly, some things became complicated in our church. Politics and people can sure mess things up! We chose to leave our church and start brand new somewhere else, recognizing that we needed simplicity. People did not understand why we left, and we lost most of our friends.

The new church seemed okay to let us sit in silence and not become involved in any way. We felt like we were invisible, and my agony was immense as we went through the rituals of Sunday morning church.

Extra tests were done on my unborn baby to ensure his heart was fine. The pain in my chest was so great at times that I felt I could not even breathe; it was like a fire burned a hole in my chest. I thought I would cease breathing and just die from the agony of pain. I asked, in all sincerity, "Is it possible to die from pain?" The doctor assured me that it would not kill me. I started to have panic attacks, all so very foreign to me.

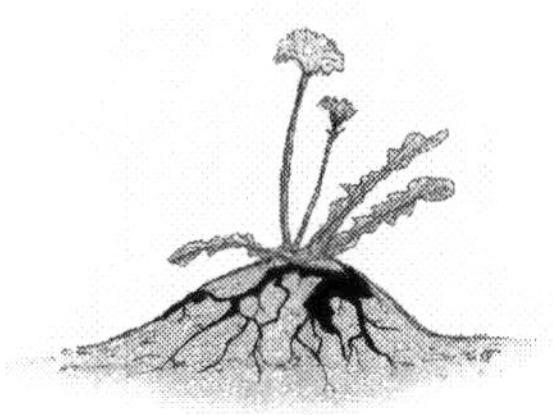

Chapter Five

Falling into a Pit

Starting with the January after Amber's birth, we had so many hard things happen. Dan's father died. Dan's job ended. His aunt died; his grandma died, too. When we left our church, we lost almost all our friends. It felt as though life had turned against us. I wrote in my journal:

> After Amber's death I stood so tall, so strong, when the Lord took her away. I tried to have all the right attitudes and to believe Him completely in all things. Since then I have been destroyed so there is nothing left of me inside. I am nobody. There is a raging wind that is more powerful than I that wants to destroy me. God is not helping me anymore so I cannot fight it anymore. I say, "Be not overcome of evil but overcome evil with good" but God is not real to me anymore. Nothing seems real. Only the pressure in me to destroy myself.

I found great comfort in Dan and the many picnics we had with our son. David was such a perfect child for us, always so pleasant and happy to go anywhere, and he loved the long car rides. These long rides in our old car were a profound comfort for me. I could not sleep in my bed, but the sound of the engine would immediately lull me to sleep in the car. The old-fashioned vacuum windshield wipers on our 1939 Chevy made the same rhythmic suction sound of Amber's breathing at the end of her short life.

As our baby grew in my womb, so did the pressure and pain in my chest. It was so debilitating that I really thought it could be the end. Then the pain would shift to crazy thoughts and I would be absolutely tormented in my mind. I couldn't decide which was worse, the physical pressure and pain or the tormenting thoughts. I asked my doctor for a certain medication that had helped me in my teen years. I tried everything I could think of to find some relief. Day and night the pain and torment would build and build until I thought I would either explode or die. I became aware that there was something else wrong with me, something other than the death of my child. This was more than just grief.

Paralyzed

I would think about Amber and then try to put the pain away to be present for my life and son. When I'd go back in a moment of privacy to look at her baby pictures, or allow myself the luxury of connecting with my love for her, something else would happen. Something sinister.

When I was six months pregnant with our second son, I began to feel like a train was bearing down on me, ready to run me over. I was stuck on the train track unable to move. Living in this horror, tormented for days, I became paralyzed in fear.

My first hospital admission after losing Amber brought back memories buried so deeply that only something as catastrophic as the death of my child could have shaken them loose. The first of these memories was triggered in the night by a most frightening dream. It was a dream like I had never experienced before—a dream that altered my life. In it, I was back in my uncle and aunt's house and their sewer backed up. It backed up and up; the pressure was extremely intense and terrifying. Eventually the whole house exploded and spewed sewage all over me. I awoke in sheer horror. Once awake I had the very first memory that I had unknowingly buried, sealed off with the intention to never have it surface again.

I remembered being severely abused by a houseboy we had in Africa—tormented, mocked and sexually abused. I became aware of unusual smells and realized I had also been drugged. I also remembered being raped by a doctor while I was in the hospital in Vancouver as a teenager.

Ironically, this doctor had believed I had suppressed memories that I was not in touch with. He claimed my symptoms could not be only from the rejection of my parents; there had to be something more. He thought there had to be extreme anger suppressed deep within me that he wanted me to express. He tried so many ways to get me to cooperate and tell him. I knew nothing and had nothing to tell him. I was extremely upset that he would not accept that the rejection by my parents was enough for me to have acted like I did.

One day he got out Styrofoam swords to play-fight with me. He wanted me to let out my anger in a controlled setting by forcing me to hit him with the sword. I felt very awkward and embarrassed and would not cooperate with him. He became so impatient and angry with me that he eventually lost control of himself. He hit me with his sword, threw it down on the floor and marched out of the room. I have always remembered this experience.

His next tactic: he gave me sodium amatol treatments to try to get me to talk. Apparently, I had nothing to say other than to cry for my mother, wanting her to come and sit with me. Then he added another drug to which I had a bad reaction. I could not get out of bed for days and they had to assign someone to sit with me around the clock; I could not be left alone. They even had patients take turns sitting with me. All this I had remembered previously. What I had not remembered until the horrible dream in the hospital that day: this doctor was so angry he could not conquer me that he came into my room in the night and raped me. After this dream and the recall of that first memory, I was no longer able to shut off the memories. Other memories swarmed back, out of my control.

The nurses heard about my memory, about what had happened to me, and I overheard them talking. "It is such a shame what is happening to that woman. A woman her age, having memories like she is having—it's a bottomless pit you fall into and never come out of." When I heard those shocking words describing me, something fierce rose within me and internally I shouted, *NO!! That will NOT be my future. I will fight, and I will win!!*

On my way home from that hospital stay, God, in His mercy and timing, had me hear on the radio that a different doctor from that very same hospital from my teen years had just been charged with sexual assault of a minor. That doctor had also come into my room at night and I had sent him out very quickly! (I have always remembered this incident). Now, twenty-plus years later, I was hearing this on the radio, just when I needed to. It was confirmation that my memories were real.

Back home, I found myself in the most terrible, lonely, and isolated state of mind. More memories surfaced. I began to remember unspeakable ritual abuse that I experienced as a child in Kenya, at the hands of bad people. When I first began to remember the horrible, evil things done to me in the name of satan, my immediate response had been to run to my pastor and my church, to ask them to pray for me. If ungodly people could conduct a ceremony with me in such evil, then certainly godly people could do the same for me in the Name of God. But what I found instead was that all the churches around me were "neutered". Nobody seemed to know what to do with me or how to help me. I became invisible, my pain unbearable. I would lie on my bed in agony, living moment by moment, watching the ticking clock on my bedroom wall, suspended in time that would not release me.

Shortly after Amber died, my pastor gave me a Scripture about God comforting me so that I in turn could comfort others (2 Corinthians 1:4). At the time, this really upset me. I had a dagger in my heart and could hardly manage to walk and talk; the last thing I had on my mind was comforting someone else. However, the hugs and phone calls from the church were of immense value. Even when we were too numb in grief to get up to answer the phone, hearing the message on the answering machine was tremendously comforting. If you think that you don't know how to help a person who is grieving, understand that any caring gesture goes a long way. Staying away because you don't know what to say or do adds to the grieving person's loneliness. A hug would go right to my soul in comfort, even when people didn't know what to say.

Andrew, A Gift from God

Our second precious son, whom we nicknamed "bright-eyes," was born to us in the middle of my worst imaginable nightmares of pain. I was gripped in the horrors and torments of constant memories. It was a living hell I would not wish on anyone.
In remembering, I would re-experience some of the torment. Walking down those mental and emotional halls, I never knew what was lurking around each corner. Most certainly it would be a monster seeking to devour me. I learned what body memory meant as I would smell strange odors, feel sensations on my skin, and feel unexplainable pain in my organs. My rational thoughts would be overridden with disturbing thoughts that didn't originate from me. But most of all, fear and terror would overwhelm me; fear that would be suspended around me like a dark, heavy cloud turning into torture and torment. Believing I had stopped breathing only to find I was still alive.

In the midst of all this, our baby grew larger and larger in my womb, taking over my body without my having any control. This, and the effect of the memories, had me in a state of continual panic. My doctor was prepared to declare me incapable of looking after my new little one, but invested great care and attention in trying to help me be stable enough to avoid that scenario. She had become my best friend. Our relationship brought me much stability.

Contractions and labour began without my having any say. Dr. Cathie ensured us that the birth would be as fabulous as possible. The epidural allowed me to be fully awake and engaged in the entire process, without any pain! Dr. Cathie brought her hook-rug to work on, and she sent the nurses away. Just the three of us to welcome this new child into the world. Andrew came with such ease, Dr. Cathie loudly exclaimed, "Look! He's crawling out right now!" as if I had to do no work at all. We received him with as much joy as we were able. Andrew was born the day before what would have been Amber's first birthday. I started out the day remembering Amber and ended the day holding my brand-new son in my arms. The next morning, I remembered my baby who was celebrating her first birthday with JESUS while I gazed at the new baby in my arms. Andrew Daniel. His names mean brave, strong, courageous, manly; God is my judge; God is my strength.

The delivery nurse was the same one that had helped with both David and Amber. When she saw me in the condition that I was in she sternly but lovingly said to me, "What has happened to you? Look at you! The only way to get out of this is to face the wind; put your face to the wind and walk out the other side!" Those words so deeply affected me; I remember them clearly to this day. They helped me focus on moving forward with my new little one in my arms.

Once home, and now a family of four, we placed Andrew in a bassinet beside our bed, so I could easily pull him up and into the bed to nurse him in the night. I had read and heard about bad scenarios of children born into stressful circumstances such as mine, but for our little miracle baby, that proved untrue. At bedtime every single night, without fail, Andrew would laugh and laugh, and then laugh some more before falling asleep.

Every time we would look at him, his eyes would shine, very quickly earning him the nickname "bright-eyes." He was a perfect baby with a personality and resilience that brought nothing but joy into our home. It was as though he was a light to shine into our dark place. I am so deeply grateful to God for His kindness and great mercy in giving us Andrew.

Crisis of Faith

One monumental day at the cemetery, about three years after Amber's birth, I had it out with God. I was beyond devastated. I had been such a strong Christian. My belief system was "God and I could handle anything." My conviction was that if I had enough faith, I would not need a psychiatrist. Now I was being told I needed one. I wrestled with God at the cemetery. I laid it all out before Him. I believed in Him, trusted Him, and yet I had fallen so *far*. I felt that God was nowhere to be found. My suffering was too immense. I talked to God and voiced my deepest thoughts. *If God is not there for me, why be a Christian*? I sincerely considered walking away from my faith, and wondered what that would mean. I had loved the Lord my entire life. What would I be without Him? An alcoholic? I would still be a wife and mother. What difference would it make to not be Christian? I sat a long time pondering everything.

Eventually I arrived at the same place the disciples had in the Bible, in the book of John. JESUS had said something the people did not like, something that was too hard for them to process, and many of His followers walked away. JESUS had turned to His twelve disciples and said, "Are you going to go away, too?" Peter replied, "Lord, where would we go? You alone have the keys to eternal life." I came to that same conclusion. I decided that JESUS giving up His life for me was enough. How could I ask Him for more? I decided that if He never did another thing for me my entire life, what He did on the cross securing my salvation was enough. I would not ask for more.

I left the cemetery that day feeling changed. I thought, even expected, that the angels were doing a happy dance for me. But to my dismay, I returned to the same hell of existence that I had endured the previous three years. It seemed nothing had changed in my circumstances, even though I had experienced that mental shift.

My psychiatrist described me as having all the symptoms of someone who had suffered severe abuse as a child. She told me I was suffering from Post Traumatic Stress Disorder. To me, psychiatrists did a good job with helping to medicate but had nothing else to offer that could help me. I turned to alcohol to help me endure. God in His grace and mercy helped me to wait until I knew Dan was on the SkyTrain on his way home before I'd start to drink. By the time I had passed out, he was home to look after the boys. Even while drinking this way, I worked extremely hard on healing myself. I began volunteering, which added much needed structure to my day. It gave me a sense of meaning, a feeling my life counted and had a purpose beyond me.

I was so grateful to God for allowing me to love being a mother. I seemed "a natural", even after such a hard loss. I was deeply grateful the Lord helped me to be there for my children, even amidst deep pain. A wonderful kind woman from our church became Auntie Sue to our children. She faithfully helped me clean my house and would just "be there" for me and the boys. For well over two years she faithfully came to support me and love my children, all the while treating me with such patience, and without any judgment.

Once I started to feel more able to cope with life, I figured it was time to fix my spiritual condition. I went for some counselling in my neighbourhood. Some of it was practical and helpful. I was told to imagine my memories as clothes hung up in the closet that I could take out one at a time to look at. Or I was to imagine the memory as an animal and then talk to it, describe it. I would see an enormous elephant that was coming to step on me, crush me. The counsellor would then tell me to describe it, his eyes, ears. Sometimes the deadness I would feel was suffocating; other times it felt like I was an iceberg, frozen; unable to do anything.

I then attempted to find a Christian counsellor only to be told that none would take on someone who had suffered from satanic ritual abuse. It was devastating to see all the qualifications hanging on the wall in the counselling office only to be told I was too messed up for anyone to be able to deal with me! Thankfully, with deep relief Dan and I discovered the wonders of a good prayer counsellor. He became very dear to our family through our countless appointments. He knew all about satanic ritual abuse and had many people come to him for help. He understood the confusion in my heart of having been raised in a Christian home and yet deeply struggling with, "How could such horrors have happened to me?" Nothing I said fazed him.

This counsellor was a wonderful, gentle man. I would have a two-hour appointment with him once a week. Usually at least half of our time together was spent praying for me. He discovered that eye movement therapy was the most effective for me (EMDR—Eye Movement Desensitization and Reprocessing). I absolutely hated it. But as I cooperated and then went home to my family, I would find things were different! I began to see the fruits of my efforts, and my family and home life became better. The counsellor's methods helped me work through past trauma without retraumatizing me in the process. Some people who tried to help me only added new trauma to the old and it would take me a long time just to recover from the new trauma. But this man was more than just a counsellor—he was a kind, patient, prayer warrior. He told me he found me emotionally mature. That was the same thing Dan and I were told shortly after Amber died. Together with this counsellor, I was able to start to process my grief and trauma. I persevered and fought, and then persevered some more. I learned so much of my prayer life from listening to him pray for me. He knew how to pray for me so my life would be different when I got home. What an immense relief. What a gift from God!

The Lord had picked a perfect man to be my husband. There are no perfect people in this world, but we can find one who is perfect for us. That is Dan. He determined long ago that he would make my mental health and well-being his priority. If we had to go into debt to have me healthy, that is what we would do. People get loans for cars and mortgages, so why not prioritize me? What a man! He is and has been such a solid stable rock.

I became numb to some of my most basic needs. I would forget to eat. It wasn't until I began to feel faint that I would then remember, "Oh, I need to eat some food!" I lost so much weight my body was like a skeleton.

I began teaching the 2 & 3-year-olds' Sunday School class. It seemed like it would be a bizarre and difficult thing for me to do but, when I looked into the faces of those precious children and told them about JESUS, I escaped my pain, even if for only a few moments. This started me on a path of understanding how I could give myself away to others and find purpose for myself. Life wasn't all about me.

But I was lonely, longing for meaningful friendships. Finally, in my lonely state in our church, I determined to stop waiting for relationships, for friendships, to happen. I had been angry that these relationships were not happening, so I decided instead to be the kind of friend that I wanted to find in others, to treat people how I wanted them to treat me. I discovered the value of considering others, and I learned how to serve, how to demonstrate what I wanted and needed, rather than being angry that I wasn't noticed. I learned to stop playing games with people and become better at articulating my needs. It saved a whole lot of time to just be straightforward with people! I needed a lot of help, and I learned how to humble myself and ask for it.

I was always a firm believer that I did not have to remember everything that happened to me. What was necessary, however, was for me to be in touch with the thought process that had caused me to arrive at the belief system that I had. What I walked away with when the trauma happened, what I believed about God, what I believed about myself, was not correct. Is God safe? Am I bad? I had to go back and rewrite the truth deep in my heart.

Professionals that could only set the stage for me to *talk* about the trauma caused me to regress. The loving arms of Dr. Cathie or admissions to hospital were the only way I could allow the memories to surface. I had to be in a safe environment in order to allow the memories into my conscious mind. They were that horrific. I often thought, in later years, I would not have survived if God had not provided my friendship with Dr. Cathie. Although I felt a complete disconnect from God, Cathie's arms of love *were* God loving me. I just couldn't see it at the time.

Interlude

My home, my Refuge. Sitting here on my comfortable couch, laptop on my lap. The house we bought in the mountains, tall trees shadowing our beautiful home. Watching wee hummingbirds coming close to touch the climbing-rose next to my window. It seems the world has gone mad. Wracked in fear, uncertainty. Violence and fear abound. Covid-19—a word we wish we had never heard. Lives lost and robbed from loved ones. Others denying it is real. Yet my home has captured a peaceful sanctuary. I am a happy and content woman. My kids are grown and flourishing in their individual homes. My adoring husband still goes to work, and life goes on as if we are untouched.

This day, a Saturday, I reach for my journal. My own recordings of my life from 1993. My eyes stare at the opened page. I freeze, catapulted back twenty-seven years in time. Finding it hard to breathe as I see words describing something even worse than the death of my beautiful daughter. Amber's death tore my heart out, but the memories of the childhood abuse had destroyed me as a person. I wanted to be stepped on and crushed like a worm on the ground, someone to please put me out of my misery! I had fallen into something worse than the death of my child. I close the journal, unable to proceed. Body shaking, heart racing.

I must move forward. I must fast-track to a healed place! I will remember to live out of my healing as I learned long ago. I will lean into His healing Spirit like this girl in this picture lets her hair blow in the wind. I will trust God to help me, to write through me out of His place of hope. I don't need to write out of pain and darkness. I can write out of my healed heart.

PART TWO

CONTRADICTIONS

Chapter Six

Prisoner of the Past

In the early years after Amber's death, I spent hours upon hours taking care of my birds and my sons, desperately trying to get ahold of God. I felt very much like I had lost God, like He had turned against me. Something about remembering old things activated new captivity inside of me. I found when I remembered something that happened to me, I then needed to grow into a new dimension of healing. The memory released another dark captivity. Another battle to be won. The experienced memory would hold me captive until I learned to walk out of it.

I had really believed I was a strong Christian. I did everything I knew to help myself. I memorized more verses, fasted and prayed, fell on my face, and begged. Nothing seemed to help. I clearly remember one day feeling a strong need to be "born-again," as if I had never done that before. So, I did. I said the sinner's prayer and invited God into my life. It felt like everything I had been taught about God, right from childhood, now needed to be relearned. I told my husband that my foundation was cracked, and I had nothing solid to stand on. I started from square one to relearn about God and how to have a relationship with Him. I figured that if I had gone so wrong, I needed to go back to the beginning and learn anew what I did not understand.

I needed to wander and be on the move like I had wandered the neighbourhood as a child. I spent endless hours driving or sitting at the ocean. Each time, as I arrived home late at night, I would find a small light on and a note from Dan saying he had left a light burning for me.

I began to see how my comprehension of God and my view of His Word had been harmful to me. My faith had not held me. What I thought was a solid rock that I could stand on did not hold me. Soon after Amber died, I had turned to alcohol and cigarettes, desperate for something to secure me, as well as needing a way to punish myself. I immersed myself in reading an informative book, *Don't Waste Your Sorrows* by Paul E. Billheimer. I wished so much that it would bring me comfort but instead felt myself excluded as the writer explained all those wonderful verses for those who were suffering for Christ's sake. I did not think my suffering was for Christ, so they could not apply to me. I neither knew why I was suffering so much nor how to help myself. I did not seem to be finding any comfort from my faith. When I looked at my neighbours I'd say to myself, "They suffer just the same as me! Knowing God is not making my pain any less than what they experience. When cut, I bleed just the same, whether I am a believer or not."

I felt so restricted and confined by "do's" and "don'ts." I wanted something—anything—to bring me relief, but nothing did. God said He would never leave me. Why did I feel that He had? All the verses I tried to claim, tried to stand on, did not help me but rather set me back. Verses that told me that God would not let the waters overwhelm me or the fire burn me frustrated me. I certainly *was* overwhelmed, felt destroyed, and burned to a crisp. In 1 Corinthians 10 it said God would not allow me to suffer or be tempted beyond what I was able, that God would make a way of escape for me. I even shouted that verse at God some days as I begged and begged Him to help me not give in to smoking. No matter how hard I tried, I couldn't seem to make a connection with the God I had learned to love. I struggled and strived trying to learn why depression seemed to affect my spiritual connection so severely. Why did my baby dying, and my remembering childhood abuse cost me a loss of connection with God? I agonized over this for more than six years. Who had made a mistake? Was God wrong, or was I wrong? My life felt like such a contradiction.

I had heard that in marriage you would only have one spouse "up" and one spouse "down" at any given time. Help each other, right? Not so with us. It seemed both Dan and I fell into a pit at the same time, especially in the early days of the intense grief. We would pray and pray and feel dashed to the ground, hopes destroyed. Dan commented that trusting God and praying could be equated to going out to start his old car. If eight times out of ten the car would not start, he would quickly lose confidence in the car. That described our spiritual state. Occasionally we would be encouraged, but most of the time disappointed.

I felt like I was drowning, desperate to cling to anything that would help me keep my head above the waters. My love for my children was immense but the pain was becoming greater than even my motherlove. At times I felt trapped by my children and my husband. If it were not for them, I reasoned, I could easily just let my life slip away. I did, however, find out that when I thought about walking away from my faith, it was like saying I didn't know how to play the piano or ride a bike. Once you know how to play or ride, that knowledge is inside of you for life. My faith stayed inside of me like that, even when my brain tried to tell me otherwise.

I felt like a prisoner of my past, bars around me that would not let me loose. No relief, no hope that I could touch. Oddly, I was able to connect with the Lord better at the cemetery. Sitting on the grass with a bottle of alcohol, I would talk to God. I could almost feel a connection there that did not seem to ever happen at church. I felt so utterly dead inside. My body longed and craved for something, but I did not know what that was or how to satisfy that need. I felt very much that my whole life had been wasted. That is a cry throughout all of my old journals, "*My life has been wasted.*"

Survival Mode

Attending church became an empty routine, a test of endurance. It used to be something that brought life to me, but that seemed no longer attainable. I put my hope in believing that what I *once* had was real. Believing that going through the motions of attending church would one day help me again, even if it appeared to no longer help me. For now, it made me far angrier; it brought disappointment to the forefront of my heart.

When I wasn't volunteering and David was at school, I would often lay on my bed and stare at the clock in endless agony: five minutes feeling like twelve hours. Time became my enemy. I went to great lengths to record details. On a calendar, I faithfully recorded how many days I had been successful in not smoking. I highlighted my good days and added them up, over and over, so grateful for anything that gave me a reason to get up and do something. I became so focused on details as a way to cope that I even recorded the date each of my birds laid their eggs and the predicted hatch date. Focusing on keeping records kept me going just enough to care for my sons.

However, the horrific memories kept coming. I remembered how my pets had been harmed and used to silence me as a child. I remembered how my beloved dog Lassie was slashed down her side with a *panga* (a machete-like African tool) by intruders one night. It took many stitches to repair her injuries. My family had blamed men coming in the night to steal parts off our car for the attack. But now I knew otherwise. It had been done by evil men to silence and terrify me. Another thing I remembered was the missing bird we thought flew away, the golden crested crane. It had its tongue ripped out to show me what would happen to me if I were to talk.

One specific early memory required a couple years of intense therapy. As a child, I had been laid on a deceased old man as an attempt to transfer gifts from the deceased to the living. Remembering the various things that had been done to me was too much for my mind to process. This was much more than the houseboys but other oppressors as well, including some women. I have never been able to recall where my family were at these times as I was taken away.

These horrors affected my ability to make good decisions. When Andrew was six months old, I overdosed on pills, a dangerous amount that could have seriously harmed me, especially my heart. It was my cry for someone to please notice my unbearable agony. My cry was not to die but to have relief from my suffering. I knew that the risk of that cry could have been death.

I awoke in ICU with a desperate need to breastfeed my son. I insisted and begged the nurse to bring me a machine to pump my milk. A nurse rudely told me I should not be taking up a valuable bed in ICU as people who respected their lives needed it. All I could think of was my baby and was immensely relieved when they brought me a breast pump. I knew that as soon as Dan took the bottle of freshly pumped milk home, he would throw it out as I was so full of drugs. But it gave me hope, gave me purpose in trying.

Alone on my hospital bed, my heart bled great drops of pain. I had loved being a mother so much when David was born. I did everything I could in caring for all his needs. Dan didn't change any of David's diapers (yes, cloth diapers) because I loved caring for him so much. When Dan got home from work, I wanted him to enjoy our sons, not work more. So I had done it all. Andrew had never had a bottle in his life; he had only been breastfed. And now I had tried to take my life and left Dan with a six-month-old baby that was completely dependent on me. I had just made my life so much worse. Thank God for Dan's mom who took care of Andrew and David when Dan needed help! My hospital stays were never long; I would quickly rebound. I was deeply grateful that I was still able to resume breastfeeding Andrew once I got home.

As I learned to enter a rhythm of mothering my two sons, the Lord started to bless me with many wonderful healing moments in between the terribly dark times. I loved my children and the fun we had together. Andrew's birthday celebration was always followed by Amber's. We would decide together whether to go to the cemetery or go for a picnic. One year, when it came time for David's birthday (the day after Amber's) he was so sad, crying, "Oh, Amber. I miss Amber. How can I be happy on my birthday when we do not have Amber?" I grabbed him by the shoulders and said in a stern voice, "David! This is your birthday and I want you to be happy. We have every reason to be happy and celebrate you today. I want you to go to the front door and throw all your sadness right out that door!" To my surprise, this little boy went to the door, opened it, and threw his hands out into the air. He came back in the house with big a smile on his face and we had a wonderful day with lots of laughter.

Welcoming Our Girl

One day a wonderful lady, a guest speaker at our church's women's event, was happily joking about how she knew deep in her heart when her family was complete, and she was done with babies. She asked the room full of women how many knew what she was talking about: "Done! You know when you are done!" The whole room erupted in laughter. But deep in my heart I did not feel done. My biological clock was definitely ticking, but Dan and I had a deep desire for another child. Doctor visits, prayer and longing had not resulted in another child. When I mentioned to Dan that all of the baby items were still in our closet, he replied that we had lots of room, no need to get rid of things before I was ready. I was not ready, so I hung on to everything, including my maternity clothes. We had figured out that we were able to get pregnant only one month out of the year–November. More Christmases rolled around, and each year I would feel "strange" and quickly go for another pregnancy test, only to be disappointed.

December 1998 it happened again, only this time the test was positive! Unable to contain my joy and not wanting to make a mistake I rushed out to buy two more tests. All three agreed. At 43 years of age, I was going to have another baby! I knew in my heart right away that this child was a girl. We found out early in the pregnancy that my hunch was correct. We were thrilled! Our home was filled with joy; even the boys were so happy. Andrew showed us a picture he had drawn of a rabbit and three tests, as if God had told him before we knew. Everyone we knew was happy for us. The Lord had helped us in so many ways and we had grown—and healed—a lot. I knew that was the biggest reason I had been able to get pregnant. So much healing and joy had come into my life. I knew well enough that this was not a replacement child and really did not appreciate people telling me so. We loved each one of our kids, including Amber, in their individual ways.

The day had long come and gone when I chose my friendship with Cathie over the doctor relationship. Cathie and I met weekly for lunches for well over twelve years. The structure and consistent faithful friendship brought much comfort. Yet when she heard I was pregnant, she announced, "No one in this world is more capable of delivering this baby than me!" I went back to being her patient for the pregnancy. What a delight to have your best friend care for you, all during pregnancy and birth! This meant that all four of our children would be delivered by her. Wow, God really loved me!

Incredibly, my due date was the same week as all my other children's birthdays. Dr. Cathie was determined that my daughters would not have the same birth dates. She admitted me to the hospital August 15 and attempted to induce labour. It felt like all of the specialists at hand had been invited to attend the birth, and maybe, because of my age and my history they had. I had previously read a fair bit about the warnings and dangers of delivering a baby at now 44 years of age. I was induced, and Dr. Cathie used all measures known to her to get that child out of me.

After three days of trying, late into that third night, I finally, reluctantly, signed forms for a C-section. Kimber would start to come down the birth canal, making it appear that all was well, and then suddenly scoot back up, keeping us all in suspense for endless hours. Just after I signed the forms, the hard contractions started with great force. Knowing that a C-section could not be performed once that happened, Dan and I shouted with glee! That meant that, even though the doctors tried everything within their power to not let it happen, Kimber was born on Amber's birthday. Seven years to the day! We were ecstatic! It meant so much to us to have the girls share the same birthdate. Seven is a special number to God and it was special to us.

That meant that David was born August 20; Amber and Kimber were born August 19; and Andrew was born August 18. My goodness. And to think we had trouble getting pregnant! We had simply needed to realize it could happen only one month in the year!

Nonetheless, I also had a significant amount of fear. I had read that many babies born to women my age died from "a failure to thrive." The words boomed in my head, especially since Kimber was born with some unusual boils and put on antibiotics. Once home, rather than gaining weight, she continued to lose weight. We went through some very anxious days, until we discovered that her darling little mouth was just too small to properly latch on while nursing! After that, we supplemented bottle-feeding her as well, and she gained weight, growing and thriving like any other baby. We were an incredibly happy family.

David and Andrew, now 11 and 6 years old, became my helpers. You would think I had planned to have built-in babysitters on purpose! When Andrew started school the next month, I missed him greatly, but that also meant that I had a brand-new baby to enjoy all to myself. I was so happy to be able to breastfeed Kimber for over two years. She was an absolutely delightful addition to our family, and we revelled in her with immense joy. I had felt a certain loneliness in our home that was dominated by males, and now I had a female to keep me company. I didn't think I could get any happier than I was at that time. I wrote in my journal that the boys did not want to even go out to play with their friends once they had a baby sister in the house. We all just "drank her in." We settled into three years of growth in our family's healing.

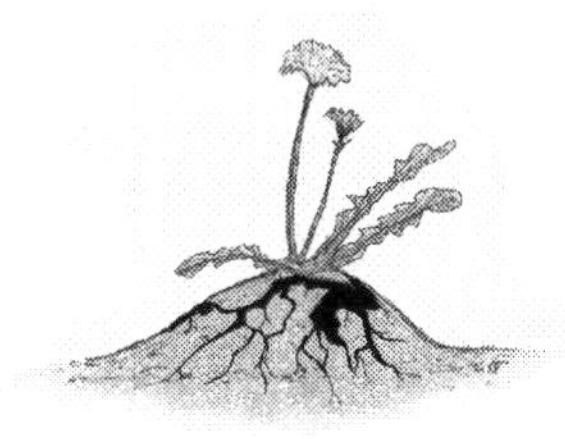

Chapter Seven

Moving On

After staying in the same church for ten years we decided it was time to make a change. When we left, I left all my pain from those years there and looked forward to starting afresh and on new footing. I had been involved in children's ministry and enjoyed working alongside my own children in clubs and classes at church. Because I had felt so very lonely in my grief and suffering, we had worked extremely hard at connecting with others. We opened our home to lots of people, always willing to entertain. One Christmas we had fifty people come to share goodies! We hosted many dinners and held Bible study groups in our home. Dan had become an elder in our church.

Now, at our new church, I felt like a scarecrow out in a field. If someone came near me, they seemed to be quickly scared away. I had spent many hours in counselling, reading books and studying, so why would this be? I would question to myself, "*I am a loving and caring person. Why do people withdraw from me*?"

I did develop some friendships, and a few of those special souls have remained good friends until this day. One day, as I was reeling in my despair, one of those friends, rather than consoling me, challenged me to write out ten things for which I was thankful. I was angry at her! How could she be so insensitive? But I finally decided to give it a try. It was a hard exercise to do, yet as I worked through my list, I started to understand how helpful it was.

Not only did I feel deformed and different from people around me, but I also realized that I was not able to learn the way most people learn. I never seemed to fit into the typical learning mode of other people. Having to learn modern technology has been a huge challenge. This same struggle with learning also seemed to affect my hearing from God the way it is formally taught. When I was (and still am) put on the spot to hear from God or when I would do the exercises in a book, I didn't seem to be able to grasp the teaching. Often my mental blocks around learning became a setback and discouraged me from even trying. So, I set out to draw close to God and hear Him in my own way. All of my learning seemed to come about in unusual ways.

Since we were in a new church, I wanted to be open to doing things differently. I also wanted to change from working with children to working in the women's ministry. I was so eager to make friends and be assertive. Thankfully, my excessive drinking days were over, but I still struggled deeply with smoking cigarettes. It felt like they were my best friends and supplied stability and direction for my life. What a crazy thing to say!! But that is how I felt. I realized that I had much in common with the drug addicts on the street and could identify with how impossible it is to walk away from the drugs. I felt that same inability to resist when it came to smoking.

But I still had so much pain in my heart and still such deep contradictions inside of me. I felt as though I had lived several different lives and they never intersected. I felt disabled, as if living without an arm and a leg, yet living in a world where everyone else had all their limbs but still expected me to function the same as them. Life was very painful for me, and a huge struggle. My loneliness was still immense. There were days I would feel so blessed and rewarded by all the ways I helped other people only to go home and reel in pain for many days. I would still get angry with people for not knowing how much pain I was in; for not understanding how hard life was for me.

One day early on in our new church, the Lord spoke clearly to my heart. He told me that He did not want me speaking to these new people. I was to be silent. If they came to talk to me, I could talk to them, but I was not to initiate a conversation. I had to give up my attempt at making friends. I was so upset with that! I wanted to make everybody my friend. However, as I obeyed and quietly watched and observed, I discovered so many new things. Some people came to me that probably would have stepped back if I had initiated the contact. I really wondered if what the Lord was asking of me was to be a permanent thing. I wondered if He did not want me involved in any ministry areas at all. I became willing in my heart to give it all up. If that was what God wanted of me, then yes, I would do that.

After I had mastered the art of being quiet, the Lord then showed me a picture of myself with a line down my center. One side of me was healed, the other side of me was still full of pain. The Lord said to me, "Now I want you to speak *only* out of your healed side, not out of your pain." A huge light bulb of understanding lit inside of me. I began to understand how many things I had been doing from the pain side. For example, saying, "Let's get together and form this group" was me speaking out of my pain. I knew what it was like to be ignored and lonely and I had wanted to form a group because of that. I understood that I was to now say, "Let us do this because I know how good, gentle and kind JESUS is. Let us meet to talk about that." What a huge breakthrough in my life! I learned to check where my words were coming from before I would speak.

The Pink Coat

At that same time, many churches started to offer courses on "Listening Prayer". It was so encouraging to find like-minded people who could help me with my hunger to connect with the

Lord. No longer would I have to rely on someone else's faith to direct me. I devoured the seminars and any contact I could get with new friends who had a like passion. The first course had great teaching on how to hear the Voice of God, but one thing stood out that became life transforming for me. The speaker taught us that, if in doubt, ask ourselves the question, "Does this sound and feel like the voice of my Saviour?"

Prior to this, I had shut my Bible in extreme discouragement for about six years. Every time I had tried to read it I felt either confused or condemned, so I had quit trying. I had so much of God's Word hidden in my heart from loving God since childhood, and I lived on that. I would pray as I went about the busyness of my day, never trusting myself to sit with the Bible and open my heart.

Soon after such great encouragement from the Listening Prayer Seminar, I decided I would try again. I opened my Bible, daring to open my heart to see what God might say to me. Within moments of reading the words on the page, my heart sank to the ground. Once again, I felt confused and condemned. Again the very thing I wanted to help me felt like my adversary. I felt such devastation; I was trying so hard. I closed my Bible. It was time to get my daughter from school. Running up the hill as I had done countless times, reeling in my own despair, suddenly words from the Seminar came back to me. The teacher had instructed, if in doubt, "Ask the question."

So, I did. I asked my heart, "*These words I just read from my Bible, do they sound like JESUS?*" Instantly I felt something dark that had been covering my entire body fall away. It was very profound; I clearly understood then that the enemy had been affecting my mind as I had read God's Word. What a wonderful breakthrough! It seemed that a greater gift than hearing God was this new ability to slam the door on the enemy! I now understood how I could be lied to even while reading the Bible. Then I remembered that JESUS himself had satan come to him, quoting a distortion of scripture as well. My life was about to drastically change. In my mind I saw a picture of hearing the Voice of the Lord; it looked like what happens when you let food colouring drop into a glass of water. Knowledge just suddenly dropped inside me.

One of the foundations for learning this type of prayer was to first find a safe place. We were instructed to ask the Lord to show us a safe place and, if we found none, we were told to pick a familiar verse, such as being in the palm of God's hand or sheltered under His wing. Just this instruction alone would throw me into panic! I felt I had no safe place. For so many years I could not quiet my heart to pray; I needed to keep my mind always focused and occupied so that the torment would not take over my mind and heart. Now I was being told to pick a safe place and quiet my heart?! That was far too daunting for me! The traumas from my childhood had utterly destroyed any possible sense of safety. I could not even imagine myself hiding inside a teddy bear or any other place of safety and protection.

Despite the insights I was gaining from the sessions, I still felt so messed up inside my heart, still felt an inability to pray and receive from God. I was desperate for help. The truth be known, I had always been desperate for help—I just hadn't found people who could help me. Now I had found them.

After Listening Prayer #1 came Listening Prayer #2, where we were to practice listening in prayer for others as well as receive prayer from them. Because of feeling so very unsafe, I was adamant that I'd have to be a fool to trust myself to the hands of people praying for me and hearing words from the Lord on my behalf, people who themselves were still learning. I sent a strongly worded letter to the instructor. In his response to my angry letter, I found him to be so gracious with me. He directed me to an alternative, one-on-one ministry.

This involved a weeklong session where a wonderful woman, with a pastor's heart, prayed for me three hours a day for five consecutive days. She prayed through my entire life, right from my birth to the present, praying about anything and everything

I wanted to bring up. Every sore spot or wound was taken to the Lord and opened for healing. It wasn't necessary that everything be remembered, but everything that caused pain must be opened and turned over to the Lord to touch and heal. I had to let it all go for healing. Paul says in Philippians 3:13, "… forgetting what lies behind and straining forward to what lies ahead…" I could not press on until those things behind received more healing. The hurts and abuse had stamped a belief system in my life that had to be changed… and change it God did! It was fabulous! It was so precious to have a caring heart want to know me, and then help in taking what burdened me to the Lord. This truly altered my life. I began finding freedom and access to my Lord that I didn't have before. Dan was so supportive and excited to have me get help that he was willing to take the week off work to be there for our daughter when she got out of kindergarten for the day. That made it possible for me to give this my full attention.

The next step was Listening Prayer #3, Ministry to Others. I sat amongst a group of people, some pastors and ministry leaders, even though I still found myself so raw among strangers. But I cried out to God to please help me. I wanted to participate; I wanted to be of benefit to helping others find freedom.

After some teaching, we were instructed to quiet our hearts and go to that "safe place with the Lord," the place where we meet with Him to commune and enjoy that personal relationship. As I tried to listen to the instructions, once again fear and panic rushed to the surface. There was no safe place for me anywhere on earth. Everything I thought of in life and on this planet was exposed to various levels of violation. There was literally no place I could think of that would be safe for me. That was the depth of the violation I felt in my life. As I pondered this, I thought of lightning. Yes, a bolt of lightning—God's power unleashed upon this earth—was safe for me. Heaven was safe.

Suddenly, as I sat there praying, the Lord showed me my pink coat draped right there over the back of my chair. Yes, that was my safe place; that was where I could go to be able to get through the rest of the seminar. As I thought about my new coat and how remarkable it was, how so many strangers and friends commented on how beautiful it was, I thought, *My husband, the dearest man on this planet, believes that I am God's gift to him and those around me. He absolutely loves to buy me things. Every time I come home from the store with a new outfit, he is so pleased for me. He adores me. As much as I've tried to tell him I would benefit from him giving me feedback on my weaknesses, he is oblivious to them. How blessed I am!*

Immediately I was flooded with a new understanding. I saw the Lord delighting in me the same way my husband did when I bought that pink coat. It was as if JESUS had been right there in the store with me when I chose the coat. I thought, *The Lord delights in me and enjoys seeing me appreciate the natural bent that He has designed in me. He likes to see me enjoy dressing myself nicely and enjoy the good things He has placed in me. He enjoys me, He loves me – He even rejoices over me.*

This revelation both shocked and thrilled me. I could hardly contain myself! I had to stop myself from laughing out loud. I shared with the people around me what the Lord had just conveyed to me. They seemed to not grasp what I was so happy about, but that was okay. I finally had my safe place—my pink coat! This coat represented my relationship with my Lord and Saviour.

Finding a safe place with the Lord would then become as easy as putting on my pink coat. With my awakened understanding, my relationship with Him only grew. The relationship would always be there. That was what I was to trust in. I found my answer to build my life on. God can be trusted. The more I got to know Him, the more I adored Him. I just needed to look for Him every day of my life. And when I looked, I found Him! And I still find Him! He is working in our lives every day, even when we can't see it. He does not abandon His kids.

When I got home that day, Andrew had a picture he had drawn at school. On dark paper, in chalk, he'd drawn a bolt of lightning. I hung this on my bedroom door for many years as evidence of how my children were affected by the deep healing that was transpiring in my own heart and life.

By the time the Listening Prayer Seminar was over, I understood that, when the Lord had previously spoken to my heart and I had not responded to His Voice in humble tears, it was because I had not yet really let His love inside of me. It was head knowledge, not heart response. Recognizing His Voice in a way that transformed my thinking was what brought about a radically changed life. When God told me, "*You are made in My Image, you are beautiful, you are worthy, my chosen treasure,*" I had to believe what He said. He doesn't make "trash people". I had the power within me to allow Love to enter my heart and belief system. I realized that it was not a good idea to disagree with God. My proper response to God needed to be gratitude and acceptance. The glory of God is man fully alive, and I was not fully alive until I let His love inside my beliefs about myself, and how I was to relate to God and the world around me. Paul phrased it this way in Ephesians 3:17–19:

"...so that Christ may dwell in your hearts through faith—that you, being rooted and grounded in love, may have strength to comprehend with all the saints what is the breadth and length and height and depth, and to know the love of Christ that surpasses knowledge, that you may be filled with all the fullness of God."

No Stone Left Unturned

Around this time there was a terrible tsunami and thousands of lives were lost. As I watched the horrific pictures on TV, I had such a strange sense that I knew what it was like to witness and be a part of a horror such as this. I had a deep awareness that, at times in my life, I had experienced my will and resistance being bypassed in forceful, terrifying ways. I felt that I had already faced the horror of dead bodies all stacked on top of each other. It was difficult to process why a big part of me could identify with such tragedy, but this helped me become aware that the depth of suffering I had endured was now giving me a far greater ability for joy and love to give out to other people. I began to learn how to bring the two together. Pain and healing. This enabled me to help other people while I was healing from my own pain.

As I was increasingly growing into my healed heart, I wanted to make sure I left no stone unturned and no conversation missed that might interfere with my having a pure heart before God. One day I sat down and wrote a letter to the current pastor of the church I had attended as a teenager. In that letter I explained what had happened to me at the time I had been sleeping in the church, specifying that the purpose of my letter was to help me in my healing journey. Writing the letter helped me sort out my experience of what had happened. I told him I was not looking for anything other than to be heard. I let him know that I would be fine if he did not respond. I had my teenage son read the letter before I sent it, just to check that there wasn't any bitterness or anything else that would make the letter unfit for mailing. This was the pastor's response:

> Sandy,
>
> I apologize for not getting back to you sooner. To be honest, I waited several weeks, prayed, and wondered how I would respond to your e-mail. Not that the response is that difficult, but my heart ached reading your story. You are right… God has not rejected you; He loves you deeply and welcomes you with doses of love and grace that I'm sure most of us can't fully grasp! I'm really glad that you stepped out and wrote. It's good for me as the pastor to hear your experience. This church, like so many others have been, still is, filled with flawed people—I suppose that will always be so! My hope is that we have matured along the way, that we keep maturing, allowing the Holy Spirit to flow through us in such a way that we embrace people, not perfection! Your story reminded me of my

> own responsibility to my four children. Being a pastor's kid is not an easy task—ugly at times! You reminded me of the care, dedication I MUST show them—thank you!
>
> In the very truest sense, I deeply apologize for the hurt you experienced at this church—my heart is grieved, and yet I am delighted to hear that you are moving on. I trust that my heavenly father will bring complete healing to you and your family! I wish I could have been there 35 years ago… so now, I will pray for you that God will continue to do the work He has started in you! Blessings on you!

I was over the top excited and fell on my face before God in gratitude. I knew I would most likely never get an apology or any acknowledgment from my father, but this pastor (even though he personally had no connection) represented an authority figure in that denomination and he was apologizing to me. He was acknowledging that a wrong had been done, and he was sorry. That was enough for me. I allowed a new fresh cleansing of God's Spirit to flow through me as I flourished further in my healing journey. Praise God for this pastor and his wonderful letter!

The Chicken that Changed My Life

Our 9-year-old son was asking for a dog, again. His persistence and desire tugged at my heart, but we *really* did not want a dog. As the months went by, Andrew did not stop trying, quietly asking again and again.

At lunch one day with a friend, I complained of Andrew's request and no possibility of a solution—we did not want a dog! My friend suggested I pray about it. She then told a cute little story from her family life of how they prayed for a dog and God sent them a very special one that none of them were allergic to. I hated those stories—the happily-ever-after ones that belonged in a book, not in real life.

The next day I found myself becoming increasingly angry toward my friend. As the emotion mounted, I wanted to pick up the phone and vent my feelings of anger and betrayal. I wanted to shout, "How dare you ask me to pray about something so trivial as a dog! How dare you ask me to open my heart and ask for anything?! If I don't ask, I don't get hurt. If I don't hope, I don't feel disappointment." At that moment I realized, recognized, it was the Holy Spirit stirring my heart. The Lord wanted me to pray about it.

So, on my knees I went. The years of barrenness, the desert of my soul, feeling abandoned by God were all in the forefront of my heart. I told the Lord how we didn't want another dog–"but I want Your will, Lord". I could see no way to please us all. How can God grant opposing requests? So, I gave it to the Lord. Not my will but Yours. Dan agreed to pray as well.

Even though I had received wonderful healing through the Listening Prayer seminars, at this time I still deeply struggled to allow my heart to trust and believe that God was actively involved in my life. I was still praying only as I was going about the busyness of life, the "God help me" prayers while I was in motion. I was more than happy to pray for you concerning a job loss, health issues, etc., but I couldn't bow my heart in personal vulnerability with my Lord. I was too afraid to open my heart and risk disappointment and hurt again.

Shortly after that, as I was busy around the house, Andrew came running in shouting, "Mom, come quick! There's a hurt bird outside!" I rushed outside to find a small chicken running in the road. She wasn't hurt but was unable to fly away like most birds Andrew was accustomed to. After all, she was a chicken! We caught her and brought her in the house to feed and care for her.

That evening as Dan and I prepared for bed, I was almost too afraid to voice what was in my heart. My voice broke as I finally blurted out, "You don't think that chicken is the answer to our prayer, do you?" It was one of those sacred moments where I felt all heaven was listening to me. My cold hard heart started to soften. As the words tumbled out, I knew something was melting inside of me. Dan was quiet for a minute, and then said, "Yes, I think it is an answer".

We proceeded to keep and love the chicken. We named her Chip and she became family, sleeping on my lap and living in our house, only going outside in the daytime. After awhile the excitement subsided and Andrew came to me: "Mom, I know God sent us a chicken, but I want a dog!!" Back on my knees I went, only this time enough healing had taken place that Dan and I bowed together. "Lord, not our will but Yours. We don't want a dog. Andrew does. What do You want, Lord?"

Soon after that, I was out with our young daughter and saw a beautiful cat run across someone's lawn. I stopped and crouched down with Kimber, marvelling at the beauty of the black with white whiskers and white feet. I said, "All my life I have wanted a cat that looks just like that." That was all. We got in the car and forgot all about it.

A few days later we were walking in the mall and a stranger came up to me, opening a large cardboard box and asking if I'd like a cat. To my astonishment, there were kittens, including the one of my dreams with the white whiskers on a black body. I didn't want a cat; I already had a nice cat at home, but I was so in shock that God had heard what I said to Kimber. God cared about markings on a cat. I was almost speechless! I took the kitten home in my pocket, hardly able to process my thoughts. When Dan got home that night, I was quick to say, "Before you go getting upset you must know that it was free!" These are stories that belong in books, not my real life. I had never experienced anything like this before.

That night as I read my Bible before I got into bed, I read in Psalms 50:11 in the Message Bible that the Lord knows every mountain bird by name, and the scampering field mice are His friends. That was it. I was completely overwhelmed at this point. I liked mice. I could see personality in their eyes. Each one was different. I bred birds for many years and God named each one? He cared about what markings I liked on a cat. The God of heaven calls the little mice His friends? I must know a God like that.

The very next day, after praying for guidance on where to look, we went and bought a puppy for Andrew. A 6-week-old puppy and a 6-week-old kitten to share a kennel together for comfort at night. I then announced to our children that our family was complete. No more praying for anything else!

The most impactful thing about this was that I learned to look for what God wanted. Not just what our family wanted. I couldn't imagine how God could honour my son's request for a dog when Dan and I did not want one. In the process of answering our prayers, He softened our doubtful hearts with unexpected, even unusual answers blessed with personal joys. A cat, a chicken, and a puppy. Father in heaven knew how to be extravagant in blessing us with intimate joy. Because Chip was brought inside our house every night to keep her safe, and released into the garden in the daytime, she took a lot of care. When I brought her in for the night, I'd sometimes hold her in my lap as I'd watch the evening news. As she would cuddle down and sleep, I would enjoy the warmth of her body and think how she was a tangible sign that God loves me. And that He could use something as crazy as a chicken to help melt my unbelieving heart.

We were overjoyed with our new awareness of faith, but many temptations came along to challenge my new growth. When we took our new puppy to the vet, he told us we had picked the wrong dog and would never be able to trust it around children. As my heart started to question, I said, "NO" *No* to my doubt. I would believe God over what the vet said. I could not be encouraged in God and grow in faith without learning to also build muscle as soon as the enemy came to challenge my new joy. Time showed that Andrew picked the best dog for our family and we loved her dearly.

Words cannot express the explosion of life and joy that came into our home at that point. The only comparison is to be born again into God's Heavenly Kingdom, where radical change comes and there is no turning back. The turning point for me came when I chose to abandon my unbelieving heart and recognize God's Hand in my life instead of explaining it away. The years of pain had robbed me of my ability to cry. The Lord went on to heal me more and more, and much joy came as I learned to cry; they were such sweet tears. Those of you who have no more tears to cry or are not capable of crying, will understand the sweetness of tears when it is appropriate to cry. God specializes in healing broken and hard hearts. He'll even use a lost chicken that needs love.

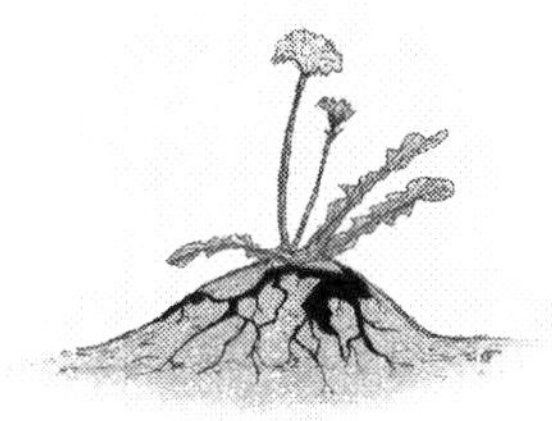

Chapter Eight

Released from My Disappointed Heart

I entered an exciting time in my life, choosing to reject the voice inside of me that was causing me to doubt and not trust. Before Amber was born, I had been naïve and didn't think terrible things would happen to me. When I was told about Amber's life expectancy, the doctor had said the chances of her heart defect happening were like the risk of being hit by lightning. Rare and likely not to ever happen again. I found my sense of identity and safety shattered in my naiveté. Lightning does strike and it does kill people. Statistics did not mean anything to me anymore. If you are the one that is struck, it means everything to you.

Since then, God had touched my heart in profoundly deep ways by resurrecting my ability to respond to Him. I had the visible reminder in front of me every single day in the form of that beloved chicken. I grew wiser in understanding what to let go of and let die inside of me rather than nurture with wrong thinking. I made many decisions to say "no" to myself and "yes" to trusting God's Voice within me. It had been lost for so long and I now wanted to pour as much water as I could on the new, tiny plant of faith within me.

Our church seemed so happy and open to anything we wanted to do, even taking the chicken up on stage one day to do a promotion for prayer ministry. Prayer was where I came alive.

I became involved in praying for people any time the church would give me opportunity. I traveled to many places to attend conferences on learning how to hear from God, or how to give out the healing He had provided for me. I stepped into ministries in the church where I was gifted with trust so I could pray for people. I would be so excited in church and would feel so full of God while taking part in the worship services, only to find it was not enough. Hungry for more, I started to pray at home on my own.

At the same time, I decided I no longer liked the name Sandra and changed my name to Sandy. It felt so much lighter. I became so full of joy; people would often comment that I glowed. I began telling people, "This is what healed looks like. Look at me! If you ever wondered what it was like for Lazarus after JESUS raised him from the dead, talk to me. I can tell you what it feels like!"

While still fiercely addicted to Nicorette gum, wearing the Patch, and smoking some of the time, I had a lengthy dental appointment. The dentist alarmed me when he commented that I was doing something that was ruining my teeth. When I told him about the excessive gum chewing, he confirmed that was the problem. I was so addicted that I would even have the gum by my bedside to chew more in the night. I was not accustomed to going such a long time without it as I sat that day in the dentist chair. Once I left the office and thought about all of this, I realized that I still could not yet put more gum in my mouth. I started remembering all the healing that had been happening in my heart. I heard the Voice of my Lord say to me, "Let Me be your sweetness." I understood this to mean instead of chewing the gum. I chose to let my heart cooperate and I started to reach out to find the sweetness in my relationship with JESUS rather than turn to nicotine gum to make me feel better. Praise God! I found I could finally walk free. Eleven years earlier, after many wonderful years free of any addiction, I had chosen to buy cigarettes. I had wanted to use them to harm myself. By burning my arm, I had hoped that the pain in my flesh would help me access the pain inside of me; the memories I could not remember. I had wanted to remember but didn't know how to make the memories come. Now I walked free. The sweet Voice of the Lord had shown me how to walk free.

I then started to pray and worship alone in my house while the kids were in school. In no time at all I found two hours turning into three, then four! Sometimes the only reason I would stop praying was because the kids came home from school. I was so filled with desire and passion for more healing, more ability to hear what God's love language was for me. I was on a great discovery that God speaks the language of our heart. I was also learning how to effectively pray for other people. One prayer time as I worshiped, I saw a large open beach. In the vision I wrote the word JESUS in huge letters in the sand, only to weep with joy as I watched Him write, "SANDY, I don't reject you. I am proud of you." Wow! To have the God of heaven speak so tenderly to my heart is indescribable!

One day when David arrived home from school, he asked me what I had been doing. I told him, "Worshipping." He replied, "I thought so." I asked him how he knew, and he said he could feel God. When I asked him what that was like he replied, "I dunno, like I can smell Him."

My morning ritual had always been staggering out of bed, grabbing a coffee, wanting no one to speak to me, and sitting in my chair to read the newspaper. One of those mornings as I reached for the paper, the Lord spoke to my heart and said, "Who would you rather hear from first thing in the morning?" This shocked me to my core. I was looking to the world news to set my thoughts for the day. From that day on I faithfully read my Bible first thing in the morning. Even if we are travelling or when I have no time for various reasons, I always open my Bible if only for one verse. I want to prove to God every single day that I would rather hear from Him. This has altered my life.

As I began to spend extended times in worship and deep prayer, I learned to start with music. I would "enter into" a worship song with all my heart, often lying flat out on the floor or dancing with great abandonment throughout my house. My animals became accustomed to my exuberance. I read somewhere that to enter God's presence one needs to begin in adoration and praise, so I would do that. As I would adore the Creator, I'd be lost in wonder for great periods of time just thanking and praising Him for how wonderful He is. Then after sometimes one to two hours, I would get to the requests that I wanted to pray about only to discover that I now wanted to pray totally differently than I thought I would pray. The big needs seemed to not matter so much anymore. I learned that I am a worshipper. That is who I am.

I also found those deep times of prayer would cause me to access the depth of suffering in my soul. These are my words copied from my journal around that time.

> **My talks with God January 2005:**
> When Amber died, I gave her willingly to You. I trusted and looked to You, God, and Your people. GOD, DID YOU OFFER A WAY OF ESCAPE THAT I DID NOT SEE? DID I TAKE A WRONG TURN? Am I mentally ill?
>
> At the cemetery, You said, "Be still and know that I am God." It did not touch me or help me. Forgive me for my anger, but what was I supposed to do? What did You expect from me? I turned to You, God, when they told me I needed a psychiatrist. "JESUS is all you need," is what I have believed with all my heart! I turned to You, God, over and over. YOU WERE NOT THERE! Why did I have to live in the hell that I did? Is it my sin/past generations? My ignorance? WHY? HOW CAN I TRUST?
>
> Is there any hope for me? I've been like this all my life, even as a child. Every day of my life I fake it. I'm NOBODY. I PRETEND. I go with

> the wind. NO IDENTITY, NO CORE, NO CENTER, NOBODY INSIDE. Is there any hope to change? My foundation is cracked. My faith does not hold me. Everything that I believed is faulty. All that I am is undermined.
>
> I have a huge hole, a vacuum inside of me. Received no mothering or what neglect? The hole has been filled with my pain. I have no idea how to give my pain to JESUS. What should the hole be filled with? I need to let JESUS empty me first before He can fill me. Just as I had that big surgery at 17 years of age, making such a huge hole in me that the nurse had to pack each day. I need You, God, to fill the hole pain has made in my life.

The next day I wrote:

> Thank You that I am important enough to need to find You for myself, not so I can tell someone about my experience. Thank You that You take time for me, that I am important enough to spend time with GOD!

Now, in my deep prayer times, I found that I could go back into my memories alone. Without a counsellor, without being in the hospital, without being in my friend's arms. I began reclaiming the little girl within me that was trapped as if lost down in a deep well, lost in pain and horror, bringing her to JESUS for healing.

One day I asked JESUS, "Why do I have to go into the well to get her, why didn't You go? He replied, "Because you wanted her dead, you need to bring her to Me." I saw JESUS bent down to me and He wept as He responded to me. I could feel His tears as they washed over my body, my shoulders, my head. What cleansing! Because I had been made in His Image: I had value. I was feminine. He had time for me. I was important to Him. I hadn't yet (and still haven't) grasped the extent of God's love for me. I had talked about Him and wanted to know Him for so long. Now I wanted Him to talk to me and communicate with me.

In the midst of one horrible memory, when I asked God how He saw my heart, I heard Him say, "Sweet child, you are a very busy active hive full of sweet honey. I went to JESUS school. He taught me—and continues to teach me—as I go to Him to learn.

Soon after these deep prayer times I struggled yet again, anger erupting and spilling over. As I was losing control over myself once again, I heard the Lord tell me to go wash the windows in my house. I was thrilled! My heart sang, "This is the first time, sweet JESUS, that I found you in the middle of my hell and torment!! Praise God! His love is amazing, and it is big enough to help me."

Then I had a vision of me and JESUS, legs tied together as if in a three-legged race like I would participate in as a child. Going back into a memory or everywhere I went, I'd giggle with delight as I imagined I was tied to JESUS and we were participating together. This brought me such comfort and joy. It also really helped when I prayed for people and offered them my help. With this picture in my mind the serious responsibilities would lighten and be fun.

Growing is Hard Work

Soon I found the courage to hear God say things to me that were really hard to hear. One day as our family was leaving church, we noticed a group of crows. Shouting to Dan to slow down so the kids could see, my heart sunk in my chest. I saw that the crows were attempting to peck one of their own to death. I quickly motioned to Dan to keep driving as I did not want the kids to witness that. Then the Lord spoke to my heart, "That's how you are treating Dan." I was shocked! It hurt, but as I pondered and opened my heart, I remembered that crows will cull their own when one is weak or sickly. I realized that I was pecking at my own beloved husband, in a way, to rid him of anything I found displeasing. The revelation was hard to accept, but I had asked God to talk to me about hard matters. I wanted to be helped, to grow, to pull in the reins on myself, to be a stronger person. I could take this correction from my loving Heavenly Father since it was done in love. The picture of the crows has helped me numerous times throughout our marriage and my life. God is kind and He is helpful.

The Lord also really helped me with defining my purpose in life. One day He called me a green arrow. Like an arrow, my job was to point—to point people to the Way. It felt so simple, so directive and good. Green is the colour of new life, hope. I liked the simple idea that all I was to do in life was to point to the One who can help. I could do that. My life felt more manageable.

I also spent a great deal of time studying about the armour of God in Ephesians 6. I wanted to feel protected by God. One day, the Lord gave me a delightful vision. I saw myself as a small girl standing close to JESUS, who was huge. Something frightened me terribly and I threw down my armour, ran to His leg and clung on ever-so-tightly. Me, a small child holding the big leg of JESUS, my armour thrown on the ground. I had to laugh. I immediately understood that God was showing me, that yes, I needed to learn how to use His armour correctly, but when life happened, when a crisis came, I could cling to JESUS' leg. It was my relationship with Him that was the solid Rock I was to build my life upon, not my ability to learn enough techniques or to practice them perfectly. This really helped me relax and trust.

Friends very dear to Dan and me lost their son in death. One Sunday soon after, they came to church and we ended up sitting close behind them. During the worship service I noticed that when everyone else stood, they remained seated, humped forward in their grief. I wanted so much to be able to help them. As I lifted my arms to worship God in song, I leaned so close to them that I could almost touch their backs. Then I started to worship on their behalf. As I lifted my arms to heaven, I said, "God, they may be too deep in the heartache and suffering to praise You right now, but I can praise You on their behalf." And I did. With all my heart I leaned in hard to praise God on their behalf. I remember that as the moment when God started to unfold understanding in me of how I could come before Him on behalf of other people. I could bring the praise of God into their circumstance. I became a worshipper for others, and saw lives changed as I praised. All I wanted to do was worship, and then worship some more, everywhere I went. As part of that worship I began to pray and symbolically open the windows of someone's house, inviting a spirit of encouragement to flood their home and hearts. I would invite light to shine and dispel all darkness. I still do that today.

This same dear couple was in our home Bible study group. Their shattered hearts made leading the group during those early days of their loss, tender. It just so happened that once again we were boarding the African grey parrot. One thing unique to these amazing birds is that they like to talk a lot when you aren't looking at them. Before our meeting I covered the bird with a blanket hoping to trick him into thinking it was bedtime so that he'd sleep. But instead, it was a perfect opportunity for him to talk—a room full of people close by that he could hear but not see. As he started up his chatter, Dan leaned over and said, "Shhhhh, Kojo! You be quiet!" to which the bird replied very clearly, "Shhhhh, you be quiet!" I was so upset. I did not know how to make a talking bird be quiet, especially in a solemn atmosphere. Our dear friend with the broken mother's heart burst out laughing. The bird then mimicked her voice, perfectly copying her laugh! The whole group burst out laughing. Our friend laughed and laughed until she said she just might pee her pants. Afterwards, she commented that it was the first time she had laughed since her son's death; she had feared she might never laugh again. God had used a talking, noisy bird to bring joy into our home, hearts, and friends once again!

God is so amazing in all His creations, including birds and animals. This African grey parrot was a most remarkable bird. He had hundreds of words in his vocabulary and the ability to copy sounds like screeching brakes on a truck, the beep of a microwave or the inflection of a human voice so you knew exactly which person he was copying, male or female. He would engage in conversation with me as if he had intelligence and wasn't just mimicking like parrots are famous for. This became clear to me, one night, as I was lying on my bed talking to Dan. Not wanting to get up yet to put the bird to bed, I tried to ignore his calling. He wanted his blanket placed over the cage, one corner left open for him to peek out, so he could sleep. The longer I delayed, the more he kept asking over and over, "Kojo go night-night, Kojo go night-night." Finally, in a most exasperated voice, this bird called to me, "Would you hurry up!" I was so shocked that I immediately jumped out of bed. I had just been rebuked by a bird! From then on, I knew he was not only copying noises but in fact understood much of what was being said to him. He loved to argue with himself, saying, "Kojo is a girl, no Kojo is a boy." Then he'd laugh. He could identify birds outside and would announce, "That is a crow, that's a chickadee," and he would be right.

Animal Babies

That spring Andrew purchased some pet rats and planned to earn money by selling the babies as pets. When I awoke that beautiful sunny Easter morning, I could hear sounds of just-born baby rats coming from Andrew's bedroom. It seemed so appropriate that the very first baby pets Andrew would experience would be born on Easter Sunday morning. What made the day an even more joyful Easter Sunday morning was David, age 12, being baptized in church that morning! New life!

What joy animals brought into our home. In my growing up years, animals were my friends and toys, and I wanted my children to enjoy them, too. I believed that children could learn so much through animals—how to be responsible, kind and patient in caring for them and how to learn in the loss of them dying. I thought it was much better for kids to learn early on that even though there is pain in life you can recover and heal from loss.

We were overjoyed when Kimber's cat finally got pregnant. We allowed her cat to have one litter before getting her spayed. I wanted our daughter to experience the birthing process. What joy this brought into our home! Even Kimber's teacher was in on the anticipation. When the time came for the kittens to be born, I only had to appear at the classroom door and the teacher quickly shooed Kimber out the door to rush home to see the birthing. One kitten was born right into her hands! Andrew also brought his friends into my bedroom to watch this delightful scene.

I truly believe it brings God honour when we stop and appreciate all of His wonders and give Him the credit, whether it's the night sky with stars magnificently strewn across it, or the wee sparrow. He must have quite a sense of humour to create a huge elephant, a giraffe with an overstretched neck and funny meerkats standing so straight in their groups. A huge part of being a healed and whole person, I believe, is to deeply appreciate all of God's wondrous design. Such diversity! I also believe God is a lot of fun. He likes it when we laugh. I can bring Him joy. I believe that the spirit of the animal returns to its Maker and am convinced that, one day, I will see the animals that I have loved in heaven with me.

My Pain

While so many good things were happening to me and our family, I would still be suddenly thrust back into the horror of my childhood. One day I saw in my mind the monkey that we would see in Kenya where we would holiday. The Lord had me see the monkey come to me, wanting to give me back my pain. I understood at that moment that I had given that monkey the pain that I had not been able to carry as a child. It now felt so awful! I felt mean. How could I have been so mean, giving that poor monkey my pain?

As I told a dear friend about this, she told me that she thought it was wonderful. "Just give the pain to JESUS," she said. As if that was a simple process! I wanted to cry out, "NO, you don't understand!" I had become very aware that I could not give anything to JESUS until I first owned it myself, owned my pain and how I had handled it. So once again, sadly, I spiralled downward.

I had seen not only the monkey, but also our trip to the coast in Kenya; me as a child, the night ocean, the beach, and sand. The tide going out had taken bottles that we had buried in the sand. We kids were going to sneak back at night to have a party, but the tide had exposed the hidden pop bottles and floated them away. Now, in my spirit, what was supposed to be covered, hidden, no longer could stay that way. Things I had not previously remembered until this experience were now being exposed, whether I wanted them to be or not. As this personal tide receded, I could see what had been hidden. I had no control. I was in an ocean of pain and torment with the new set of memories that were unearthed. However, I had the ability to force myself to function as if nothing was wrong, and I resumed my responsibilities both at home and in ministry. To me that ability was a gift from God. Most people had no idea there was anything wrong. Pushing myself to present well helped me to cope.

Around that time, malls in our area started selling items from Africa. Something as simple as a small drum or an item of clothing would send me into such a full-on panic that I would need to run from the mall. I could not look at anything from Africa without an extreme reaction in my body. I also found that, as my children grew in age, I would sometimes have a new memory surface of myself at the current age of my child.

One time while in prayer, the Lord let me see again one of our houses in my childhood; the backyard where some of the worst memories happened with a houseboy. I did not want to look at that darkness, but the Lord showed me that there was fresh green grass growing where I remembered only pain. Then I realized that by now, my abusers would have died of old age. I allowed more healing to flood my heart and mind.

During the time these memories were all coming out, my family told of an incident when one of our houseboys came at me with a knife to attack me—right in front of my family. My parents immediately dismissed him. Later they found out he had succumbed to some kind of brain disease.

A movie came out around that time called *The Passion of the Christ*. I had gone with a friend, and all my attention was focused with concern on how she was processing what she was watching. I later hurried back to the theater to watch the movie by myself. It was a brutally hard movie to watch as it depicted the violence that happened to Christ when He was crucified. As I watched, I allowed myself to see and accept deep in my heart, that Christ's sufferings were far greater than my pain. I had been so overwhelmed with my own stuff and found it immensely helpful to see up close that JESUS paid the ultimate in suffering. He hurt more than I did.

Something that has bothered me for many years is when Christians say that JESUS took our place so that we don't have to suffer. I believe that to be wrong thinking. He paid the penalty for our sin, not for an escape from pain. I do suffer; I suffer the same as people with no faith suffer. If I am cut, I bleed just the same as others. Knowing JESUS grants me new life and a future and a hope; it doesn't dissolve my responsibility of picking up my cross and following Him in surrender to God's will. The sooner I die to my own "stuff" and pick up my cross, the sooner I attain peace.

One day as I was in prayer, I saw myself with a huge, wrapped gift so big that I staggered under the weight of it. My spirit responded to the Lord, *My pain, my problems are a gift*?! At first, I resented this and was angry towards God. "How could my pain, my anguish of soul be a gift from You?" But then I responded, "Thank you, Lord, for Your gift. I accept. I'm starting to understand how You restore my soul."

Joy in Gardening

We were blessed with such a nice big house and yard but neither Dan nor I had any interest in gardening. Keeping the grass cut was the best we could do. It was wonderful to be able to visit Dan's mom so frequently and we loved going to her house for frequent dinners. She was the world's best gardener, and she loved her flowers. Many times, when we'd leave to go home, I'd have a bouquet of fresh flowers in my lap from her garden. I'd wonder what was wrong with me as I had absolutely no interest in the flowers. I would have liked to have been able to say, "No, thank you," to taking her flowers home, but I didn't want to hurt my mother-in-law's feelings. Over the years I would try again to garden. People would say how something magical happened to them when they worked in the dirt. So, I'd turn over the dirt and wait for that wonderful feeling, but it wouldn't happen. I'd go back in the house accepting that I had no desire or ability to appreciate plants, trees, or flowers.

We had joined a small group in our church and the senior pastor just happened to be part of that group. One day he and the group offered to come and help me garden. I was very embarrassed to have friends come over and work in my yard, especially since I have never been good at having people work alongside of me, even in my kitchen. When they arrived, the pastor had kindly brought extra kneepads, which he gave to me. I had never seen them before and shyly put them on. These wonderful people worked for many hours cleaning up our yard. I was so humbled that my pastor would get down on his hands and knees and weed for me.

To my surprise, before the end of that summer, I was out in our yard working on my own. I found a new healing—an awakening happened in my heart. I began to notice the beauty of plants. It was as if a light of awareness had been birthed in my eyes and my heart was now capable of appreciating beauty.

A few years later when the kids were older and the garden gorgeous, there was a time of some intense conflict in our house. In my frustration I went outside to sit in my garden and fume. I had previously transplanted one of my favourite dahlias and, as I sat near it, saw that it had died. Perhaps it had been too large to transplant at that stage or I had done something wrong in re-planting it. Already feeling so angry and sorry for myself, I blurted out to God, "God, why are you not answering my prayers?! I have prayed so long and so hard over this family issue. If my faith amounted to anything, I should be able to … to say to this dahlia 'live' and it would live!" As I heard the words coming out of my mouth, I had a strange awareness that, if my faith was real, I should be able to do just that. I could not understand why God wasn't answering my prayer about the conflict in our home, but I now felt challenged to apply my faith like I had never done before. I got up off the ground from where I had been hiding under a bush and I spoke to the dead dahlia. "In JESUS' Name, live! I speak life to you, I speak hope. You are now to live. God has made you to live and give beautiful flowers and that is what you will do." I went outside the next day, too, and breathed my breath on this plant and prayed, speaking life to it. After the third day I started to see a slight change. Immensely encouraged I kept praying and speaking life to this plant.

That summer it grew incredibly large in front of my bedroom window. I could lie in my bed and see the gorgeous white-pink blooms from this once dead plant that had come back to life because God is real. He is real and He was helping me to know how I could be a part of speaking life into dead places. He showed me hope in dark places; He showed me that my words could also speak life into people. In the beginning God's breath created us all. These many years later, I took this photo of the very same plant we brought with us to our new home. Many friends, as they have heard this story, have taken a bulb and planted it in their own garden.

Stepping into Ministry

As soon as I received a new breakthrough in my healing journey, I couldn't wait to pass on what I learned to somebody else. People seemed eager to hear of my joy and I found many more opportunities to pray with people. About that same time, we decided it was time to start attending a different church, one in Langley. We eagerly made the half hour trip, each way, especially as we were pleased to find some of the main goals of this fabulous church were to serve and to pray. Right up my alley!

Even though we lived in the heart of Whalley, considered by many to be an unsafe—even dangerous—neighbourhood, we were great walkers and regularly walked through areas of poverty, drug addiction, and homelessness. I did not believe I had anything to offer these people. Officials had warned, "Do not give them money." Others had said, "Don't ever make eye contact." Year after year we included our kids on our walks, ignoring the suffering around us. One time I had tried to help at a community meal that our church hosted for people struggling, and felt I really "bombed out" by making a fool of myself. I couldn't relate and didn't know how I could be of any help to them. I concluded that I couldn't do everything; that we all have differing gifts and abilities; that working with street people was not my gift. I gave money to those who could help and decided that working with the homeless or drug addicts was certainly not my calling. I was confident and settled in that belief.

One day as we were once again walking, a thought troubled my heart. I had seen people sleeping out in the open, so dirty, and seemingly destitute. I wondered, "*What would JESUS do if He were walking through that neighbourhood?*" This troubled me; I did not know the answer. In Christ's lifetime on the earth He did not rid the world of poverty. In fact, He said we would always have the poor with us. This unsettling question came to me over and over.

In time, I felt the hand of God moving me towards helping in a ministry that was close to our home, called NightShift Street Ministry. Many churches and groups took part in this ministry, undertaking the amazing provision of a hot meal every single night of the year, served outside whatever the weather. NightShift also ran a clothing truck that provided clothing, toiletries, and other essentials a homeless person might need. At this point, the ministry had been running for well over ten years. I paid them a visit but was still so sure I had nothing to offer. To my great surprise, our new church in Langley was also helping NightShift in our neighbourhood. I started to serve in this ministry through our church in Langley that took me back to my own neighbourhood in Surrey!

Things certainly were coming together. It was as if God was telling me He had thoughts that superseded mine. The story in the Bible from Acts 3:6 became so real to me. Peter, one of the disciples, said to a crippled man, "I have no silver and gold, but what I do have I give to you." I had no abilities to work with street people but what I did have, I could share.

During volunteer orientation and training I heard about the ministry's purpose, goals, and passion—the heart of the ministry. When the founder explained that they required a hot meal to be prepared every night, cooked as if we were preparing for guests in our own home, I was hooked. I was amazed at the heart attitude that would treat people living on the street, people who sometimes were eating out of garbage cans, with that kind of dignity. This really captured my interest. After learning the boundaries and expectations, I started to serve meals and take part in a large prayer circle that followed every meal. Live worship music would play while people were eating, setting the atmosphere for an enjoyable evening.

I was struck to my core one night as I observed the participation in the prayer circle. As our large circle held hands, one young man shouted out in loud sobs, "God, I'm so sorry! I have "used" again. I didn't want to mess up. Will You please help me?" I was so surprised with how open and willingly vulnerable these people were. I was further hooked. I loved honesty and I loved learning how I could be useful.

One night early on, dinner was over and the after-meal lingering was happening. I gathered all the courage I could and approached a group of men talking. It was a cold time of the year and most of the men had a hoodie up over their head, faces looking to the ground. I quietly slipped in and tried to enter their conversation. I heard one man say he had just gotten out of jail. To this day I can hardly believe I did this, but in my insecurity and fear, I blurted out, "Oh, so did you learn your lesson?" He replied, "#%@& no! I have been in Oakalla Prison four times!" I knew that this prison in Burnaby, B.C., was one of the province's most notorious prisons and that it was eventually shut down.

I was so horrified with myself and quickly tried to slink away into the shadows to lick my wounds. How could I have been that stupid, that tactless?! After a short while, to my surprise, the same man approached me, wanting to talk to me. The strangest thing happened. The more we talked, the taller he became. He, and I soon knew his name, now looked me in the eye while talking ... and we had a great conversation. It felt no different than talking with my neighbour down the street. After he walked away, I was dumbfounded. What had just happened? Had he changed or had I changed? I saw him as a person much like me and I enjoyed our conversation. My fear had drastically fallen away.

I served there with a team from my church once a month. After a while I was asked to be co-leader of the team and eventually a team leader. I asked Dan if he would always make sure to also be there if I was the leader—more for support than safety. It was obviously my passion and desire but, being the wonderful husband that he is, he wanted to support me. It was still a very daunting thing for me to be leading a team of volunteers out on the street to do ministry. We were never sure what we would find. Soon I became a church team leader, overseeing all of the NightShift teams from our church. Eventually we had three teams consisting of eighty volunteers. Considering the cooks, sandwich makers and all the prep work we had to do before we even got to the street, it was a huge undertaking. We needed to organize, prepare, and serve a meal for anywhere between 50 to 150 people, depending on the time of the month. My role also included arranging for live worship music and a speaker, and then conducting a prayer circle at the end of the meal where we would pray individually for anyone that wanted prayer. I loved it! I love showing people they have value. A person does not become less of a person when their circumstances change to what looks less desirable to me. I loved treating people with dignity and giving to them, especially when they had already received so much rejection.

I came alive in this ministry, finding purpose and meaning in my life. I could go to bed at night and feel that I had made a difference in someone else's life. What a great feeling!

NightShift

Soon I began working in the ministry's office, helping with various tasks such as assisting with volunteer training, working at the front desk, and leading a staff prayer time. I loved to help people pray together, people who came from many diverse backgrounds or different views in theology. It was an amazing feat to have so many different church denominations agree enough to bring about successful ministry on the street. Such diverse opinions yet all wanting the same goal in helping people.

I planted flowers in the large cement planters in front of the office. It was so enjoyable to have flowers grow in such a spiritually dark place. However, these planters became a favourite place to hide drugs or weapons, and plants were regularly pulled up when people wanted to see if there were drugs hiding underneath. I would have to regularly buy more plants and often had to replace the dirt as the planter was sometimes used for a bathroom. Where do homeless people go to use a bathroom? I had not considered that before. Where do they keep a toothbrush if you give them one? How can they go to sleep at night and keep their bike and possessions safe from theft?

One morning as I opened the door a man swore at me, telling me how stupid I was to plant flowers in that area. He shouted, "Do you really think anybody here really cares about your "#%@& flowers?" I knew God cared, I knew God saw value in each human, each flower. I cared because God cared. And so, as I smiled at the man, I continued to care for the flowers.

Another day a man came in, very distraught and crying. He had gone into the thrift store across the street and asked for a pair of shoes so he could wear shoes for an important meeting that was coming up. The manager had thrown him out and told him not to come back. As he cried out his pain, explaining how he was trying so hard to change his ways, trying so hard to not steal, he shouted, "Do you realize how easy it would be for me to walk into that store and steal shoes?! But I chose not to. I chose to ask the manager if he could show me some kindness and give me the shoes I needed." The more he talked, the more I wanted a pair of shoes to give him. I looked at my feet wishing they were bigger, so that my shoes would fit him. But I had nothing to give him; I could only sit there and listen. Before he left, he gave me a great big smile and said how much I had helped him. I had given him nothing! I had only stopped what I was doing and tried to listen to his heart. That was enough for him. I could give what I had, and I had done that. I felt valued.

Some days, going into work in the morning, I would find the office door blocked by a horrible mess left by someone who had spent the night sleeping there. Just as I had learned to not mind changing my children's dirty diapers, I did what needed to be done in uncouth situations. I discovered there were no easy answers; everyone had a story that could make me cry. Some people had bad situations happen due to no fault of their own. For others, their mental illness kept them on the street. One man had never found a way to manage his deep grief after his wife's death. Sometimes families would come for one of our evening meals; they simply did not have enough money to last the whole month and were genuinely hungry. Many people wanted the fellowship and interaction of people who cared enough to be there to listen, and to laugh at their jokes. Loneliness was a driving force in much of their interactions. Addiction was prevalent: a crazy thing that steals and pulls you in and under to places you never thought you would go.

One night, when it was my turn to give the short talk after the meal, I spoke about how immense the Father God's love is for each of us and how we all needed to feel valued. The crowd received it well; I felt so full of God in that moment, like God was speaking right through me. But just as I finished speaking, a fight broke out right in front of me. Watching this fight unfold, I decided to go against the training I had received as a volunteer and by the police. When dealing with conflicts and conflict resolution, the "do's" and "don'ts" were clear: never get in between two people who were fighting. But that night, I did just that. I walked in between the two fighting men, turning towards the one that seemed to be the perpetrator and repeated the same words I had just said over the microphone. "We all need to feel valued," I said. And then I asked him, "Do you need to feel valued, too?" He reacted as if I had thrown icy water in his face. "You're right!" he admitted. "That's what I need." And just like that, the fight was over. I asked a volunteer on our team to pray with this man. It turned into a wonderful prayer encounter and another opportunity to show love and compassion, diffuse anger and build relationships. The man then started to strut around the crowd loudly announcing, "This is church! You need to listen! This is church!"

One man on our volunteer team had served as a police officer for many years. He wanted to avoid any stigma or judgments about himself from interfering with his reason for being there, so on his first night out with us he dressed in disguise. I didn't even recognize him! He was kind and was so pleased to not have the social restrictions his career placed on him; he could pray, hug and love people as his heart longed to do. I loved it that we were all on the same footing. It wasn't too many weeks later that I asked him to speak after the meal. Plucking up his courage he told the crowd he was a police officer. The crowd responded in immediate silence; everyone froze. They had already come to know him and never expected this disclosure from him. Then this dear man shared deep things from his heart, his very real and relevant struggle to know God and be known by Him. Tears rolled down his cheeks as he spoke from his heart of love to a hurting crowd. What a wonderful privilege it was to be part of a moment like that! What meaningful joy!

I learned so much working with the homeless—about respect, authority, boundaries, limitations, compassion and why we need to be patient. I saw how a dedicated team that yielded to authority and respected boundaries functioned. I learned more about the spiritual authority of a believer. I also grew to understand the power that music has over a crowd and how to set an inviting atmosphere. I was surprised to find so many people we met there already had a faith and were Christians, or were open to being prayed for, no matter what the faith.

Some of the things we experienced while working at NightShift were hard to process. During the winter it was difficult to go home to our warm beds when people we knew and cared for were sleeping out in the elements. One frigid winter I worked some shifts in our Emergency Shelter; there I learned that all our friends had some sort of weapon. One night one of the women was tied to a tree and severely beaten. Our street family had their own sense of street justice and would often police themselves but at the same time were also very protective of us, insisting that we be treated with respect. Even amidst the violence and stealing, they would look out for each other.

Oldest Brother had taught me many years previously that if you wanted to be a good manager, you had to intentionally work yourself out of a job. All you had to do was ensure that everybody else did their jobs. That was what I tried to do with my teams. I learned how to do everything and then released the responsibilities to someone else. Driving the truck was no problem but backing it up with a trailer behind was no easy task! I spent hours communicating with the volunteers by e-mail, always checking and ensuring they were going to follow through on their tasks. I really enjoyed staying in touch with people to ensure the tasks were done well. It was rewarding to collaborate with people who took volunteer work seriously. Someone started to call me a professional volunteer. It seemed I had more than a fulltime job with all the volunteering I was doing.

Since we lived in the worst part of the city, everyday when I walked to work, I walked past the heartache, suffering, and plight of the drug-addicted and homeless. It was on one of those walks that I was stopped dead in my tracks. I noticed a vibrant yellow dandelion, blooming ever-so-brightly, that had pushed its way up and through hard asphalt. I marvelled at the sharp colour, the strength and tenacity of life itself that was not held back by its situation, by its circumstances. As I paused to appreciate the beauty of a weed, I also admired its inherent desire for life. In a few more steps I'd be at work with dear broken, hurting bodies and souls that were eating out of garbage cans, living on the street. Castaways of our culture; those we don't want to touch or be near; parts of ourselves we don't want to look at. And my eyes would see the beauty, the vibrancy of life in their eyes. Just as I could love the beauty and tenacity in that dandelion, I could see and love that in hurting people.

I am a Dandelion

I, too, have pushed through that hard, hot asphalt that looked impossible. I, too, have been loved when I seemed unlovable.

I am a dandelion, a weed with little perceived value finding the tenacity, the strength and determination to grow through impossible places. My miracle is not only me learning to love myself, but the greater miracle of allowing God's love to redeem me, allowing others to love me. Taking what felt unattainable to me, making healing my reality.

I burst out
through the hard asphalt of my struggle
into a bubbling spring
of refreshing, life-giving joy.

Because I have heard
The Voice of Love.

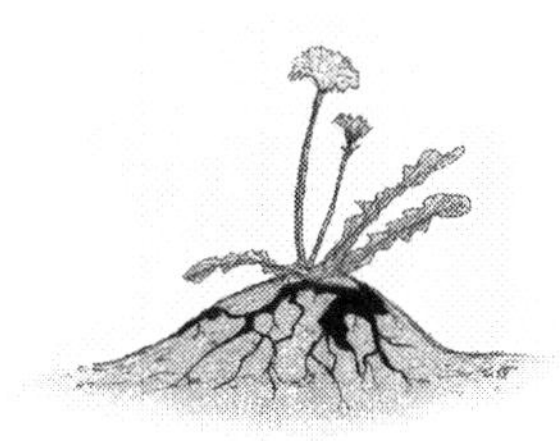

Chapter Nine

Breaking Out

Around the same time that I was being "set loose" to serve, love and care for people living on the street, I also became increasingly involved in our church. I absolutely loved that church and to this day think it was one of the best things that happened to me.

During one of my early days in this church, as I sat quietly in a service, I heard the Lord speak to my heart. As He showed me the scars on my arms from my self-inflicted wounds, God showed me a glimpse of heaven and said to me, "One day you will no longer have those scars" I was pleased but acutely aware that I was not overwhelmed in tears and love. I felt nothing, as if only my brain heard God. My emotions did not respond in any way. I was very troubled by this and asked for prayer to be healed of my numbed heart. People thought I was crazy; they saw me as this dynamic Christian on fire for God and told me I did not have a hard heart. But I knew otherwise. I lived in massive amounts of emotional pain and suffering that no one knew about. A kind woman who prayed for me said I should start writing, that I should write and write and write. I kept a journal before but had not written in the way she was suggesting. I had never thought of myself as a writer.

This church prayed about everything! No program started up without first having a time of prayer. It was a large church with two morning services and a prayer room staffed the whole morning. It was a place that knew how to give people many opportunities to serve, helping each one grow into their own giftings. It gave me a platform and opportunity to learn how to let my light shine and run free from the chains that had held me back for so long. The support I received was tremendous and I obviously gravitated to the prayer room. Dan and I really enjoyed being ushers at the door, welcoming people and then making ourselves available to pray for them before they left. I had found my element!

As I became increasingly able to offer myself in meaningful ways to pray for people, I found myself one day at the front of the church as part of the prayer team. We were there to offer prayer for others and all eyes were on us. In my insecurity, the Voice of the Lord broke through and I heard Him say to me, "They are coming to receive from Me, not you." I was so relieved! Heaving a big sigh, I internally laughed at myself. "*Of course, they don't want what I have to offer. They are coming because they want to hear and receive from God*." The word the Lord had told me a few years earlier became so real, once again. I was a green arrow; all I had to do was point people to JESUS. It felt so simple, so doable.

Yet I would get so frustrated and upset that I wasn't able to recall scripture when I needed to and wanted to. I would be so blessed as I read my Bible only to completely forget what I had read. I would want to bless a woman as I prayed for her with verses that had spoken such encouragement to me, only to have my mind go blank. She would tell me her name and I would immediately forget it. Eventually I decided that I would just plough forward anyway and not let my forgetfulness disqualify me. God had qualified me, and I would agree with Him. I learned to pray for people even when I forgot their names. I started writing down many verses that I found meaningful. Before long I would find someone to give the little paper to, someone who would weep with joy, saying that it was exactly what their heart needed at that moment. I forgave myself for not being able to memorize and recall scripture as needed and just wrote verses down instead where I could look at them when I wanted one. I started to carry my enormous Bible everywhere I went, full of little notes to give away.

Women's Prayer Team

One of the wonderful programs the church offered, the Wednesday morning ladies' time, had an organized prayer team. I quickly joined the women's prayer team. Since everything that was done at that church started with prayer, we as a group did just that. I had certainly found a place where I felt fulfilled. I had found my niche.

Joining the women's prayer team also involved a secondary ministry called e-prayers. So many people were so busy, and the best way to connect with them appeared to be via e-mail. I committed myself to learning how to effectively pray for and communicate with people that were asking for prayer by e-mail. Always, without exception, I would pray, "Lord, open the eyes of my heart!" in line with Ephesians 1:18. As I prayed for them and their request, if a picture or a scripture came to my mind, I would include that in my response. I would look to scripture to find insight from God's Word as to what the picture in my spirit meant, and God would deposit knowledge in my heart. For example, if I saw green, I would look in the Bible for a verse about green grass and then mention in my e-mail that the Lord leads beside still waters and green pastures.

Before sending out my response to each person, I would re-read what I had written and imagine what it would sound like to the reader, often someone I didn't know. How would it sound to someone sitting all alone at home, someone perhaps not yet of faith?

Then I would look for confirmation from the person as to what direction to take in any follow-up. I would receive an overwhelming response from people affirming that God had touched them through my e-mailed prayer. This catapulted me into a pattern that is still strong in my life today.

I learned so much while on the prayer team. As the women responded back to my e-mail, I learned increasingly more of how to connect with people. It was also very exciting to later meet up with them in the prayer room when they would come and find us for further prayer and to talk with us in person.

It was much easier to take risks in my learning curve while in safe circumstances, such as with my fellow prayer team members. One day, I e-mailed a prayer to a team member and included an encouraging scripture. I also told her that as I was praying for her, I saw in my mind an accordion being played. To my surprise and joy, the next time I saw this dear one she explained the significance of the accordion. She told me through tears that her mom had passed away and that she was missing her terribly, and one of her favourite memories was of her mom playing her accordion. I was overjoyed! Overjoyed that God would tell me something that specific and that it would touch my friend's heart in such a deep way.

A while later, as my confidence grew, I e-mailed someone else on the prayer team and told her I really had no idea what this meant but I could see a kohlrabi as I prayed for her. It was a real stretch for me to tell someone something like that, especially since I wasn't even too sure what vegetable that was! A few days later she told me about the good laugh she and her husband had over my e-mail. She had previously dug up a large kohlrabi from her garden and had left it on her kitchen windowsill for so long that her husband kept warning her it would go bad if she didn't do something with it soon. As she read my message the Lord touched her heart with the understanding that the kohlrabi was like the spiritual gift within her. She was not to let it sit and go stagnant but was to use it for God. What joy this brought our hearts. God is fun!

Connecting a felt need with a relevant scripture was powerful. Every e-prayer response was copied to the leader, creating accountability and firm boundaries. It appeared that I was designed for this. The more e-prayers I responded to, the more practiced I became. The more I honed this skill, this ability from the Lord, the more I heard the Voice of my Lord for myself. My courage to listen to God's Voice for my own heart also grew. I found Him to always be so very tender and so truly kind. There is no condemnation in the Voice of the Lord. And yes, it does take courage to hear God's voice.

This prayer team would also go other places, like other churches' women's retreats. It was so exciting to see how easily women would open up and ask for prayer from strangers! I had certainly found a place where I felt fulfilled.

One year the prayer team attended a large women's retreat and the speaker profoundly affected my life. I don't remember her specific type of mental illness, but she stood in front of us all with boldness and confidence. She had us laughing and crying, and challenged us to the depths of our hearts, all while allowing us to see the severity of her illness. Frequently she would forget what she was saying halfway through a sentence and ask us to help her remember. We had all fallen in love with her and would eagerly shout back a reminder of where she was in her train of thought. The women were totally engaged! Rather than disqualify herself, the speaker brought dignity to someone on medication, someone struggling on such a deep level yet still choosing to use the gifts God had given her to affect the world around her.

Sitting and listening to this wonderful woman gave me courage to go ahead and follow God with all my strength even when I felt like such a misfit, an oddity. I knew that moving forward, I would make many mistakes but somehow, as I listened to this speaker, I gave myself permission to be okay with that. That was a defining moment in my life. For my whole life I had felt out of step with the world around me. Born in Africa, having so much trouble adjusting in Canada, marrying later, being older in my childbearing - I always felt out of step. When I had tried to speak it always seemed to be the wrong timing, or people acted as if they didn't even hear me. When I wanted to be known, I had faced rejection. I had deep pain and could never understand why people talked right over me and didn't seem to notice me. I went home from that retreat feeling released to serve, even when I made mistakes.

At a different retreat, I had an experience in God as I was worshipping and swept away in adoration. I heard these verses:

"Then those who feared the Lord spoke with one another. The Lord paid attention and heard them, and a book of remembrance was written before him of those who feared the Lord and esteemed his name. 'They shall be mine, says the Lord of hosts, in the day when I make up my treasured possession, and I will spare them as a man spares his son who serves him." (Malachi 3:16–17)

As I praised and worshipped, I had a vision of the entire room of women being letters of the alphabet. Each woman was one letter and to make up a word, she needed to go stand next to someone else. All over the room women, each with their individual letter, came together in unity to make up many wonderful words. I needed to be with someone else, too, to make a word; I was not a word all on my own. God's book of remembrance was us making up all these collective words.

Prayer Team Leader

As time went on, the dynamic, Spirit-filled leader of the prayer team stepped away and I became the leader. I bonded with them, we bonded with each other—twelve women passionate about prayer, forming lifelong relationships. I'm convinced that one of the main reasons we developed such strength was the many times we gathered together and prayed. Here we could practice praying and feel safe, knowing that these dear ladies allowed lots of mistakes. Over the course of time I needed to apologize to each gal on the team! I had worded something poorly or I had appeared careless of feelings, or I had cut someone off! I discovered that I often cut people short when they were speaking. Together with these ladies, I now had a safe environment with boundaries where I could be real and honest while practicing my developing skills. Here was a place where I could have the humility to say, "I am sorry," and be mature enough to accept an apology. I wanted to be held accountable; I wanted to be open to feedback and be able to accept correction. All of this did wonders for our relationships.

Our prayer team would regularly gather for what may have appeared to be a social time but in no time at all, I would outline how I saw our evening unfolding. To me, it was important to have a clearly defined purpose for the evening and a set time to end. As much as it was wonderful to hear the women talking a lot and becoming excited, I also felt there always had to be a firm, clear direction of what was expected of each person and why we were meeting. I also endeavoured to give each woman an equal opportunity to share and to receive prayer. And then, if we were in someone's home, I wanted us to be respectful of the hostess and not overstay our welcome.

In the early days, as we approached summer and became concerned about "disconnect," I organized what we called Girls in Touch. Throughout the summer, I assigned one week for each of the prayer team members to be loved-on and prayed for by the rest of the team. Any thoughtful way we could imagine making our sister feel loved and cared for was acceptable. It was a powerful thing to know that a group of women were praying for you for that whole week. It also brought much delight when a note was found attached to our car or fresh baking left on the doorstep.

I so appreciated the numerous guidelines and standards developed in that prayer ministry. I had learned in my early years of parenting, that prayer should never be used as a platform to tell your child what you thought. When my kids were little, I tried so hard to never use a prayer to discipline. That was a fast way to turn a child against God. If I used God's authority to back up my viewpoint and my child feels it is unfair, they could very well end up thinking God is unfair. This was also applicable in our prayer ministries. Praying for someone was not to be used to express an opinion.

Another guideline I greatly respected was that of not giving advice or recommending a book to the person coming for prayer. The team's main focus was prayer, and prayer is what the person would get. I also knew from personal experience that a woman made herself vulnerable when she asked for prayer and I wanted us to treasure that as a sacred moment and respect her heart. If I or any team member felt that the woman could benefit from a referral to a pastor, counsellor, lawyer, or any other professional or had an obvious need, those things were outside of the prayer encounter. Our role as a prayer team was one thing only - to pray! This felt like a wonderfully comfortable boundary for our team to function in. Our church had other structures in place that could aid those diverse needs. My hope was always that if the prayer team had a limited role and stayed within that, they would not suffer burnout. This also fostered our great friendships. It felt good to know that when I wanted prayer I wasn't going to get someone else's opinion of what they thought I should do! The world is full of opinions but how often do we receive genuine caring prayers? One great verse that grounded us comes from Romans 1:11–12.

"For I long to see you, that I may impart to you some spiritual gift to strengthen you—that is, that we may be mutually encouraged by each other's faith, both yours and mine."

An additional helpful guideline was that the team was discouraged from rubbing backs or acting motherly in wanting to comfort the woman who came for prayer. This could potentially shut down the beautiful encounter the woman was receiving from JESUS. That was our goal—for the woman to receive from

God, not us. Overly touching a person could stop the flow of the Holy Spirit doing a deep work. If the woman lacked a mother's love, the greatest gift we could give her was to help her receive love from the Lord, not us. A hand on the knee or shoulder was enough to connect in healthy ways without being a distraction or a threat.

A Church Women's Group

It was amazing how much the church's Wednesday morning women's group impacted so many people. There were months when the attendance swelled to over 200 women. Some professional women purposely scheduled that morning off so they could attend.

Since I was the prayer team leader, I would arrive well before the meeting started and go to the prayer room to begin praying for the morning with whichever prayer team members came. I never pressured them to be there every time; my hopes were to have team members delighted and wanting to come to serve. Some women from the team would arrive shortly after I did, and many mornings the guest speaker would join us. I always was compelled to first stop and ask God what He wanted from us rather than barge ahead presuming that we knew what to do. That was one thing I insisted on - that we always asked God to speak to us with scripture and direction.

By the time I released the prayer team so we could enjoy the meeting, the rest of the women were already seated at the round tables. Walking into a room of 200 women was always such a delight! The music was wonderful; worship always speaks to my heart.

After the guest speaker, great food, and during that second hour the women could choose from a variety of workshops, sometimes as many as seventeen different ones. The choices varied greatly—walking, knitting, how to use your computer, photography, crafts, Bible classes—and were led by the women themselves.

Typically I didn't attend any of the classes myself. My role was to oversee the prayer room where the prayer team gathered with any women who wanted prayer. That was where I usually spent the second hour of the morning—fostering the deep relationships of the prayer team while we prayed over these precious women and their needs.

One year I started a class myself that I called *Praying the Scriptures.* I didn't know how many women would be interested in the class, but the numbers didn't really matter to me. I just wanted to help women know how to become better listeners to God and receive the answers their hearts needed to hear.

After an opening prayer and a few simple instructions, I gave these women an explanation of how God speaks to us. I had already chosen and had printed out a Psalm so each woman would have the same translation. Then beginning with my trusted prayer team, I had each woman read aloud one verse, going around the circle one by one, letting them become comfortable with each other and their own voice. I continued around the circle several times, verse by verse, repeating the Psalm, until it felt like the women were relaxed and at ease.

Just as I had to take baby steps in my healing and my journey in hearing the Voice of God, I knew these ladies need to take baby steps, too. I asked them to continue reading, only this time, after each woman read her verse, she was to turn that verse into a prayer for herself and pray it. I read the first verse of the now familiar Psalm and turned it into a prayer for myself. The women were nervous at first but soon caught on. I was shocked to discover how seldom women prayed for themselves and never aloud. As we continued to go around the room praying scripture over ourselves, we would feel the Presence of the Holy Spirit settle in with us. The tears flowed. Reading and praying scripture is always powerful! I was overjoyed! God is always faithful to His word. And now, these women were experiencing it, too.

Then I read from 1 Corinthians 14:3 (NLT), "But one who prophesies strengthens others, encourages them, and comforts them." I explained to the women that this was already a very firm guideline for the prayer team to work within, and it applied to this class as well.

"You can strengthen, encourage, or comfort someone in the room but nothing else. That is God's heart for us," I told them. I had found there was immense value in helping people know they were in a safe setting and that there needed to be a spoken understanding and agreement of what safety looks like. This was part of that safety.

Once I felt they were comfortable again, I told the women that we were going to read through that same Psalm again, but with one change. "This time, pause and focus on the woman who just read her verse and ask God what He saw in her, what He thought about her. It might be as simple as seeing a white dove over the woman's head or it might be having a completely different scripture come to your mind," I instructed them. "But whatever it is, speak it out loud, as long as it is encouraging, strengthening, or comforting."

Women who felt they had never heard from God would burst into tears as they realized the little picture they were describing was exactly what that other woman needed to hear. There were tears, laughter and very meaningful God moments. The women in the room felt deeply affected by God's love for them.

I, too, was profoundly affected by this. I wasn't sure why this was so successful, why this was so astounding. These women were being touched deeply by God's Word as it became personal and relevant for their life. As I pondered over this, I concluded that it was because we were reading scripture in an atmosphere where we could safely open our hearts and be real. To be humble, to pray for yourself in front of witnesses, to apply God's Word to your life personally—together they were a mighty and powerful force that brought us all to tears.

Lunch with JESUS

Oh, how the women's prayer team loved our times together! There was always laughter and deep conversation ending in praying for each other. One day the team was scheduled to meet in my favourite restaurant. As I sat and waited, one after the other, each woman messaged me that they could not come for various reasons. I sat there all alone, not wanting to leave as I loved the food served there. It seemed odd to eat in a restaurant all by myself, but I decided to do something that seemed so radical. I invited JESUS to have lunch with me! I talked with Him, asking Him what food He would pick, and I told Him that I felt He had not finished making me, that I was not a whole person. He impressed on me the verse in Colossians 2:10 that says that I am complete in Him.

Afterwards, I found this experience was too personal to share with others, and in some ways, I felt embarrassed about it. But a remarkable change happened in my life. After this experience, every time I had a meeting with other women they would walk away and make comments to me like, "Being with you was like being with JESUS." The Presence of Christ stayed with me wherever I was, whether it was laughing and walking with a friend or in serious prayer encounters. I was different, and people could see it. A Presence of God was lingering wherever I went.

I was asked to speak at a lady's group and decided to read them the story I had written for my children— "The Chicken that Changed My Life." I had wanted my children to have a written copy of the story of our pet's role in my healing. They will always remember their mother and her beloved chicken and how much their lives changed because their mother found her joy. It was a time when I was so in love with my Lord and Saviour.

I told the group that, yes, we enjoyed fresh eggs from our family pet for many years, but sadly, only a few months after I wrote out this story and read it with tears to my family, the time came for me to say goodbye to Chip.

"I don't think you could have found a more loved chicken anywhere," I explained. "She'd lived out her life and it was time." I went on to tell the ladies, "There are very few times in my life that I have wept such deep sobs and cried as hard as I did that day. We buried her in our back yard. I was not just saying goodbye to a pet. She represented the catalyst that enabled me to shed that hard, unbelieving heart that was far too afraid to open to anyone, even my Saviour. And you can testify with me today that I am a happy person that can give out to others because I, myself, have received."

Then I prayed for those beautiful ladies that morning. I prayed that if any one of them needed a special sign from the Lord, that He would speak to each of them in His own unique way specific to that lady. My prayer for them was that they would hear Him, that they would open their hearts to hear His Voice, that they would choose to have the courage to believe and to let His love inside of them. Since then, in several churches we have been a part of, I am known as "the chicken lady."

Fruits of a Prayer Life

New life was also being birthed into our prayer life as a married couple. The first time we prayed together beyond the usual prayers for our kids and families, was one New Year's Eve when Dan and I chose to get on our knees and "pray in" the new year like we remembered doing as children. Both of our childhood churches had held Watchnight Services where people would gather for a late-night service to pray through the hour when the calendar changed from one year to the next. That one hour felt so long but it started us on a new path of learning to pray in more focused ways.

This was confirmed by an incident we had with one of our kids. One night I felt so troubled about our son who was out with friends. As alarm grew in my spirit that things were not okay, I finally phoned the home where he was staying, embarrassed to be calling just after midnight. When our son's friend answered the phone, I asked to speak to my son, wanting assurance that all was well. Our son reported that all was fine, there were no problems at all, and he'd be home in a while. Puzzled, I tried to go back to sleep, wondering if I had been a little foolish in calling the home to check. But sleep eluded me as my concern only grew. Dan and I sat up in bed and started to pray. We prayed about everything we could think of that might possibly be wrong. As I started to pray about our son driving home, I suddenly had an awareness that the danger was him driving his car. So that is how we prayed. I imagined every single intersection coming home, every potential drunk driver, while trying to think of what scripture to pray that would be relevant to our son and to our anxious hearts.

On the way to church the next morning I didn't immediately ask questions, so as not to appear as an overbearing, anxious mother. Finally our son, in the back seat of the car, spoke out. "Do you want to know what happened last night?" We were all ears! He explained that I, his mother, had a reputation among the teenagers. They believed that I heard from God and that if I got a warning from God, they'd better listen up. When I had called, these kids, mostly with new drivers' licenses, had been on the verge of going out on the freeway to race and see who could go from 0 to 60 miles an hour the fastest. Because of my phone call they decided to stay in and not go out. Wow! What a jolt this gave my level of confidence—confidence that God loved my son, that I had heard from God and that He had directed me in how to pray.

Another night, a similar thing happened. I was very alarmed in my spirit and awoke to pray. I even went to our other son telling him that something was wrong, and we needed to pray. The phone rang, and I heard my son on the other end of the line. "Mom, we've been jumped. I'm okay," he quickly assured me, "But my friend is going in the ambulance and I want to go with him." At the time I didn't know what he meant by 'jumped.' I soon learned that his group of friends, girls included, had headed out to walk to the corner store. A carload of strangers stopped, got out of their vehicle, and beat on my son and his friends with a skateboard, baseball bat, and tire iron. Our son reported that he grew long legs and ran faster than he had ever run in his life. As he later recounted the details to me, he appeared electrified with an awareness that an angel had helped him to run that fast. Thankfully, all of the kids recovered fine.

Another time one of our kids left home in unsettling circumstances and I was sick with worry. There is nothing like the ache of a mother's heart when conflict divides her family. It also struck me to my core that this child was close to the age I was when I had become homeless. I was so incredibly grateful when my child came home soon after but not before the Lord hit me square between the eyes with the need to examine my own heart. 1 Corinthians 13, well known as the Love Chapter of the Bible, explains what real love is in verses 5–7 (MSG):

"Love never gives up.

Love cares more for others than for self.

Love doesn't want what it doesn't have.

Love doesn't strut,

Doesn't have a swelled head,

Doesn't force itself on others,

Isn't always "me first, "

Doesn't fly off the handle,

Doesn't keep score of the sins of others,

Doesn't revel when others grovel,

Takes pleasure in the flowering of truth,

Puts up with anything,

Trusts God always,

Always looks for the best,

Never looks back,

But keeps going to the end."

I was convicted deep in my heart, especially with the words, "Love doesn't force itself on others." I became acutely aware that I had been using my mothering skills to try to force what I wanted. I could not wait for my son to come home so I could humbly apologize. We had a celebration steak dinner when he arrived!

Such wondrous joy I experienced by learning to hear direction and encouragement from our Father in heaven. He was helping me with all my affairs, teaching me how to pray, when to humble myself, when to stand tall and strong, and how I could better discipline with love.

One Sunday morning before church I asked the Lord to show me how He sees each member of my family. I saw a picture of Dan and then each of my sons, and when I asked about Kimber, I saw a picture of a deer with her fawn pulled in so close and intimate. A very comforting picture. When my family got up, I shared with them what I had seen. On our way to church we approached a busy intersection right by a large mall. Kimber shouted, "Look!" There on the side of the road where deer should never be, was a mama deer with her adorable fawn. We were amazed to find how loudly God was speaking to us. He gives such great comfort, hope, and direction.

For many years we enjoyed Family Camp in Hope, B.C. It was always a highlight of our year. David had a habit of staying under the water at the lake for prolonged periods of time. In the beginning it would alarm me but over the years I adjusted to him doing this. One particular year we had been standing on the dock watching the kids jump in, swimming and playing when suddenly David came shooting up out of the water and collapsed on the dock gasping for air, his skin a blueish-grey colour. When he could finally talk, he told us that he had gone deep under the water; he had wanted to go right to the bottom of the dock structure. He had wrapped a rope around his leg to help him stay under so he could go deeper. But when he wanted to come back up, he couldn't get his leg loose; it was caught. He knew he was drowning, when suddenly, somehow, his leg came loose, and he emerged. God did a miracle and had an angel release his leg. I couldn't stop thanking God for days! I still thank Him whenever I think about that!

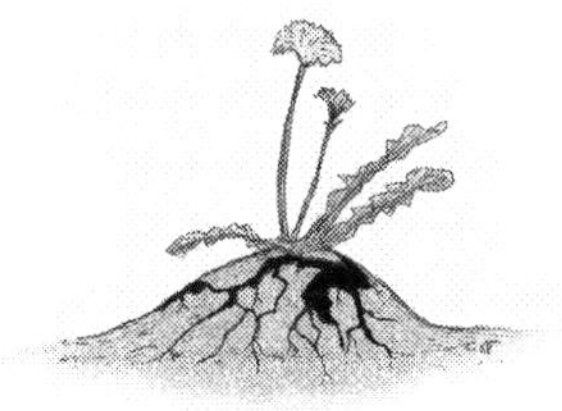

Chapter Ten

Identity in Christ

But I still had so much pain in my heart and still such deep contradictions inside of me. I felt as though I had lived several different lives and they never intersected. I felt disabled, as if living without an arm and a leg, yet living in a world where everyone else had all their limbs but still expected me to function the same as them. Life was very painful for me, and a huge struggle. My loneliness was still immense. There were days I would feel so blessed and rewarded by all the ways I helped other people only to go home and reel in pain for many days. I would still get angry with people for not knowing how much pain I was in; for not understanding how hard life was for me.

A big part in my healing journey came through something I read in *The Bondage Breaker* by Neil Anderson. In the book was a "My Identity in Christ" card that became one of my standby tools to help in a time of need. The card has three columns; the title of each column is an identity statement to declare that I am accepted, I am secure, and I am significant. Each column then lists Bible verses to affirm the truth of each title. Experts tell us that if we want to learn a new habit, we need to repeat the desired effect every day for three weeks. The goal was to read this whole card aloud, twice a day for three weeks. Some of the time you were encouraged to look in the mirror, to read the card to yourself. The first time I did this I felt so foolish, especially if I thought somebody in my house could hear me talking to myself! Even though I felt silly, I had made a commitment, so I persevered.

A different part of your brain is activated by reading aloud than by just reading it to yourself. After a while, as I read, I would find myself disagreeing with what I was saying. *That's not right*! I'd tell myself after reading the words "I have not been given a spirit of fear" or "I am free from any condemnation said against me." Some days I felt very condemned, or insecure and even fearful. As I thought about why I was reacting negatively like that, I realized I was disagreeing with God's Word. As I persevered in trying to develop this discipline, I began to notice other lies I was believing about myself. When I said the truth aloud and found my heart disagreeing, I knew where to focus on building up my confidence and strength that day. I finally had a tool to help me retrain my brain from the trauma of things from my childhood, or like the harshness of teachers and the embarrassment that I would feel. I have given out hundreds of these cards and to this day I have them in my Bible. Whenever I enter a tough time in my life where I am struggling, I will pull out the "My Identity in Christ" card and read it aloud. It helps me center myself in correct thinking. I find this so valuable.

One time I took one of those personality profiles to help me know myself and find the right fit with ministry positions. The results of that test told me I was not cut out to do anything that I was doing! I was so grateful I had been teaching myself who God says I am. He knew me better than a test did.

A Miracle Happened Today

All throughout the years I would occasionally go back and visit my parents, taking the kids with me and testing the waters to see if they wanted a relationship. I would always leave disappointed. Nothing changed until they got too old to remember to be mad at me. After so many years of distance and strain with them, I felt prompted by the Lord to pick up the phone and call my father. The words unexpectedly tumbled off my tongue as I spoke to him: "I love you." I wrote in my journal, *"I feel love in my heart."* I cannot remember the last time I had told my father I loved him. It must have been as a child. As I listened to his voice over the phone, I felt a pang when he described his and my mother's joy in still being able to eat their meals together, even though they were in different levels of care in the same facility. Mom was in 24-hour care and dad was in a more relaxed part of the same facility. She had said to him, at 93 years of age, surrounded by dying people, "I'm learning to not resist a situation I can't control." What an attitude! My dad, too, was so positive, in such a healthy way, telling me what the good parts were—she was using her walker and getting up. Her mind was still sharp, but her heart was failing.

The next day I carefully prepared my heart and cut fresh flowers out of my garden. Excitedly I went to go to see my mom. I would surprise her! I had not shared my flowers with her before. Over the previous couple of years something had changed when I visited my parents. As they aged it seemed as though the friction had gone. They no longer needed to make comments that hurt my heart. At first, I attributed this to frail minds that forgot to still play the game of "who is at fault." After searching my heart, I decided that I would not look at whether an aged mind was a factor in causing them to forget to hold me at a distance. I would accept whatever love they gave me and would not question "why."

As I entered my mother's room, I was surprised to find her sitting up in bed and very alert. I had imagined her lying in bed waiting to die, not aware of much. I sat close and showed her the pictures I'd brought of my family. As her eyesight was so poor and she had no magnifying glass, I described each picture. I stayed a long time and enjoyed it. There was a lot of love in the room. She shared the things she was learning, and I determined I, too, wanted to still be a learner in my final days.

She said I had been a good mom. I did not remember her ever affirming me before and it felt good.

As I got up to leave, planning to go search out my father's room, he entered my mother's room. What joy erupted as my parents saw each other! After a hello and brief hug with my father, I sat down again beside my mom. My father pulled his chair in so close he pushed up against my leg, stretching over me hungrily, greedily reaching out to touch the one he loved and rub her arm. My parents acted like lovers who had not seen each other in an awfully long time. It had been three hours. They could not stop touching, loving, smiling as their eyes embraced in longing. The man that I had so much trouble touching, being physically close to all these years, was leaning over my legs to show the woman of his dreams all the love he could muster. And I allowed a miracle to happen. I allowed my body and spirit to be overwhelmed with the love in the room. The love that had caused me to be created in the first place. Love I could choose to allow inside my heart. Love that came from outside of the three of us.

A few days prior I had attended a prayer gathering with some wonderful people, and the teacher had challenged us to ask a question of the Lord and of our own hearts. The question was, "What lies am I believing? What truth or name do you want to call me, Lord?" After this encounter I wrote in my journal

> God is good. He can be trusted, and He sometimes answers prayers that we have never even prayed. He shows evidence in my life of deep healing from a heart that has truly forgiven. Thank you God for helping me to do the impossible.

This miracle in my mother's room was bigger than I had ever imagined.

After this visit with my parents, I asked the Lord the question, "What lies am I believing about myself?" In response, He gave me a clear vision of myself as a baby, and the band around my ankle when I was born—the band that identifies the child. I heard the words, "Not wanted." So, like my teacher had instructed a couple of days before, I asked the Lord what He wanted to call me, and He said, "Beloved; cherished." This was so strange to me as my mother had always loved babies, especially baby girls. I could not imagine what might have happened for me to be branded as not wanted, but this was an underlying thought that I had experienced my entire life. As I attempted to file this away to work on later, it suddenly came to me. The miracle!

Sitting on that bed between my parents and their love had allowed me to see the lie I had been harbouring about my identity. A whole lot of life had happened between me and them that made me feel rejected, even despised. I now allowed a healing to take place deep in my heart. I was wanted and I was loved. I moved on from that day believing people would now see a difference in me; a different heart response: New eyes of love responding from a deeper healing.

Making Decisions, Becoming Whole

NightShift Street Ministry also had a Care Center where counsellors were available. A professional counsellor named Laurel Hildebrandt had been invited to conduct a training workshop for these counsellors at the Care Center. She would be teaching a unique method of prayer counselling she had designed called the Levelling Prayer Technique. Laurel had already been successfully using this gentle method of counselling in her own private practice for years (and she would certainly add that it is a gift from the Lord and not her own idea). I was so excited and held my breath in anticipation as I asked if I could please attend. Although I was not a counsellor, I was involved in prayer ministry and I was interested to see how she used prayer to go deep and heal a person spiritually, cognitively, behaviourally, and emotionally. I was thrilled when I was told I could attend this weeklong class, and eagerly agreed I would not use the technique since it was to be used by trained counsellors only. I knew too well the damage that could be inflicted upon someone through prayer ministry when it was done by people who did not understand their limitations. It can be very tricky to discern between mental illness, trauma, and effects of drugs or demonic influence, not to mention the complication of fractured personalities.

I devoured every minute of this rich teaching, already somewhat familiar to me from studying about our identity in Christ in Neil Anderson's books. An incorrect view of God, theology that is "off," undermines a person's happiness, freedom, and mental health. This was such a highlight in my life—to be grounded in correct thinking. At the end of the course, I concluded that the only thing standing in my way of having that free and victorious life was whether or not I believed God. I determined to believe as I had never believed before.

Little did I know that only one week later my mother would die. I had dreaded that moment for many years, worrying about how it would affect me. So much unfinished business. So much never said, never settled. Several years previous, I had told my parents in a letter about the Africans in relation to abuse, but we had never discussed it.

My plan had been to have a conversation with my mother about my abuse from a houseboy, and I figured the easiest way to face that topic would be to first talk about me and my siblings. Appropriate boundaries and safety were not something established in our home. I plucked up the courage and attempted to talk with my mother about incest in our home amongst the siblings while I was growing up. Sadly, my mother's immediate response was to say, "You cannot hold a child responsible for normal discovery as they are growing up." This response, I felt, showed me it was not safe for me to proceed in a conversation with my mother. If she could not handle me talking about incest, how could she ever handle me telling her about all the rest? I was sad that these things would never be worked out with my mother.

I decided to make an appointment with Laurel and was greatly relieved when she agreed to take me on as a client, even though she knew my background. She was so gentle of spirit, wise and astute. I felt encouraged that she wanted to listen well to me before deciding what course of action to take. I had much experience with people wanting to categorize me in a slot that was not a good fit, assuming that a certain procedure or line of practice was what I needed. It seemed that what had worked for others simply didn't work for me, and Laurel seemed so willing and able to listen to what God was saying to her heart, as well as to what I was saying. At that point in my life I had reached a place where I was content and fulfilled and had chosen to close the door on going back into my past. I figured I had healed enough to be happy and to continue forward. I could not live my whole life going back and working on myself! Yet my relationship with my daughter, now 10, had become somewhat volatile, and I believed that going back to work on my past some more could potentially help. This new counsellor seemed a good fit.

Courage to Heal

Even though I was happy and fulfilled in my mothering, marriage, friendships, and ministry opportunities, I continued to struggle on a very deep level. I had grown beyond feeling like I was missing limbs but still felt inadequate and not whole as a person. In my journal I would draw myself as a large circle with only a part filled in as if I were taking up only a portion of my life.

There was an unexplainable strange sensation I had experienced for many years: feeling like nails were being driven into my hands. A sense of shame would wash over me, and I would interpret this to mean that I needed to be punished, or I needed to punish myself. I would have such wonderful ministry encounters and feel so good about God using me, only to feel these strange sensations. I often asked God if it had anything to do with identifying with Christ's suffering. Was I to die more to my own selfish heart? Was I not giving God the credit for all the wonderful things He was doing through my life?

One day, in one of my deep healing times with the Lord, I had a new memory from my childhood. I remembered the tormentors, my abusers, hanging me upside down and acting out a mock crucifixion with my little body. It also felt like my eyes were gouged out—like my spiritual eyes were destroyed at that time, preventing me from understanding that God loved me. These abusers did what they could to harm the good that the missionaries were doing. My dear counsellor walked me through the horror, the depth of shock and suffering, and into glorious light and healing. I never again succumbed to those horrible memories of nails in my hands and the mocking voice in my head that I hadn't recognized as not being my own.

Another memory came to me that overwhelmed my human ability to process. I had struggled my entire life with finding fault in myself when things went wrong. For every problem that happened in life, I could find some way that I was responsible. As I became capable, growing in courage and strength, I was able to recall the time I was forced to witness, as a wee child, a ritual human sacrifice where a baby was murdered. My abusers, grown men, intentionally caused me to feel and believe that I was to blame for the death of that child. Memories such as this required professional help, and I am so grateful I had the support I did. With Laurel's help I was able to get to the root of why I felt such self blame and shame.

It's hard to comprehend that even today, some people participate in these rituals. There are many other horrific things that I've remembered that I do not want to write about. There would be no benefit to anyone to read about such things. I have received healing in stages, with each new memory, even though many people told me there was no hope of recovering or being able to walk free from this.

Pastor Janet

I grew to greatly value my Pastor, Janet. She was the overseer for both areas of ministry that I was involved in. Even when I helped facilitate Freedom sessions, she never seemed to tire of my excessive desire to always hold myself accountable. Our church was not necessarily familiar with my wild ways and unconventional ideas of what I thought it meant to walk in and live by the Spirit. I sent her countless e-mails and reported to her my thoughts and plans. I saw her as someone I could make myself accountable to as I felt a deep need to be held accountable.

During one of my counselling sessions with Laurel, I saw myself as resembling a globe, the world. Internally I was separated like the world is separated into countries. I truly did feel like those separated countries. I felt like I had lived many different lives that never intersected, that there were parts of me that never connected. The fracture was so severe. The more healing that I received the more the land took over the water until I became one whole world, a whole ball. As I thought about this, I felt compelled to tell Pastor Janet my whole story. Up until this point I had never told anyone other than my counsellor my whole story. I asked Pastor Janet for an appointment with her where I could share. I told her it would need to be a two-hour appointment.

Spring Break was approaching, and I asked my kids if they would release me to shut myself up in my bedroom to write my story. It was awfully hard to do, but I wrote down everything I wanted to tell this dear kind woman about all that I had experienced. I realized that it in fact would take more than two hours to read what I had written. My story turned out to be 33 pages, typed! It was such a big event for me that I asked my counsellor to come and sit with me while I read to Janet. It took extreme courage and lots of water and deep breaths as I ploughed through my written words and poured out my life to two beautiful, caring, responsive hearts. Afterwards I drove home in a daze.

The next Sunday at church there were tables set out in the entrance where people could sign up to volunteer for an upcoming event. I took my place behind the table as one of the leaders. Pastor Janet slipped in beside me and as we worked together, she didn't shy away, didn't change her behaviour, didn't act any differently towards me. At one point she did lean close to me to say, "How are you?" I was thrilled. I was not rejected, judged, or treated differently. She now knew all my "stuff" and I still had a place in my church. I had not disqualified myself by "telling it all." This was momentous for me in my healing journey. A most precious valuable gift had been given to me—not only her time and a listening heart, but her continued acceptance of me. She did not treat me any differently once she knew the things in my past that were so hard to come to terms with. This really helped me with bringing myself together as a whole person.

From that time on I moved forward with a greater confidence in God and in myself. The sky was the limit with open-ended potential for me to grow into all God had created me to be. I had found a place of support, the structure of accountability and the encouragement to grow. I felt so useful and loved all my opportunities to give out of the overflow of love and joy that bubbled up and out of me. The depth of joy was certainly increasing far above the depth of pain I had suffered.

Growing in Leaps and Bounds

Christmas Day, I wrote in my journal:

> PEACE in our home for Christmas. It's 10 a.m., turkey is in the oven and all are still asleep on the living room floor.

We started this family tradition when David was only two years old. Everyone would sleep on the living room floor on Christmas Eve, and attempt to keep the fire burning in our fireplace all night long. Once the gifts had all been opened, amid the mess of paper all over the floor, Dan would tell stories.

Copied from my journal in the new year:

> Dear God,
>
> It's January 2012. This year has never been lived before by anybody else … and I get to live it. This is awesome, frightens me and thrills me all at the same time. What a privilege. As I enter your Presence … enjoying your heart … Lord empty me, the rooms of my heart, sweep me, the spent experiences, sweep the residue left out in my heart. Let light come, enter, cleanse, and purify me. Empty my mind of thinking of all those people. Purge me. Burn up what does not belong in your daughter.
>
> The Lord responded to me by telling me, "You are too pale. Expose yourself to Grace; take a daily shower in My Grace." I saw myself with white skin lacking colour and I understood I needed to get out in the sun. Like I needed to expose myself to sunshine for a healthy body, the Lord wanted me to expose myself to Grace. Without Grace to warm and colour me, I am lacking, am even weakly. I want to feel it, give it away, expose myself, internalize the Grace. Taste it, share it, grow in it, bathe in it.

I accepted that I wasn't showing myself enough grace, and found direction in these verses:

"So be content with who you are, and don't put on airs. God's strong hand is on you; He'll promote you at the right time. Live carefree before God; He is most careful with you." (1 Peter 5:6–7 MSG)

I had heard countless sermons throughout my life and would allow myself to be challenged to the core, especially by sermons that would encourage us to take a leap of faith. The preacher would build up the sermon, eventually saying, "Take that leap and jump off the cliff. God won't let you fall." I'd respond and do that. I wanted so much to have all God had for me. Yet it seemed that every time I took that leap I'd fall flat on my face and have to pick up the pieces once again, trying to figure out where I'd gone wrong. Now the Lord was encouraging me to believe again, to trust again. I was growing into a new relationship with Father as well as with other people. I was growing in leaps and bounds in seeing JESUS strong in my weakness. There was so much encouragement all around me amid the glimpses of torment from the past.

Furthering our growth and increasing our learning curve, Dan and I discovered a prophetic conference held every January near Portland. Travelling down to Portland became a highlight of each year. The purpose of the conference was to hear and discern what God was saying for the upcoming year. This became a cornerstone in my life as it caused me to examine my own heart at the start of each year. I decided that I would ask God to give me a specific word at the beginning of each new year, to be my focus for that year. That particular year He showed me Job 36:16–18 (TLB):

"How He wanted to lure you away from danger into a wide and pleasant valley and to prosper you there. But you are too preoccupied with your imagined grievances against others. Watch out! Don't let your anger at others lead you into scoffing at God! Don't let your suffering embitter you at the only one who can deliver you."

God was showing me how to not get tripped up and derail my healing journey through being mad at people who misunderstood me. He told me, "Let go and build anew."

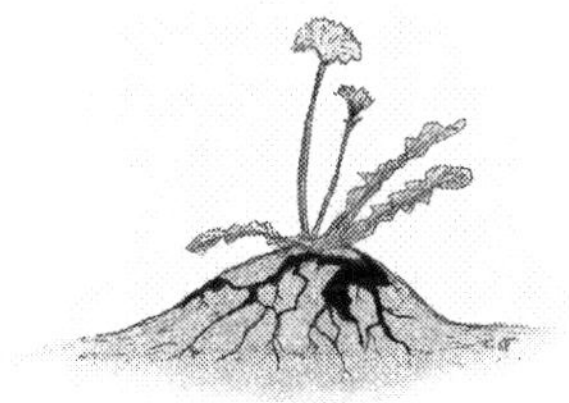

Chapter Eleven

New Territory

The moment I believed that I could live in victory is when my new life began. As I said, I had determined to believe with all my heart as never before. The ONLY thing standing in my way was whether I really believed it. Now I had help (with Laurel) to remove my obstacles. My personal paraphrase of Ephesians 2:6 is "I am already seated with Christ in heavenly places." It was time to live like it was true.

Laurel instructed me to guard my heart and do a study on what that could mean to me. Guarding my heart was a boundary that I could set. These were familiar verses to me:

"Behold, I send an angel before you to guard you on the way and to bring you to the place that I have prepared. Pay careful attention to him and obey his voice; do not rebel against him." (Exodus 23:20–21a)

I will not drive them out from before you in one year, lest the land become desolate and the wild beasts multiply against you. Little by little I will drive them out from before you, until you have increased and possess the land." (Exodus 23:29–30)

I identified with the account in the Old Testament of the people of Israel taking over the land God had for them. It was to be their inheritance and they had much work to do and many battles to fight and win before they were ready to live there. If

God had given them the land all at once, they never could have maintained it and potentially could have been overcome by the wild animals. This made so much sense in my personal life. I had to grow into my healing bit by bit just as a child learns to crawl and then takes tiny steps, little by little. We are not born at the teenager stage ready to drive a car and act like an adult. We grow into maturity. My life certainly has taken this route in my own healing journey. As I grasped a new truth, gained a new victory, I had to grow into my healing, take ownership of new thinking and claim it as my own. I had to "take over the land" bit by bit and establish myself there before I could move on to the next part. Now I had additional territory to take over with this new counsellor. Something so remarkably wonderful about my appointments with Laurel was that at the end of every session she would ask JESUS what He had to say to me. When she told me to ask, I would always say, "I hear nothing," as I never do seem to hear in the way others expect of me. Laurel would always hear from Him and would write the beautiful words of God's love for me on a piece of paper so that I could take it home with me.

This is one of the first ones she gave to me. This is what she heard God saying for my heart:

> "You are My radiant and beautiful bride, My daughter. How I love you! Let My love fill you to overflowing so that you can love yourself, too. From My love flows rivers that cleanse you. I am so proud of you. Wear your new robe of righteousness and truth and do not pick up the old shame one again. I will burn it in the unquenchable fire. I love you."

The technique Laurel had developed was so comprehensive; so powerfully effective, and it supplied a framework for me to safely open the door and go back into the old memories. I could totally fall apart in her office and then be put back together again before I left because of her way of praying for me and her way of having me pray for myself. However, it did take a two-hour appointment each time. I was beginning to feel like David says in Psalm 124:7 (emphasis added).

*"We have escaped like a bird from the snare of the fowlers; the snare is **broken**, and we have escaped."*

Battles

As we progressed, I found myself falling into a pit. The horrors I experienced that previously would have hospitalized me—frozen in fear, paralysis and inability—were now faced in Laurel's office. I came up against a power far greater than I could stand against alone. However, I saw that Laurel had the power (from God), knowledge and position in God to stand with me. I learned to trust as I had never trusted before. Together we were able to deal with the terrifying oppression. She later told me she thought I received so much from God because I had made a choice to trust her. That was a decision I chose to make over and over. My life verse once again:

*"Trust in the Lord with all your heart, and **do not lean** on your own understanding." (Proverbs 3:5 emphasis added)*

I had studied Ephesians 6 about the full armour of God many times throughout my life, but now I gained an understanding of it like never before. The full armour of God is not for a "flesh and blood" battle. My enemies were not people. My enemy was spiritual darkness, rulers in heavenly places, authorities that were not God-ordained in my life, cosmic powers. Or, as it says in Ephesians 6:10–13 (TPT):

"Now my beloved ones, I have saved these most important truths for last: Be supernaturally infused with strength through your life-union with the Lord JESUS. Stand victorious with the force of his explosive power flowing in and through you.

Put on God's complete set of armour provided for us, so that you will be protected as you fight against the evil strategies of the accuser! Your hand-to-hand combat is not with human beings, but with the highest principalities and authorities operating in rebellion under the heavenly realms. For they are a powerful class of demon-gods and evil spirits that hold this dark world in bondage. Because of this, you must wear all the armour that God provides so you're protected as you confront the slanderer, for you are destined for all things and will rise victorious."

I was beginning to see what my battle was really about. I had put so much effort into learning how to put on the armour of God, to have correct thinking, the right belief system, to walk in faith and truth. Now I realized I had been putting the armour on over top of the wounds and hurts and wrongs that had penetrated my heart. I had to first get those thorns out of my spirit before the armour over top could fully protect me. I figured out that evil could reside in my pain. Now I found myself sitting with someone truly knowledgeable who could help me face what felt to me like an evil force far too great for any human to withstand—and she did not appear to be afraid. She was patient and kind and yet a mighty force that could stand with JESUS on my behalf and show me how to walk into freedom. I realized that the horrible separation from God that I would sometimes feel was now something I could address and work through. I wanted help so I could make my pain count for something!

"Put on truth as a belt to strengthen you to stand in triumph. Put on holiness as the protective armour that covers your heart. Stand on your feet alert, then you'll always be ready to share the blessings of peace. In every battle, take faith as your wrap-around shield, for it is able to extinguish the blazing arrows coming at you from the Evil One! Embrace the power of salvation's full deliverance, like a helmet to protect your thoughts from lies. And take the mighty razor-sharp Spirit-sword of the spoken Word of God." (Ephesians 6:14–17 TPT, emphasis added)

I ran to scripture like I had never done before. During most sessions with Laurel, I would clutch my huge Bible to my chest and cling to God with all I had. Words in the Bible would take wings and leap off the page, coming to life in my heart and understanding. I found a Rock on which I could stand, while I opened the door to the memories and experiences that had robbed me of my childhood; stolen my life from me; and programmed me to be something other than who God had made me to be. I learned that the process of walking free is not a power encounter with satan. He is not so big that I have to fight him. I don't wrestle him. It is a Truth encounter. I apply God's truths and satan shrivels up. Psalm 18 became so special and one day Laurel read the whole thing aloud over me. These verses especially spoke to me:

"He sent from on high, he took me;

he drew me out of many waters.

He rescued me from my strong enemy

and from those who hated me,

for they were too mighty for me.

They confronted me in the day of my calamity,

but the Lord was my support.

He brought me out into a broad place;

he rescued me, because he delighted in me." (Psalm 18:16–19)

I would have the most incredible and wonderful experiences with God and His immense love as I would take part in these sessions moving towards healing.

From my journal:

> I am a book. My book looks like some of it is bunched together. Like a book that has been stored out in a damp garage. As He (God) leafs through my pages, He finds some stuck together, almost like black with mold. I ask Him to protect my lungs, protect Laurel's lungs, as my pages are leafed through, exposed to love, exposed to light. This mold is why someone should not try to help

> me that does not know what they are doing. I watch as JESUS leafs through my book and plants kisses on every single page. Separating, kissing—healing me from the inside out.

Early on as I had sought help for healing, I found very few people willing or able to try to help me. I had become so discouraged, especially when I learned some new counsellors were graduated with instructions not to take on any clients who had suffered from satanic ritual abuse. Where were we supposed to go for help? As the Lord unfolded this picture for me of the book, the mould, I understood how the black mould from unveiling my life to someone else, could potentially cause them harm and me further harm. I was immensely grateful for Laurel's professional knowledge, skills and ability to hear from God and follow His leading. It took knowing her position in God and being firmly grounded in scripture to unveil what needed to be seen by the Light. People with big hearts that liked to do prayer ministry could potentially cause more harm than good, by opening the lid to the darkness while not having the skills to walk a person out into freedom.

Going Back to Go Forward

As Laurel would pray for me, I would become aware of a separation inside of me where, as a child, I had stored parts of me in different places. It was as if the trauma was so great that I had to hide a part of me where the event happened. Many times over recent years, I had wanted to pull out all my teeth as I had felt that evil had been planted inside them. One time sitting in Laurel's office, I connected with myself as a young child and was totally convinced I had left a part of me hiding under our dining room table, tucked up tightly against the underside of the tabletop. Another time, as I remembered a mission compound in Kenya, I thought I had left myself hiding inside the big water barrel that was used to store rainwater. I also remembered being lured off the mission station and taken away to a village while my parents were at a conference. Another time I found part of myself in a brick, outside my childhood home. Laurel would help me release these parts of me that felt trapped and left behind, allowing them to go with JESUS to heaven for healing. It seemed so bizarre and too hard to believe, yet as I cooperated, tremendous healing and growth transpired in my life. This occurred countless times, every time I went for more help over many years.

In the little bit of reading I have done, people who have suffered the amount of severe trauma that I did have developed multiple personalities. Here again, I proved to be different, which was why I needed someone who would not categorize me according to what they had learned but would be willing to adjust their thinking. I had not experienced multiple personalities, but I did have deep fractures that needed to be healed before I could become one whole person.

Sometimes I would come home in a state of shock. In fact, I would go into shock at times as I faced the things that had happened to me. They were so "over the top" and overwhelming, when I'd come home and enter the world of my family, children and the mundane things of life such as making dinner, I would sometimes need to go to bed for a whole day to recover. Then I would slip in and out of thinking that all of this was too much to be real, too bizarre to be my real life. Many times, I wondered if I would have ever remembered those suppressed memories if Amber hadn't died.

During this time, the family dog that I wrote about in my story *The Chicken that Changed my Life* suddenly became ill. Andrew woke me up soon after we'd gone to bed one night. Saber was terribly ill. We rushed her to an emergency vet only to discover that by the time Andrew laid her on the vet's table, she was gone. She had died in his arms. Apparently, she'd had a tumour that burst.

Driving home was heart wrenching. I was very concerned for Andrew. This dog was his dog and slept in his bed with him every single night. Still a young teenager, he was devastated. This was so sudden, so brutal and final. We talked about heaven and if he would see her again. We cried and comforted each other.

What I experienced next was a real eye-opener and a shock to me. Even though I had dearly loved Saber, it was as if her death had never happened. I had completely disconnected and distanced, separated myself, from that reality. I had not been aware that could happen to me. As I proceeded in my counselling, I found so much became unreal in my life. At times I felt that someone could even convince me that I never had children, that they were just something I had made up in my head. The fracture in me was so great it was like there was nobody inside, like I was just an empty shell. My entire identity and personhood had been wiped out. As if my fingerprints were gone. What was real? How could I not be in touch with having given birth to our four children? This experience with our dear dog really helped me start to understand myself to another level in my healing journey.

God in His great mercy provided so many wonderful things in my life to help me. I would feel absolutely destroyed in some of these sessions with Laurel and then need to re-enter my life as a leader in many areas. I was mentoring women, leading a prayer team, working with the homeless and leading a weekly prayer walk through the streets of Whalley. I needed to pull myself together so quickly to do this. Several times I helped teach the Volunteer Training at NightShift only a few hours after coming out of these counselling sessions. It was like I was living two lives. Only it wasn't two lives, but the miraculous way God provided for me to stay on my feet and not be swept away into insanity. Forcing my brain to think of my children and the need to lead a group saved me from slipping into another reality that might destroy me. I never could have done this without someone walking through it with me, someone who knew God to be bigger than anything else.

Laurel never seemed afraid, defensive, or troubled by what I had to say. She seemed to always know what to do. Her utmost confidence in God and her relationship with Him boosted my courage. She would always take me to JESUS, and He would handle all things. Many times, I found myself completely unable to speak when she asked me to repeat prayers after her. When I prayed them for myself it helped me "own" them, rather than just let her pray for me.

For more than a year, I was stuck on the alphabet. The letters would go over and over in my head.

Aa Bb Cc Dd Ee Ff Gg Hh Ii Jj Kk Ll Mm
Nn Oo Pp Qq Rr Ss Tt Uu Vv Ww Xx Yy Zz

When I was a child and learning the alphabet, I had been programmed by abuse to think differently about my life and who I was. This programming had given me a compulsion to live by a distinct set of rules, and now I wanted to free myself from these directives. Night and day, I would be working myself through the alphabet. I would spell and work through the word J E S U S over and over and over, as if I needed to work my body through each letter. Once, I saw myself as a typewriter, only every time I struck the key I wanted, something different would come out. Sometimes in session with Laurel I would lose the ability to speak or even breathe properly. Or I would ask if I could spell my answer, as if stuck in the letters.

God's Words written in the recesses of my heart were coming to life to heal all of me. I fell increasingly in love with scripture and wanted to live inside those special verses that had come alive for me. I was so grateful that I had become a worshipper. Day and night I would live in songs. The sessions were brutally hard but the healing … oh … so … sweet!!

In the beginning I saw JESUS in that ocean that stood for such pain and torment for me. He stood, arms open to me, and asked me to come to Him. Walk into that Ocean of Pain! My fear was debilitating. In anguish I cried, "What have I done by opening that door into my past again!?" When I told Laurel that it would destroy me, she made me look at her and then said, "It already has destroyed you. Now it is time to get healed." In time I grew to understand that she was right: the worst had already happened; it was now time to heal.

"Talitha cumi"

I had so many experiences with God. I heard JESUS come to me and say, "Talitha cumi," which is translated as "Little girl, arise." In the Bible, JESUS raised a child from death and in Mark 5:41, He called her out with those words. He was calling all parts of me to arise from death, too.

One session was significant in helping to release my personal shame. It took a tremendous amount of effort and cooperation on my part, only to see myself at the end of the session picking the shame back up to take home with me, as if it were a familiar cloak I needed to wear. I discovered how much work, self-discipline and retraining of my brain needed to happen for me to keep the healing that I gained. I saw myself as a cup, full of shame, and I needed to hold myself upside down as long as it took to drain every last dreg out of my cup. I wanted a clean cup to hold whatever God had for me! I needed to empty *me* of all that negative harmful stuff.

I learned that God did not want to make me a better *me*. He wanted to transform who I thought I was into what His wisdom had crafted me to be in the first place. Before I was born, I was a thought in God's mind (Jeremiah 1:5, also Psalm 139:13-14, Ephesians 1:4-6). Before life damaged me, I was perfect and beautiful in God's eyes. I needed to find out who God says I am.

After one of my counselling sessions I accidentally stumbled upon a dead duck while walking in a park. Seeing it catapulted me into remembering death—the times I had tried to take my life, the times I had been taken to the point of death by abusers.

Then I saw a mental picture of the bridge that was part of the view from my house.

From my journal:

> So much talk of DEATH, duck at Mill Lake, taken to the point of death, all the times I have "romanced death," played with it.
>
> As Laurel was praying to remove all those bad thoughts and things from my life I saw myself on the bridge as I have envisioned so many times. Walking over, driving over … I would imagine and wonder … if I went to jump, would anyone come for me, would anyone rescue me …would Cathie actually leave her work and come for me? Over and over those years I would wonder. I was now thrust into this scene while Laurel was praying for me. Seeing myself wondering if I had the courage to jump. As a teenager on the street no one had come for me.
>
> Then, I saw the Lord come for me and He said to me, "I will rescue you." I melted into His arms and as Laurel continued to pray for me I watched as the things she was praying about started to fall off of me and tumble into the water instead of me falling into the water. The heartache, suffering, evil curses, and harm done to me was falling away, far down into the water. Not me.

The next day I wrote:

> I AM FREE! Praise God! I am back to my normal self; my foundation does not feel cracked anymore.

As time went on and I received increased healing, becoming stronger and stronger, I went back to this scene at the bridge the same way I had gone back to the scene of me at age 15 when I had attempted suicide. I had re-lived the scene where I was being taken out of the house on an ambulance stretcher. The Lord let me see that when my mother's voice had called me back to life, not all of me had come back. I had allowed a part of me to stay dead. The girl in me needed to be rescued by JESUS, taken to heaven to be healed, and then returned to me as a healed part to be reintegrated into my body. Now at the bridge, again I saw that I had imagined jumping so many times that a part of me had already done it. I could not be healed and whole until I went back to that spot in my memory and asked JESUS to forgive me and take that girl to heaven for healing.

As Laurel prayed me up and out from under that water, death, suicide, I spoke to those parts. Laurel spoke to those parts. I would not have been able to do it if she had not touched me, placing her hand on my leg, and holding my hand. I felt too small, too weak. I couldn't speak but she gently called and coaxed me until I was finally able to do it. I sent death and suicide away. I told them to go away from me. Then He came! JESUS entered in the middle of it all and He dropped a key into my hands. A key to LIFE and I unlocked my heart, my will for Him.

"Behold, I stand at the door and knock. If anyone hears my voice and opens the door, I will come in to him and eat with him, and he with me." (Revelation 3:20)

In between these earth-shattering experiences, I received tremendous encouragement from God and found I was becoming much more effective in my ministry opportunities. More and more, I was being asked to speak publicly and lead people in their own healing. I truly found that the well of joy inside me was much deeper than the depth of suffering I had endured. People would tell me I was shining, that I had a glow about me. As I walked through malls, I noticed people would look at me and smile. Something about me was making strangers smile. Others told me they were drawn to a peace they felt coming from me. I knew that I was being called to let my light shine.

"Is a lamp brought in to be put under a basket, or under a bed, and not on a stand? For nothing is hidden except to be made manifest; nor is anything secret except to come to light." (Mark 4:21-22)

I was learning lots about walking into that Ocean of Pain to be with JESUS, and then growing in the ability to release my pain so it would not live with me. One day I experienced this as a transferring of my pain to a ball.

My Journal:

> Let us play Ball. My parts are with JESUS and I find I still have some pain today, not in my heart but my mind. JESUS invites me to put my pain in a ball and play ball with Him. I try a small hard ball. I throw it against a wall, sometimes clapping in between the bounces or twirling my body around before it bounces back to me. Then a larger ball. I find the courage to bounce it out into the dark, but I do not see JESUS throwing it back to me. How do I find JESUS to play ball with Him? He tells me to put all the grief from the loss of each part I ever had, put all that pain into the ball. I try to remember each part.
>
> One of the balls is so large it looks 5 feet in diameter. Will I play with other people? It is so large! JESUS, Your ball, the world, the globe ... is that your pain? It becomes a ballroom, dancing with a monster, my pain ... becomes Beauty and the Beast, dancing, twirling, and enjoying, the monster pain turns into a ballroom dance with JESUS. I am back in my house at 13 to 15 years of age and I bounce the ball up and down the hallways, into the rooms, bouncing and playing with JESUS. And I remember each pet I had lost as a child, every pain and heartache as I play with JESUS. Playing until I realized I had placed my pain in

> the ball and JESUS was not throwing it back to me. I had learned how to separate my pain from me and let it go.

Something very deep was also happening to me as I learned how to allow love inside of me. I knew in my head that God loved me, no doubt about that. But I felt like I was so ugly, untouchable; someone to repel and reject. I had never been a physically "touchy" person as far as hugs and coming close to people. I accepted that as normal since that's how my mother was. As I increasingly allowed more of God's love inside of me, accepting the Love Words He was saying about me and at times allowing Laurel to touch me as she prayed, I changed. Something happened. I wanted to touch people. And then to my shock, I was all right with people touching me! My kids knew they could love me all they wanted by sitting on my lap or rubbing my arms, but they knew to never touch my face. After one of these deep sessions with Laurel, I knew I had received a new healing. When I told my family, Kimber could not stop coming up to me, and touching my face to see if I would react. My kids were so proud of me! It no longer bothered me at all to have my face touched.

That Christmas I wrote,

> I see JESUS has lots of gifts for me under the Christmas tree. Each one is a piece of myself.

In one session, I told Laurel of my desire to go back to Vancouver and walk the places where I had become homeless, look for the buses I rode and find the place where I had made that fateful decision to end my life, before God overruled it. I could hardly believe it when she agreed that I should go, but she insisted I let her know when I would do this. She thought it would be better if someone went with me, but these were things I needed to do alone. Being the impulsive person that I am, I immediately got in my car and drove straight to Vancouver. I found the house we lived in when we first arrived in Canada. From there I went to the high school steps where I had slept some nights. My old church building no longer existed. I went into the restaurant where I had worked and was shocked to find that it still looked the same after all these years. The washroom, the position of the booths—everything was the same. As I sat at the counter, I became acutely aware of how close I was to the alcohol behind the bar. Memories flooded over me. Then it happened … JESUS came and sat across from me. Instantly I relaxed and felt fine. Driving home, I felt so much more complete and a new peace and acceptance filled my heart.

I discovered that I would slip back and forth between revelling with joy in my new-found healing and getting sucked under the water in darkness and pain. Some days it felt like I was engaged in a fight with the legendary monster Ogopogo in the lake. Who would win? Other days it felt as though I had been run over by a truck and needed to be in ICU. I still found times when I thought I would not make it. I fought a battle in my mind many times, telling myself over and over, "I choose life, I choose to live," rejecting the thoughts that would say otherwise. Healing with JESUS was wonderful, yet I still needed to retrain my brain to stop thinking the old way. The old way wanted to destroy me, claiming that I was not worthy of life.

Once again, my Journal:

> Dear God, this pain feels unmanageable. You ask more of me than I can bear. My lot seems unending. If this is what You want for me, if this is what I am to embrace … then my life You can have. I surrender, I give up the fight. I will accept the pain and suffering. No longer seek release. You are my release and if You don't give it to me, I will stop running away from pain and walk into it and accept it. So I commit spiritual suicide, I give up the fight, I accept my lot, my share and accept if You want me in continual pain. I am Yours.

I was drawn to this verse in Acts 9:5 (NKJV):

"Then the Lord said [to Saul], 'I am Jesus, whom you are persecuting. It is hard for you to kick against the goads.'"

Saul's resistance to God caused him much pain and anguish. I no longer wanted to resist God but wanted to humbly cooperate with all He had for me. I wanted to not only believe in God—I wanted to know Him. And I wanted to die to myself like JESUS had died, and put to death the hurtful painful things that tried to take me down.

One day while I was going back into my memory, the Lord told me to "look for the flowers." In every memory and every thought about a person or event I was to look for God's flowers, look for what beauty was there mixed up with the ugliness. Also, when I asked Him what to do with my old photos, He said, "Put them in My washing machine," and I'd watch as God washed my life to make it something I was capable of looking at.

I understood that I was to grow into learning who He made me to be before all the pain from life happened. In 1 John 3:20 we read that even if our hearts condemn us, God is greater than our own hearts. He is greater than my own self-condemnation. Wow! I am hard on myself, but He is greater and knows the truth about me.

Soon after this new learning curve, while I was at a wonderful worship service where there was freedom to sing and dance with abandon, JESUS appeared to me again. I was taken in my spirit to the cemetery, Amber's graveside, where I had done so much grieving, soul-searching and … drinking. JESUS came to me and gave me a wineskin to drink from. It was so refreshing! Drinking from His jug satisfies. I wrote in my journal:

> I think now, if I have a desire to drink alcohol again, I can go back to this experience and drink from my relationship with JESUS.

After that time, I never again succumbed to the need to drink alcohol in an excessive way or from a craving in my body. Praise God!

The Lord's Covenant of Peace

"I will make with them a covenant of peace and banish wild beasts from the land, so that they may dwell securely in the wilderness and sleep in the woods. And I will make them and the places all around my hill a blessing, and I will send down the showers in their season; they shall be showers of blessing. And the trees of the field shall yield their fruit, and the earth shall yield its increase, and they shall be secure in their land. And they shall know that I am the Lord, when I break the bars of their yoke, and deliver them from the hand of those who enslaved them. They shall no more be a prey to the nations, nor shall the beasts of the land devour them. They shall dwell securely, and none shall make them afraid. And I will provide for them renowned plantations so that they shall no more be consumed with hunger in the land, and no longer suffer the reproach of the nations. And they shall know that I am the Lord their God with them, and that they, the house of Israel, are my people, declares the Lord God. And you are my sheep, human sheep of my pasture, and I am your God, declares the Lord God." (Ezekiel 34:25–31)

I was God's sheep, His little lamb; and I could take Bible verses like these and apply them to my present circumstances. The beasts of the land that wanted to devour me were my old thought patterns, inner turmoil, and torment. God could help me banish nations out of my present land: my body that I wanted to own for myself without having foreign thoughts invade my mind.

Still, I kept finding myself taken back in my memory to the mission compound in Kenya, where we used to go for meetings every year. The place where I had believed as a wee girl that I could store a frightened part of myself in the large overhead drum that held rainwater. Over and over I would revisit this place in memory, as if it called to me to try to find myself. I would think about the multitude of spiders and webs that hung through the trees, and now as an adult, wondered why I was not afraid. I thought about the public path that went through the compound. All day long there would be a trail of people walking through on their way to a village. And then I recalled a small black boy with a wheel. The children loved to play an African game of turning a bicycle tire with a stick. They would run for many miles keeping the wheel going. And I then remembered that was my cue: I was to follow this boy off the compound—an unspoken call I was not able to deny. People had used the overwhelming power of ritual abuse, drugs and torture to mar my young life; to give me a script to follow, like the alphabet written in my understanding.

Now in my present life, we again attended the yearly conference in Oregon that we loved so much. Every session began with an extended time of worship; a minimum of three hours of worship each day. This particular day, as an amazing flute player trilled God-anointed music, I found myself swept away in the wonder, the grandeur of God. As my heart and whole understanding were enraptured by the beauty of JESUS, I saw again the African boy that I would follow as if hypnotized. Only now, as I worshiped God and thought about this memory, that flute playing became God writing on my soul. My Father in heaven was rewriting any script that had been placed within me. I could feel the evidence of permanent change within me, as I was allowing God to rewrite my DNA.

Once as a child, I had watched as those bad people branded the black skin of Africans; other victims of the ritual abuse. When they came to brand me, someone said, "Not on her white skin. We will do it on the inside." It was one of the ways they took ownership over me. Through torture, drugs, manipulation and domination, a person can be overcome and have their own sense of self destroyed. You can experience overriding of your will, losing your own identity—especially as a child.

Laurel knew how to let me see that God had written my story first, before anyone had taken ownership of it, and that everything that had been overridden could be reclaimed. She knew how to help me have "healed memory," diffusing the bite of pain, coming to a place of resolve. Abolishing the power that darkness held with it. This Scripture was timely:

"He has put His brand upon us—His mark of ownership—and has given us His Holy Spirit in our hearts as a guarantee that we belong to Him and as the first instalment of all that he is going to give us." (2 Corinthians 1:22 TLB, Life Recovery Bible).

JESUS said in John 14:30 that, "[satan] is coming. He has no claim on me." As I wrote that, everything within me arose to shout *NO! That's not true, he does have a claim on me, and I can't be released!* I continued to pray the truths that God says about me. "It is God who made me and put HIS BRAND UPON ME. HIS MARK of OWNERSHIP sealed, guaranteed, that I BELONG TO HIM." He has the true claim on me! I spent endless hours in worship, allowing God to flood me internally with His Spirit and His Words of Truth to overwrite all that had previously been put in me.

It was around this time I wrote in my journal that I was making so many people cry. All I had to do was start talking about how real JESUS was in my life and they started to cry. I began to see JESUS as a Lion and sometimes I would see Him walk into church, up and down the aisles. He looked to be about three feet high. I would find this so comforting and sometimes imagined climbing on His back for a ride, my arms wrapped around His neck.

I entered a season where I often pondered about what JESUS meant when He said the eye is the lamp to our soul.

"The eye is the lamp of the body. So, if your eye is healthy, your whole body will be full of light, but if your eye is bad, your whole body will be full of darkness. If then the light in you is darkness, how great is the darkness." (Matthew 6:22–23)

I read all the verses I could find about light; eyes; and how to get God's love and light inside of me. This search lasted almost a whole year as I desperately tried to get God's truths deeply rooted in me. To our utter surprise, one day after an intense session with Laurel and releasing a wounded part of me to JESUS, my eyes changed colour right in front of her! They had always been green/hazel and now changed to a pretty blue.

I went to my doctor and asked her to examine me. I told her, "I believe I have looked into and examined God's love for me to such an extent that it has literally caused my eyes to change colour." I went on to say, "Please examine me and see if you can find a different reason as to why my eyes have changed colour." She had been my doctor for a few years, and I had never said anything like that to her before. Surprised, she sat back in her chair awhile and pondered how to respond to me. She said that in all her years of experience she had never seen anyone's eyes change colour this way. Darker, yes. She had seen colour change related to depression, but always going darker. She had never heard of anyone's eyes going a lighter colour, especially blue. She said, "Whatever you have been doing, Sandy, keep it up!"

I was thrilled! It seemed that now there was physical evidence of the deep healing done in my life. I couldn't show people what had happened inside of me, but I could show them my eye colour! Around this same time Dan also noticed the pitch of my voice had changed and I sounded different, too.

As the years progressed and our children grew older, one of our kids went through a crisis and I stayed at their place for a few days. I had not been able to communicate with Dan to update him on what was happening, and he later told me he went to bed that night feeling very distraught. Not knowing anything can sometimes be worse than knowing facts. As he worried, prayed, tried to sleep, and worried some more he discovered that my special cat had come close to his ear and started to purr. That steady rhythmic humming sound seemed to be saying to Dan, "Trust God, trust God." That is how he eventually went to sleep. Soon after he had one of his occasional appointments with Laurel. At the end of the session, as is customary, she asked God to speak to him. Laurel then said to him, "This is very odd, but

I hear this purring sound as if a cat is purring the words "trust God, trust God." I found it most remarkable that she had the ability to hear from God on such an intimate level. My confidence only grew in God and His ability to heal.

From my Journal:

> In my struggle, aware of huge expectations and responsibility on me (teaching a breakout session at the upcoming women's retreat), the Lord in His kindness showed me … me standing on JESUS' feet, just like my children would do with me when they were small. I was leaning into His big body behind me. He held each of my hands as He steadied me so I could walk on top of His feet. When He moved, my feet moved with Him. I could lean back and feel the comfort of His body behind me.
>
> Verses on TRUST are powerfully impacting me. Over and over God is giving them to me to see how TRUST can literally define the borders for my life and my experience. "TRUST in the LORD, and do good; dwell in the land and befriend faithfulness." Psalm 37:3
>
> The Lord is saying to me … I have lived at His feet for many years now. I am to allow my Trust to define the boundaries of my land. Befriend the boundaries of God for my life through trust.
>
> I saw JESUS with all the children gleefully playing around Him, skipping, laughing, throwing water. I went to the River [of Life] Laurel talks about.
>
> I saw JESUS holding me as a trophy. He went to the gates of hell, found me, won me and I am His trophy He presents, gives, to the Father.

I started to fall in love with my husband all over again. We have always had a solid, stable relationship, but my love was rekindled, and once again he could make my heart skip a beat. Another fantastic miracle that the Lord has done is in our sex life. It is vibrant and healthy! That was a surprise to me as I thought old people no longer experienced this. I marvel at this now as I read about how people who have suffered abuse, especially sexual abuse, have had such struggles in that part of marriage. When I was in the worst of my memories, Dan, being the kind, gentle man that he is, was always so patient and understanding. There were periods, though brief, where I would want to sleep in another room and Dan was okay with that. He gave me complete freedom to do what I needed to do to feel safe and good about myself. It would not be long before I was able to rejoin him in our bed and enjoy intimacy. This was a merciful miracle from God, as well as a testament to a wonderful caring man that has consistently treated me with kindness and respect. A promise we made at marriage was to never allow thoughts of divorce to enter our heads. A commitment of 100%. Not a 50/50 but each giving 100%. Nothing less. The Lord helped me learn how to "take my thoughts captive" (2 Cor 10:5), and I made great efforts to train my mind to think correctly so I could engage in sexual intimacy with my husband. All those years of feeling I had no safe place; my eyes were blinded to the fact that my husband has always been my safe place.

One way for me to understand the effects of trauma has been to imagine an old-fashioned camera that used a flashbulb. When the flash went off it would temporarily blind your vision. You had to wait for the effect to subside before you could see again. Trauma affects a person like that internally. It happens too quickly to be able to even close your eyes against it. Our bodies are naturally designed to heal but many times we need assistance to bring about healing.

PART THREE

THE PRAYER CABIN

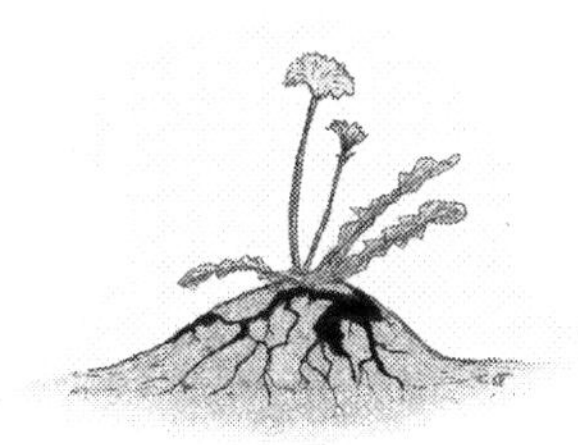

Chapter Twelve

Climbing the Ascent

I had read about something like this—a place where one could go to spend time in prayer and meditation. My heart thrilled to think people could experience being alone with God like that, but I never imagined it would happen to me. I was ecstatic when I had the opportunity to do just that and I excitedly packed my bags, deeply grateful that my husband and family agreed with me going. Three days and nights completely alone with God. I chose a new journal that would be solely for my experiences at the Prayer Cabin. I took my Bible, clothes, paper, and lots of music. Nothing else. No food, no books, no access to Wi-Fi. Just me alone with JESUS to hear what He had to say to me. Before I left, I heard a nudge from the Lord telling me to take my camera.

It was a well-built log cabin on twenty acres on the side of a mountain, the property of Lifeteams, an organization that trains young adults to go out on local missions. The large main house was usually occupied so I felt safe yet still alone, able to find the solitude and sanctuary that my soul desperately craved. After an incredibly good sleep I set out to explore the grounds even though it was raining. I was running down to the canal that runs near the freeway when I spotted a horse. To my surprise, as I approached the horse, I saw a cat sleeping curled up on the horse's back … in the rain! I quickly took out my camera and took some great pictures. The Lord had known ahead of time that this would bring me such delight. It really warmed my heart to see how well God knew me.

My Prayer Cabin Journal

> I weep with humble gratitude. This place is so beautiful. So quiet. I do not even want to turn on music. I must have value; I must have worth … or I would not be the guest in this Prayer Cabin. It is so cute- adorable- darling. It is warm and cozy. The scenery is amazing. Nestled in amongst the trees, part way up the mountain- yet still so close to the freeway. A hollow in the middle of the crazed business of life. A shelter in the storm. I must have worth; I must have value—or I would not be the guest here.
>
> JESUS would you please rock me- for a very long time. I have been through a storm. It feels like my whole life has been a storm (I know it has not really) but it feels that way right now. Laurel rocked me (with my permission) for a few minutes and my life was forever changed. I want you JESUS to rock me now- for an awfully long time. Rock me until there is no more pain in my heart. Rock me JESUS until the pain goes away.
>
> I thought the first thing I would do is turn on my music, but no. I want quiet. How will I manage myself in all this time …? It has only been half an hour. Teach me Lord. I have changed so much these last few years in my healing journey. So much so, I need to adjust to myself. Show me Lord. Separate me from the crowd Lord JESUS, separate me—and return me different. I want to return a different person from the crowd. I need to let Him take me away—sweep me away in His love. I cannot pray for others yet. He wants to

> "love on" me. I will pray for others tomorrow—not today. I must separate from the crowd.

The second day I climbed up the mountain. Many friends had given me their prayer requests and I had written them out on paper. I took their names with me to the top of the mountain. Finding a rock to sit on, I talked with Father about all the people near and dear to my heart.

The next day I wrote:

> I thought I was coming here to bring myself together—to organize myself. My healing has been coming so fast I need to catch up with myself. Instead these first 26 hours I have been in the embrace of God. Enveloped by His PEACE. His loving caress. Nothing thrills my heart more than to be with JESUS.

Joy Like a Child

Arriving at the cabin for my second stay, my time of settling in was most delightful. Feeling welcomed by God, I had fun throwing my pillows up into the loft that held my bed. I was aware of angels laughing and gleeful as well. I sat in the chair and soaked in the pleasure of uninterrupted time with the LORD: three days and three nights with nothing more than my Bible, paper, and music. My plan had been to visit the cabin once a year, yet I had been reluctant to return. As I examined my heart as to why, I realized I was hesitant to be alone with myself. Why would I want that? Then, it struck me: I wasn't coming to be alone with me! I was coming here to meet with God! That flooded me with excitement!

I worshipped, telling the Lord it had been so long that I was forgetting even how to have endless hours of nothing but sitting in His presence. Many friends had prayed for me, and one dear friend had had a vision of me in the cabin surrounded by angels that looked like large warriors, their backs to the cabin, facing out. As I soaked that in, I wept and wept with the realization that it would take several angels to surround that darling cabin. How could it be that the God of heaven would send several angels to protect me? Was I that important to Him that He would do that for just me? I cried and cried and just sat. I just *was*, just lingered in His Presence, very aware of feeling as though I was in the palm of God's great big hand with His fingers curled over me. I felt so safe. Those healing tears were so amazing and even extra special after years of not being able to cry. To be able to know God and feel known by Him—that was worthy of crying about.

After a while I realized I could do absolutely anything I wanted. I could cry for 24 hours if I wanted. I could sleep for 24 hours if I wanted, or not sleep at all ... stay up all night! I was like a teenager who was left home alone for the very first time and tasted freedom. It was so exciting! To think nobody would know and nobody would interrupt my thoughts! Just me and God.

I slept. My first big discovery was that I was so very, very tired and didn't even know it. I slept eleven hours the first night, followed by many naps. It was a rest like I hadn't known in a very long time. Deep REST. What a gift!

On my first hike up the mountain I lingered a long time at a stream and sat totally still for so long, drinking it all in. I asked the water to flow inside of me like the River of Life described in Revelation 22:1, cleansing me, healing me deep inside. I sat so still the birds eventually accepted me as part of their landscape. A small bird flew close and started begging her mate to come and join her. She was ready to start a nest! They took a bath and came within four feet of my foot to check out what was sitting in their yard. My eyes and ears took in all the sights around me; I was at peace with it all. The pleasure of His company made me unable to ask anything, made me just enjoy, just feel so very special, privileged to have such uninterrupted time, and then more time.

When I did eventually climb all the way to the top of the mountain, I laid everything out before God. My deep struggles, my unanswered questions. Asking Him to help me not lean on my own understanding. I wanted so much to do that; I wanted to understand. And I wrestled with God on a very deep level of surrendering my need to understand. God seemed so upside down to my thinking and I attempted to give up my need to know. I wanted to trust Him without having to understand why He does things so opposite and difficult for me to figure out.

I asked Him if He would please take the pain out of my heart. I wanted to be healed of my pain. I wanted to understand suffering. Yes, the big question—why do we suffer so? How could it be that my parents gave their "all" to God as newlyweds and went to Africa to spend their entire lives as missionaries—they dedicated me to God as a baby and trusted me to Him. But it was as though satan robbed me from my nest and then returned me back to it again, spoiled, damaged, and programmed for life. How could it be that ISIS was presently slaughtering our Christian brothers and sisters in the Lord? There must be something about suffering that I don't understand! "Let me know the purpose in suffering," I cried, "Let me understand! I was a thought in your mind, God, long before I was born. I was yours before satan got to me." I also gave Him my fear. Fear of the future. Fear of aging. I faced it with God and surrendered it to Him.

The next day I was part way up the mountain when I realized I had forgotten my two sticks. I wasn't a hiker and needed all the help I could get! I muttered to the Lord, "Why didn't You remind me to pick them up?! You could have easily told me that." I stopped to rest a moment, to catch my breath. I looked back down the steep incline that I had just come up. It was a long way down and oh so beautiful. As I looked, the Lord opened my eyes to see Him, JESUS, as a Lion walking along behind me. I stood there in complete awe of God. After regaining my composure and attempting to carry on, I glanced down and there, partially hidden by some leaves, were two large sticks, perfect for helping me ascend the hill. I would never have seen them if

I had not stopped and lingered. And then I felt ashamed of my flippant attitude in demanding that the Lord should have reminded me to bring my sticks.

From that moment on, for the rest of those days at the cabin, God revealed understanding to me. Many times over the previous weeks, I had heard Scripture in my heart that spoke about hearing the Lord's Voice coming from behind us. Just like the Lion was walking behind me.

"Therefore the Lord waits to be gracious to you, and therefore he exalts himself to show mercy to you. For the Lord is a God of justice; blessed are all those who wait for him ... you shall weep no more. He will surely be gracious to you at the sound of your cry. As soon as he hears it, he answers you. And though the Lord give you the bread of adversity and the water of affliction, yet your Teacher will not hide himself anymore, but your eyes shall see your Teacher. And your ears shall hear a word behind you, saying, 'This is the way, walk in it, ' when you turn to the right or when you turn to the left." (Isaiah 30:18–21)

I could see how I had been fighting God and resisting Him, and remembered some verses from Isaiah 30:15-16a:

"For thus said the Lord God, the Holy One of Israel, 'In returning and rest you shall be saved; in quietness and in trust shall be your strength.' But you were unwilling, and you said, 'No! We will flee upon horses.'"

My defenses had been a stumbling block. I now understood that my answers lay only in going to the Lord and seeking Him in His Word. Hearing the Voice behind me was the only way my path could be illuminated ahead of me to show me the way.

Suffering

I returned to the cabin for another nap. I let God rock me like a child, cradle me. I was there to show my love for Him; He was there to show His love for me. I let myself rest in His comforting arms.

Again, I saw JESUS appearing to me as a Lion to walk with me, escort me as I walked the grounds. These three days were centered around trying to understand the purpose of suffering. Once again, after all these years, I was reading *Don't Waste Your Sorrows* by Paul E. Billheimer. This time I gleaned many nuggets of wisdom:

> "The answer lies in our reaction to the discipline. Resentment and rebellion only waste one's sorrows. Whereas humble acceptance and brokenness leads to peace." (p.100)
>
> "Nothing that can come to one from any source can injure him unless it causes him to have a wrong attitude. It is one's response that blesses or burns." (p.100)
>
> "Sorrow comes to stretch out spaces in the heart for joy." (p.112)
>
> "One is not broken until all resentment and rebellion against God and man is removed." (p.75)
>
> "Before Job suffered, he knew God by reputation only. Afterward he said, 'Now mine eye sees you.' Before his suffering he argued with God, then He knew Him face to face." (p.102)

God in His mercy helped me to accept, not reject something just because I didn't understand it. I don't understand electricity, yet I use it. I chose to forge forward in my healing journey even when it made no sense.

One night in the cabin I was saddened by two bad dreams. I was so upset that I asked God, "Why?" Why in this hallowed place, enveloped in God's Presence, would I have such bad dreams? Then the Lord started to unfold for me a new understanding of how miniscule satan really is in comparison to God. How God uses satan for His purpose. Look at how satan lost when he thought he'd won by killing JESUS on the cross. Satan must have done a happy dance that day JESUS died, only to find it was all in God's plan! God allows the tricks and attacks of satan, in order to train us, give us muscles, and build our character.

"You (satan) were blameless in your ways from the day you were created, till unrighteousness was found in you." (Ezekiel 28:15 ESV)

I wrote in my journal,

> "Wow! I always thought God created satan bad.
> This says otherwise."

At the end of my time at the cabin I asked God to allow me to understand what exactly evil is. I had been taught that the power of the enemy was in the lie. It's the lies we believe. Yet I knew that satan is an entity, so it's not *just* me believing a lie.

I asked God, "So where does evil come from?" I needed to comprehend how it had played out in my life. I heard, "Choice." Evil is in our choice. I suddenly understood that every human, including me, has equal opportunity to participate in the enemy's plan or God's plan. The power is in my ability to choose. I also understood that I could participate in the growth of evil by throwing sticks into the fire, in a manner of speaking. My participation in fear, judgmental attitudes, criticisms and so on had assisted the enemy's plan in my life. I had a lot more power in my thought life than I had previously believed—both for good and bad.

I only went back to the prayer cabin when I felt the Lord calling me to return. My goal still was to go once a year. It was with immense joy that I was able to share it with my kids, too. On one mother/daughter trip we spent a night in the cabin before continuing on with the rest of our plans. My son also came to spend some time with me in prayer. There's no experience quite like it.

Candy and Math

Upon arriving at the cabin for another stay, the Lord showed me that I was like a Werther's candy. He was unwrapping me like I would unwrap a Werther's. The gold wrapping—the peeling of my past. My pain and past were like a small wrapper in comparison to the sweet, wonderful candy inside. The main thing was not the wrapper but the pretty gold sweet candy. I was the candy, JESUS was the candy, we were inseparable. So cool!

The Lord also told me to make my problems a mathematical equation, not to think of only my problem, nor only my faith, but put the two together like an equation and then see what it equals. PROBLEM + FAITH = ___. For example, I would identify the problem of feeling overwhelmed with the weightiness of a struggle. I would add my faith that God says I can do all things through Christ who strengthens me. But it was not enough to just camp on those thoughts. I needed to look for what that equaled when I put the two together. As I tried this, I began to see how it pushed me beyond a stuck place into living out God's promises. He told me to get out of the boat called Disappointment and get into His boat called FAITH.

In my attempt to understand why people are at so many varying places in their walk with God, He showed me steps going up and up. On the first step, the first understanding of Christianity, some people are so thrilled and settle for that place. It is possible to live your whole life on that step. I saw it as a step you could stay on and keep moving along. Other people would go to a second step, or a third step and keep moving along it, or even a fourth. They became happy, content, with that level of God and stayed there their whole lives. Others, not satisfied, would climb higher and live on that level. I really appreciated this picture as it helped me to not push people or wonder how someone could be satisfied with their comfort level and not move on. It was as if some people say, "Give me a little of You, God, and I will be happy." We believe in the same God but have quite different views and expectations.

Chapter Thirteen

At the Cabin with Kimber

Early one morning, as I was spending time with the Lord, I heard Him call Kimber and I to the cabin. With joy we packed our bags and went.

Leaving Kimber behind at the cabin, I set out for a walk. I climbed up to the water falling off the mountain. It was much stronger than I had seen it before. I sat for a long time, more aware of wanting to experience God in nature than I was of sitting on a wet stone in the lightly falling rain. The water was amazing. I imagined the River of Life that flows from the Throne of God. I wanted to sit under the water and let it cleanse me and wash out all the horrible stress, anxiety and fear that was gripping my heart and making me feel separated from God these last few months. Cleanse me God! Forgive me for allowing this level of anxiety in my heart! As I expressed my angst and struggle, feeling failure and separation, I suddenly became aware of my thoughts being lifted. Just as my eyes were drawn up high to watch the falling, rushing water, my spiritual awareness suddenly became higher than my struggle and pain. I had a new perspective. God was helping me to rise above my feelings. His thoughts are higher than my thoughts. His perspective was what I wanted and needed and could enter. I then realized that what I was seeking in my own home was not nearly the same as getting away from everything, and making a pilgrimage to show God that I was seeking Him.

I asked Him, "What is it that each of us are to know? What do You want me to know? What do You want Kimber to know as she prepares to graduate?" I heard Jeremiah 29:11–14: (NIV, emphasis added)

"'For I know the plans I have for you, ' declares the Lord, 'plans to prosper you and not to harm you, plans to give you HOPE and a future. Then you will call on me and come and pray to me, and I will listen to you. You will seek me and find me when you seek me with all your heart. I will be found by you.'"

Bingo! Just what Kimber's Grade 12 heart needed to hear as she planned her future! There was so much stress in Grade 12, with so many decisions to be made. She needed to find confidence for her heart. God wanted her to know that HE KNOWS and has good plans to bless her with a future that is full of HOPE! "Yay God!"

I was so encouraged in God that I went ahead and made the hike all the way to the top. The view at the top made for a most amazing place to sit and pray. I lingered a long time as I told the LORD all the concerns that were on my heart. My time at the top of that hill helped my heart come to a place of rest.

For me, having a personal relationship with JESUS CHRIST means that I need to die to my own selfish nature, and humbly participate in the new life forming within me that is God breathed through His Spirit. It is not a journey of self-discovery, but the opposite.

I had been hearing teaching that God is already inside each of us and we just need to connect on a very deep level to discover our own goodness. I was grateful to the Lord for helping me see that goodness is not in me. If this teaching were true, that God was already inside of everyone, there would have been no need for Christ to come and offer His life in death and resurrection.

Stairway of Stones

Again, I was enveloped by the Father's embrace; just completely caught up in such incredible peace and love. There is nothing like feeling God's love and being able to receive it! It was then I realized that in all that time at the mountaintop, I had not yet asked Him for anything that I wanted to pray about. I smiled, laid back in His embrace, and enjoyed Him some more. If there was one word I could have used to describe my time with Him, it would be PEACE, God's peace. I lived to worship and was satisfied beyond words to have endless hours to do just that. I listened to a CD of a prophetic musician, soaking in the beautiful words of praise and adoration. She was singing about an experience where they saw colour coming up and around the drummer. She invited the revelation of God to come into their praise and worship. Then she went on to describe how she was taken to the heavenlies—all this in song as she described what she was seeing in her spirit.

As I asked God for the same experience—visions of angels; a supernatural encounter– God showed me what I actually needed: to learn to be triumphant in the here and now. I saw in my spirit a stairway going up and up. It wasn't so much a stairway but more like steps hewn out of stones, covered in moss and grass. It looked to be many years old and I thought about the ancient paths of the forefathers. We are told in Romans 4:12 that righteousness would be counted to those "who also walk in the footsteps of the faith that our father Abraham had". The Lord had also shown me a piece of fern and as I was having communion with JESUS, the fern was put in the communion cup. I was communing with JESUS in nature.

"Come Away with Me, My Beloved"

Taken from my Journal (written for friends I was praying for):

> What an absolute thrill to be back here! So completely unexpected! So entirely God's idea. It is

the first time I have had an "intercessory rising up to rebel!" I had not had that thought before but felt compelled to take an action that says "no!" to the stress of the present culture of go, go, go, more, more, more. Needs and demands that seem to never be satisfied, and a lonely ache that is not seen or heard. The unmet expectations. I defy that pressure and ...

"Come away with Me, my beloved"

Christmas is fast approaching, and I was wanting to rebel against a culture that robs our peace and joy while claiming to celebrate that very thing! As I prepared myself at home, I was telling the Lord how hungry and thirsty I am. The Lord said to me, "Hungry, yes, but you are not very thirsty." I longed to get to the cabin to find out what on earth He meant by that! Most of you have already read the delightful times I have had in the past in this most darling cabin that has been used exclusively for solitude and prayer for many years. My plan was, once again, 3 days and 3 nights with nothing but praise, worship, walks and reading my Bible. I don't seem to know how to pray unless I first worship.

I was very excited that my oldest son was able to come in the evening to have a wee look at what I was experiencing. As I eagerly looked out, excited for his arrival, I noticed the lamp just outside the cabin had some sort of a hood or covering over it.

It is one of my very favourite things at the cabin. The tall lamppost stands just outside the front door and is high enough to shine not only all down the path, but also into the bedroom loft up in the roof of the cabin. My own little night light! I love it. I was so sad to see it covered and after considering my options of getting permission to change it, finally went out to see if I could do it myself. From a distance it looked like the covering was well secured. When I got closer I was so surprised to find it only a cloth bag strapped over the light. I quickly removed it and so happy it was in time for my son to have light to see the path.

You may ask, what I do with all my time. Well, the second day I climbed what I call The Mountain of the Lord. I took your written requests, climbed to the top and sat on the big stone and presented your needs, one by one. I lingered wherever I felt like stopping. There are no time restraints or people to consider. Not even food to interrupt my time and draw me away (although I drink as much as I want of any liquid). I just stop, rest, and look for what the Lord wants me to notice. I love the water.

The first morning, as I started to wake up, I was pierced with such sorrow in my heart. This is frequently my favourite time of the day. Many days of every week in my life the Lord uses this time to talk to me. As I fall in and out of sleep, He tells me things—scriptures of where to read, how He loves me, who to pray for. This is what I was expecting. Even more so in the Prayer Cabin.

The Lord is my chosen portion and my cup; you hold my lot. The lines have fallen for me in pleasant places; indeed, I have a beautiful inheritance. I bless the Lord who gives me counsel; in the night also my heart instructs me. Psalm 16:5–7

But there was nothing! I was so disappointed. How could this be? I was setting aside special time to be with the Lord. Where was He? It made no sense. Drifting in and out of sleep, I agonized over why this was happening. I felt terrible. I felt blocked, something in the way of me and my Lord.

The last few weeks the Lord has said things to me, like showing me that picture of a baby lathered in kisses and saying, "That's what I am doing with you." My Father God loves me that much that He kisses me all over like a baby He is proud of!

Another time I saw myself again as a young, beautiful girl with long hair flowing, blowing in strong wind. The Lord let me see His Spirit flowing through me to such an extent there is not one strand of hair, no past of my life, that He is not blowing through with His refining and healing Spirit. I am a book the Father God leafs through and plants a kiss on every single page of my life telling me, "Don't rip out pages of your book." This is the intimacy I was expecting.

As I drifted in and out of sleep and cried out to the Lord, I was suddenly struck by what I was to do. I vividly saw the lamppost that had been covered. I had taken action to remove the cloth bag myself rather than go to people living on the property to do it for me. In the same way, I was to take action again as I lay in my bed feeling blocked and hindered from accessing my intimate personal relationship with JESUS. So, I confessed my sins, those done knowingly and unknowingly, sins done to me or anything else I could think to repent of while thinking of Psalm 51. I applied the blood of Christ to myself and invited the Holy Spirit to once again invade every part of my being, to flood every part of the cabin so much so that anything opposing God would be driven out of the cabin in JESUS' great Name! Then I was able to pray.

Pray I did, thrilled I could make the breakthrough myself. I prayed for all of you in the same way. Do you feel blocked, hindered? I made a breakthrough on your behalf.

It amazed me how many prayers came out of me on behalf of so many people, churches, movements, denominations as a result of this experience with the lamp being covered. Some of us are inclined to cover up the Light because we don't want to be exposed. Some of us do not want that disinfecting light that burns up the distasteful things in our life that we are not supposed to want. It's hard to be seen when we want to hide in shame. It's hard to do the self-discipline to grow strong and healthy. Sometimes choosing not to. It can be hard to be exposed. Some of us are covering the Light to make the Gospel more appealing, palatable to our culture. The problem with this is that now you no longer see the path to walk! God forgive us and help us! I love the Light, I love JESUS. I want Him to expose me and lavish me in His love! Give us the ability to blush. Jeremiah 6:15 says they lost the ability to have a conscience, to blush.

The last morning was Sunday, my favourite day of the week. Every time previously I have awakened at 5 a.m. with such excitement to have one last experience with the Lord. To my dismay I awakened at 7:30 with a heavy heart. No praise, no excitement, no words from the Lord. Once again, I agonized as I fell in and out of sleep. Wondering how it could be that it would soon be too late to even go to church. It was so not like me to feel like this. I love to go to God's house on Sunday. Once again, in time it hit me. I started to once again remember all the prayer requests I was given. Many depressed, some of you struggling in marriage, suicidal, confused, unbelieving hearts, physical pain that makes you unable to get out of bed or crippled in fear, paralyzed in feeling not effective in ministry, or even no purpose in your life. Many too depressed to get up. I prayed for you all! One by one the Lord helped me to remember all the names of the people I was to pray for! I symbolically "took the covering off the lamp" on your behalf, interceded for you. It was a few hours before I could get out of bed! Isn't this amazing? I love God so much!

This time in the Prayer Cabin was like none before. All the other times were special and meaningful, intimate times for me. Sure, I prayed for others but this time I was called as an Intercessor on behalf of others and to rebel against how like the world the church is becoming. Sometimes it is hard to tell the difference between Christians and nonbelievers. What an honour and privilege! Thank you so much for asking me to pray for you.

He did tell me the answer to me wanting to be hungry and thirsty for more of Him. I pray lots that God whets my appetite for more of Him. When I think of being hungry I think it applies to eating, digesting God's Word. Rightfully applying the truth. However, thirst to me represents the Holy Spirit, worship, praise, abiding in Christ, sitting in His River. As I asked the Lord what He meant by me not being thirsty enough, He showed me that I need to be humble to be thirsty. Wow! I need to come in humility. Guess I need to work on my pride.

Thanks, my friends,

Sandy

Have I a Story to Tell!!

I found a very sad horse that lived near the Prayer Cabin. On a previous visit, I had been moved with sorrow by the sadness in his eyes. The next time I returned his eyes were still so sad. He came to me, but every time I tried to pet him he would pull away. I knew almost nothing about horses and was very frustrated that I could not pet him or give him comfort. I ended up talking to him, asking him out loud if he would teach me how to pet a horse, show me where he liked to be touched. And then I found myself speaking to him as if I was really speaking to his spirit. I asked him why he was so sad. Had he lost someone he loved? Why so lethargic? All the while he kept stretching out his neck so long and shaking his head in a strange way, as if trying to get something out of his mouth. Next thing I knew I was praying for the horse, asking God to heal what was hurting him inside. Then I left.

Soon after, Kimber and I stopped in to visit the horse. I could hardly believe my eyes! The horse seemed thrilled to see me and ran to us, thrusting his head into my neck, trying (ever so gently) to devour my whole hand in his mouth and prancing around kicking his back legs together like a joyful kid. Then he'd run back to me to play and enjoy our visit. The way he gazed into my eyes made me think that he was looking at me like I was a long-time friend that he was glad to see. I truly believe God answered my prayers for this horse, and that the horse knew it and attributed it to my visit. God does amazing things, and He does answer prayers!!!

Push Back Time

At another visit to the cabin the Lord said He would help me let go of the past… and that He did! As I agonized and questioned God, I thought, *I can't just stop thinking about it.* At times it feels like I am drowning. Other times my soul aches like a bad toothache. Letting go could turn into pretending the abuse and trauma never happened and that is the very denial I lived in most of my life. Memory had not been accessible to me. It took Amber's death for me to be able to start to remember. I could not figure it out. Some people say just burn your memories. Well that would burn up my life. I want to own my life and remember who I am and where I come from. What sheer pleasure to have a place to come where I could be alone with my own thoughts! A place where I was capable of entering deep into listening: Listening to God, listening to what my own heart wants to say.

As I worshipped and prayed and read God's Word, I came to more understanding. The Lord told me to say "NO" to suffering. "NO! PUSH BACK!" And then I fell in love with the word "NO" as I began to understand what I was to do. I wrote the word over and over in my journal and had so much fun writing it every way imaginable. I even started to shout it aloud. Nobody else was around to hear me, so why not?! As I entered into what it meant to say no to suffering and found it very manageable, I remembered the word my dear friend gave me as she prayed for me before I went on this trip to the cabin. She told me that she saw me like Joshua in the Old Testament, and I was standing strong, able, and ready to take the land. She said there was much land for me to yet take. Bingo! It made so much sense to me. Unlike Joshua, my land "to take" was my own life from my birth to now. I was to take it by PUSHING BACK and reclaiming what was lost but now found. I have had so much growth and healing and was now able to take the land that belongs to me, the land of my own life. I needed to say no to suffering and PUSH BACK what wanted to overwhelm me, scare me, depress me.

I wrote,

> As I do this, I believe I will start to remember the good things that I have not remembered, like what my parents' personalities are like, my two sisters and two brothers that I hardly know. I want to

> know that; I want to know the good things that are mine to own.

I believed this was a word from the Lord for more than just me, and once home I heard someone with a respected prophetic voice also say the same thing about how God was wanting to work in our lives. It is PUSH BACK time and if you want to claim this as your own, go for it. Not aggressively pushing against people or wanting your own way but push back where the enemy is using your weakness to gain advantage in your life. PUSH BACK darkness, oppression, fear, depression, feeling failure, loss. Wherever your struggle, push back and in its place let the Lord take up that spot in your heart and your understanding. Push for more of Him and His truths about His great love for you and His desire to have you fully alive, in and for Him.

Now I knew to say no to suffering when the enemy comes knocking at my door, wanting to cause me pain and heartache. I would not only say to him, "No! Get away in JESUS' great name!" but I would also say no to myself. I would discipline my own thought life and no longer slip into the type of thinking that causes me to suffer. I grew to understand authority comes through believing what God says. Anointing comes from intimacy.

That I May Know...

There are life-altering things that happen in all of our lives. Things that set the pace, redirect, or flood us with life-altering hope and direction. The prayer cabin has become such a place for me. One stay was such an extremely personal time that I found myself unable to write about it. I was challenged to the core of my being by my loving Father. I stayed the typical three days and nights, without my car. Dan had dropped me off and would come to get me at the end. I was liberated from the ability to leave if I wanted! The Lord challenged me on a very deep level, or rather I questioned Him with wanting to understand what my rights are. Do I have the right to be heard, to be understood, to have my voice respected? Are these things I should fight for and demand? (Our culture says, "Yes") I explored whether JESUS demanded those rights when He walked on this earth. I came to this scripture:

"...that I may know him and the power of his resurrection, and may share his sufferings, becoming like him in his death... Not that I have already obtained this or am already perfect, but I press on to make it my own, because Christ Jesus has made me his own." (Philippians 3:10, 12)

I lived in these verses for a few weeks. Lord! Please! I want to know you! I am madly in love with you! Not only in the joy but also in allowing death to happen in me. Death to my own wilfulness and my need to be heard, my need to be right, my need to have the other person always agree with me. I received great comfort pressing in to make these verses my own—finding purpose in my suffering like JESUS suffered—because JESUS has already made me His own.

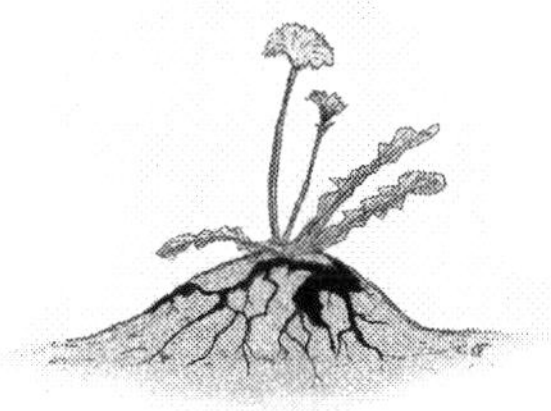

Chapter Fourteen

Fasting

There came a time when the Lord repeatedly directed me to read and reread about JESUS going into the wilderness, where He fasted for 40 days and was tempted by the devil. I thought about this passage on and off for days; I couldn't stop wondering about it. We know He ate no food but there is no record in the Bible about him drinking water. I had so many questions. As a young woman I had been taught the value of fasting for spiritual reasons. JESUS said, "When you fast..." (Matt. 6:16) as if it was something we already knew to do. I never enter a fast without first feeling the Lord calling me to do this. It is for spiritual reasons only, never for punishing myself or motives other than getting closer to God and surrendering my will.

I have faced some criticism and much resistance whenever I've talked about this. People have sometimes become very defensive and uncomfortable. I didn't want this to interfere with something dear to my heart, so I have avoided talking about it. But it is a practice that has brought me much reward. I have struggled with self-discipline and wanting my own way. In fact, I want my way all the time! The Bible says the hardest thing to control in life is our own tongue; curtailing what we say. I have found fasting to be the most useful tool to help me say "no" to myself as I grow in God. Saying no to myself is hard to do! I do not like "no." Previously the Lord took me through learning the beauty of saying no and pushing things out of my life that didn't belong. This use of "no" was different. It has been challenging to get control of myself. I completely understand there are situations that make it impossible for some people to fast, but I do believe there is tremendous value in finding an alternative, to deny one's own wilfulness and the need to satisfy every desire.

My kids grew up with me fasting and I always tried to act normal while doing so. I prepared meals just the same and sat at the table with the family as they ate. They got so used to me abstaining from food that they didn't even notice any more if I wasn't eating. When certain training was coming up for the prayer team, or important things were happening, I would fast. I would fast on behalf of other people for their personal breakthrough. I always fasted before a women's retreat to prepare my heart and pray for the other women's hearts.

When I'm fasting and start to get hungry, I use that hunger to propel me to God. I try to make my desire in prayer larger than my desire for food. I ask myself, "How badly do I want breakthrough for that person. How big is their need?" The hungrier I get the more I press in and pray! It really helps. My mind becomes sharper and I understand more of what I read in scripture. I feel like I have many more hours in my day to be productive, and I become aware of how much time we spend on food: growing it, buying it, preparing it. It also helps me to get the upper hand on my own self-centredness. When I'm fasting, I have so much more time and space inside of me for God. Do you want to hear God's Voice? Become more hungry for a relationship with Him than with food for your body; We all need help in conquering our own wilfulness that fights God's best for our lives. We all need to have some form of self-discipline in order to grow well.

Isaiah 58:6–8 tells us the difference between a right or a wrong motive in fasting. Fasting breaks yokes, sets captives free, releases the oppressed, breaks bondages:

"Is not this the fast that I choose:

to loose the bonds of wickedness,

to undo the straps of the yoke,

to let the oppressed go free,

and to break every yoke?

Is it not to share your bread with the hungry

and bring the homeless poor into your house;

when you see the naked, to cover him,

and not to hide yourself from your own flesh?

Then shall your light break forth like the dawn,

and your healing shall spring up speedily;

your righteousness shall go before you;

the glory of the Lord shall be your rear guard.

I also like to honour the Sabbath, which in our culture is Sunday. I find it interesting that Isaiah 58 says that the Sabbath is such a special day for God that the people were to honour it by not even "speaking your own words." It's a relief in our marriage to try to refrain from talking about any stressful things for one day. In Hebrews 4:9–11, we are told there is a rhythm of grace and mercy, a rest for the people of God. We are to fear that we might miss entering His rest. I do not want to miss anything God has for me! God set a pattern for us with creating the world and resting on the seventh day. There is a rhythm, a timing on the earth, including a time to rest. I want to enter that rhythm of timing, grace and mercy that brings great blessing and abundance into my life.

"If you turn back your foot from the Sabbath,

from doing your pleasure on my holy day,

and call the Sabbath a delight

and the holy day of the Lord honourable;

if you honour it, not going your own ways,

or seeking your own pleasure, or talking idly;

then you shall take delight in the Lord,

and I will make you ride on the heights of the earth." (Isaiah 58:13–14)

40 Days

Soon I clearly heard the LORD ask me to do a 40-day fast. I was thrilled to discover it coincided with our church asking us all to do 14 days of fasting and prayer. I will be honest and admit this was a very daunting task. I had done 40-day fasts, and learned a life of fasting and prayer as a young woman in ministry in early years, but I had not embarked on anything like that since. I questioned whether I was too old for this!

All was well until Day 6. I was doing what I typically did—drink lots of different beverages (water, fruit and vegetable juice, tea and even milk) while attempting to live life normally. Surprised with my physical weakness when I awoke, I stayed in bed for the day. I surrounded myself with worship music and pressed in to find the Lord, begging Him to show me what His words in these verses meant:

"And [God] humbled you and let you hunger and fed you with manna, which you did not know, ...that He might make you know that man does not live by bread alone, but man lives by every word that comes from the mouth of the Lord." (Deuteronomy 8:3)

"But [JESUS] said to them, 'I have food to eat that you do not know about. My food is to do the will of him who sent me and to accomplish his work." (John 4:32, 34)

I understood my hope was to find out what it meant to literally live off God's Word, to have His words sustain my body; my life-giving sustenance. How could I live without food and apply scripture appropriately? I also understood that before JESUS went into the wilderness, He submitted to baptism and was filled with the Holy Spirit. This told me He was both walking in obedience and full of the Holy Spirit. If these two things were not in place, it would be very unwise to embark on such an undertaking as this long fast.

As I lay in my bed that sixth day, I let all my thoughts and fears come to the surface. What had it been like for JESUS? Did He take a backpack, pillow, blanket? Did He fall over in weakness and pass out? If He did, He didn't abandon the plan. One of my sons expressed concern that my organs would shut down. I asked my own heart, "Who do I think I am, and what on earth do I think I'm doing?" I wrestled it out with God looking for scriptures to draw direction from. Yes, I had successfully lived a life like that as a young woman, but I was now old! I evaluated what were real concerns, how my family fit into this and what they were telling me. What is God really asking of me?

Day 7 I awoke early, leapt out of bed energetically and rather than walk, I ran some of my usual daily walk. I was flooded with encouragement and energy. I proceeded to live in a normal fashion and dug deep into scripture, understanding what it meant to take anointed words and have them supernaturally give me sustenance for my physical body. I was prepared to drink bouillon if I got weak, but it never came to that. Whenever I was overwhelmed with wonderful smells of good food or with the desire to eat, I'd immediately tell God what I desired so much from Him. I wanted to see Him manifested in the life of the person I was praying for. "God, we need miracles!" I'd make that need greater than my desire for food. I would allow His strength and energy to become greater in me than my desire for food.

"And [JESUS] said to all, 'If anyone would come after me, let him deny himself and take up his cross daily and follow me.'" (Luke 9:23)

The more I did this, the more I understood denying myself to mean not simply denying certain things but denying personal control of my life. Saying NO to me! Some religious practices require self-harm or flagellation but there is no comparison between those and what JESUS requests. Picking up our cross and following Him means a denial of our own selfish heart, not demeaning our bodies. I started to understand how much He was calling me to not get angry when I feel justified. How to "bite my tongue" and listen rather than make my voice heard. How to give up myself to benefit another person. How to let God's anointing inside of me get bigger than the oppression the enemy wanted to overcome me with. And I found myself seeing oh so clearly that the hardest thing to change in my life ... is me!

"It's not sacrifices that really move your heart.

Burnt offerings, sin offerings—that's not what brings you joy.

But when you open my ears and speak deeply to me,

I become your willing servant, your prisoner of love for life.

So I said, 'Here I am! I'm coming to you as a sacrifice,

for in the prophetic scrolls of your book

you have written about me. I delight to fulfill your will, my God,

for your living words are written upon the pages of my heart.'"

(Psalm 40:6–8 TPT)

I thought Day 6 had been very hard, but then came Day 24. It was extremely difficult! Stresses and challenges in my life got the upper hand and I felt overwhelmed and crushed by them. The last straw was a physical ailment that caused great pain. I'd taken such pride all my life with how healthy my body had been. I would hardly get a cold or a flu. Now suffering from extreme pain, Day 24 became worse than Day 6. It drove me for a second time to the end of myself. I crumbled under the weight of problems I was not able to fix or change. I went to bed that night wondering about Elijah in 1 Kings 19:4, where he was so discouraged and depressed that he wanted to die. An angel came and gave him two meals. He ate and went 250 miles to Horeb (Mt. Sinai) and then lived another 40 days without food! Did he walk, have a donkey? How had he managed that?!

Over the years the Lord has been faithful and kind to meet me in the wee hours of the morning before the sun comes up. Now as I started to awaken, so sad and overwhelmed, I didn't want to allow myself to fully wake up and face my present reality. I felt as bad as Elijah might have felt. He had seen God's miracles and now, where was He? Suddenly a thought went through my head. *I've come to the end of myself.* The more I awakened, the more I repeated those words. I thought, *God has brought me to the end of myself. God has brought me to the end of myself!! This is God's doing!* That knowledge flooded my being, and I was thrilled. It was God's hand that all this pressure had come against me, pushing me to the end of my ability to fix and help myself. I leapt out of bed with delight, eager for my daughter to wake up so I could greet her with joy. I was filled with great anticipation in spending the day with my husband and finding out what God had for us that day. It was God's doing and I was so glad! That was a real turning point for me. Breakthrough day!

The Cabin in Winter

Things continued to go well with my fast, and I was thrilled with the opportunity to go back to the prayer cabin. So soon! I was so grateful for family that were willing for me to abandon them in my pursuits. Thrilled for the courage to now make my stay four days and nights! Once again, no car, no books, only my Bible and paper and lots of music. Now I felt the need to maximize my efforts in pursuing much greater intimacy with listening to and seeking God. It can be hard to do in the middle of a busy life and family. I was thrilled to share my experience for the first time with some friends that came for a few hours. What a treat to share the sacredness with others!

I was not prepared for the cold and terrible windstorm that came my second day. I had never witnessed a wind up close like that day. The huge trees around the cabin shifted and swayed. My fear rose as I saw the trees bend in different directions as if they couldn't agree which way the wind was blowing! It was very frightening, even ferocious. I plucked up my courage to go down the hill and walk the dyke. When I saw others walking, I figured it may not be as dangerous as I had first thought. However, I was sure some of their dogs were going to literally blow away in the wind! The force was so strong I felt as though I would be pushed off the path with each step I took. It was thrilling and frightening all at the same time. I was plunged in to trusting God on a different level as I faced unfamiliar elements.

Later that day the owner knocked on the cabin door to check the water pipes, informing me that since it would drop to 10°F that night, I needed to keep the water running so the pipes would not freeze. He seemed concerned with the pipes, not my safely. I thought, *If he's okay with this, maybe I can be okay with this too*. So, I set out to hike to the top of the mountain, Day 36 of my fast! I sent Dan a text to tell him what I was doing, and approximately what time I would message him that I was safely back.

The Lord had provided a wonderful walking stick and I headed out. It was difficult to find the path as snow had covered much of the ground. After asking angels to walk with me, escort me, buffer me from the wind and cold, protect me from any trees falling, I headed out. I became aware of the angels as they laughed and jostled with me in a delightful trek out into the elements of the wild. Finally, I was at the top of the mountain, too afraid to venture out close to the drop-off! I was thrilled with the courage and ability the Lord had given me to conquer my fear, push past my physical limitations and trust Him to show me what He had for me that day.

The cabin was not able to maintain the heat in those temperatures, and when combined with my own inability to maintain my body heat while fasting, I slept that night in my clothes and four blankets. The next morning, I texted my friend to tell her how I couldn't get warm and was delighting in a hot drink between my hands. She told me how she was seeing me being held and comforted by God Himself. He was holding me like I was holding that warm cup!

There is something so incredibly wonderful about being all alone with your own thoughts and having time for them. Time and more time. To not only think something through but to work with it long enough to find solutions and answers. Freedom to think. Freedom to sleep all day long or stay up all night, whatever I wanted. Rest that gets deep into your bones. Nobody to notice or care.

I spent most of one day worshipping along to an artist that sings and reads scripture. This was Psalm 91 about dwelling in the secret place of the Most High. What struck me so much was wondering if all the promises of being kept from the evil one and God's protection were linked to ONLY when we dwell in that secret place. What is that secret place and where is it? I spent most of a day pondering this question. The Lord helped me see that for me to dwell in that secret place, I couldn't have any resentment inside of me. Two people from long ago in my past came to mind; I still had feelings of disappointment and resentment in my heart toward them. It became confession time for me as I flushed out the need to forgive and let these dear ones go from my feelings of entrapment and disappointment. I prayed blessings of God to be showered onto their lives that day. So, God's secret place for me was abiding in a pure place in my heart that's free of resentment. Cool!

I then found myself entering a difficult mindset. I connected with the God I thought I wanted in my childhood, but who didn't seem to parallel the God I now knew. As I began to spiral, the words flew off my pen into my prayer cabin journal. It started out great.

> "I need you, God, to be the softest pillow on which to lay my head and the strongest rock on which I can stand.

The spiral continued. My despair felt immense.

> Where are you Lord?!!!! I find you in church, I adore you—am thrilled to worship you. Where are you when I am angry with my husband or under attack from people who are cross with me? I need you to be more evident in my life! I need more help than you are giving me to change me. I can't change me! How many times am I going to come to the end of myself? How can I possibly trust you?! I was stolen from my nest (as a child), ruined, spoiled, damaged, and returned for my parents to finish raising me. Now my children struggle too!! How can I trust you? My parents trusted you with me (on the mission field) and look what happened to me. I trusted you with each of our children and look at how they struggle!

After I got that all out in the open, honest with where my heart was at, I reached for my Bible and opened to First John. As I read, God's truths caused a remarkable shift in my brain. Yes, I strongly felt the reality of my childhood, the deep impact it still has on my life today. But as I read God's word, I accepted His truth as the true reality. The Rock that endures and knows the end from the beginning; the One who has a plan and knows far better than I ever will.

I was flooded with the ability to accept God's reality to trump and triumph over what I thought was my reality. Just because my little tree (my life) formed, grew crooked and possibly became deformed in some ways, it had nothing to do with who God is and how He is working in this world and what He is up to. My brokenness does not change who God is. I will accept who He tells me He is, from His reality, not my skewed view of

Him from my life experience. My life experience doesn't dictate what's real and true. God gets to do that, and I will accept that.

The weather had improved, and I went for another hike up the mountain. During the whole fast, I had been so overwhelmed with an acute awareness of how hard it has been to change me—depressingly so! I came to the same place on the path I had been 9 years ago where God first profoundly spoke to me, when He let me find those two walking sticks. As I looked back down the mountain to catch my breath, I saw the spot where I first saw JESUS as a lion walking behind me, and heard those wonderful verses from Isaiah 30:20b-21 NIV (emphasis added):

"...your teachers will be hidden no more; with your own eyes you will see them. Whether you turn to the right or to the left, your ears will hear a VOICE behind you saying, 'This is the way; walk in it.'"

As I walked to that spot there was another shift in my thinking. I remembered how much I *had* changed. I had thought I could never work with the homeless but look at what I have done. I had thought I'd never marry and look who I have! One by one I reminded my heart of the many, many ways I had changed over the years and of all the accomplishments I had enjoyed. By the time I got back to the cabin I no longer had that pain in my heart of how impossible it was for me to change. One more battle was fought and won.

The next morning I was awake at 4 a.m., up and praying. Sorrow overwhelmed my heart. I was just so sad, and eventually went back to bed to sleep some more, only to wake up to such heaviness. I had no strength to hike and my brain seemed to be going to sleep from a combination of being cold and not eating food. I cried out to God, "What shall I do?" He answered, "Praise." So I praised. I had lost all joy and had no strength anymore, but the moment I started to defy what I was feeling and chose to praise, I had to laugh at myself. The truth was so very simple. Nehemiah 8:10 says that the JOY of the Lord is my strength. I had no strength because I had lost my JOY. The way for me to get joy was to praise God and remind my brain what I was forgetting. God is good. He is kind. He is worthy, patient ... I could go on and on with all the wonderful things God is! I was flooded with energy once again and able to go out and thoroughly enjoy my day with enough strength and energy to do anything I wanted!

Drink Offerings

Once back home again, the day very quickly came when I was at the end of my 40-day fast. I was thrilled with my family wanting to celebrate with me. I acknowledge I'm weird and different in many ways and feel like I should say, "Do not try this at home!" I chose to break my fast in a Chinese buffet and yes, I even had ice cream, and resumed a normal diet right away.

The day after was another learning curve for me. I'd spent so much time and effort studying JESUS' fast, Moses' 40 days up the mountain, Elijah etc. The Bible tells us that when JESUS was finished, the devil left Him (until an opportune time). That morning Dan and I had our usual prayer time together (and prayed about *everything*!) but we just couldn't seem to get past arguing. We'd pray some more then get into another conflict. Later as we were driving in the car, it struck me that the temptation was over for JESUS at the end of His fast, but I was being troubled even more. Why? If that had happened for JESUS, why was it not happening for me? Dan and I prayed again, only this time I became very assertive in my authority in Christ and I told satan to get out of my life! Go! In JESUS' great name. I realized I was passively looking to God to take care of the enemy for me when I needed to exercise my own authority in Him! I wanted to no longer be a passive Christian, and instead take the authority and privilege I have as a daughter of the King of Kings and Lord of Lords. After this, the peace was restored!

My next surprise was a couple of days later, when I had "come back" and the fast was starting to feel surreal. It was almost as if

I'd been away in another country and now returned home that seemed strange after being away so long. I became aware that the fast was much harder than I had realized at the time. I had been so focused on endurance, hearing and responding to what God had for me that I hadn't even realized how hard it was until it had ended. I now saw this as wonderful opportunity to be new and different and rejoin my life in new ways with new thinking. I didn't have to return to the old if I didn't want to! Denying myself took on a whole new, rich meaning. Deny myself, take up my cross daily and follow JESUS.

I did a study on drink offerings. In 2 Samuel 23:13-17, David was hiding from Saul and under enemy attack. His three friends broke through the enemy's camp, risking their lives to get him the water he desperately longed for, from the well near Bethlehem that he loved from his childhood. When they gave David the water he so desired, he poured it out as a drink offering. Paul, in Philippians 2:17, talks about pouring out his life as a drink offering. Mark 14:2-6 so beautifully portrays a woman's love and devotion as she pours out her all to JESUS even amidst criticism.

Saying "no" to my selfishness, to my will and my desire to be right, heard, understood, and respected are gifts I can deny myself in order to pour out my life for others. I want to be that sweet-smelling aroma of sacrifice for God and others to smell and savour! God is good and I feel more privileged than if I'd won the lottery. Truly. It was worth every single effort and every ounce of energy and tear spent. Why wouldn't I want to come to the end of myself? I realized that only then can I truly start to abide in Christ and learn how to live out of His heart of love and not out of my depleted self.

Chapter Fifteen

Meat

During one prayer time, the Lord showed me Himself out in an open field by a campfire. My first response was that I was frightened, as it felt so exposed. As months went by, I'd occasionally visit and revisit fleeting moments of this scene, this invitation, and gradually I was no longer afraid of this open exposure.

The morning before I left for another visit to the prayer cabin, I saw that scene once again. JESUS leaning over this campfire. He had meat for me. Fresh meat to roast on the fire. He also spoke to me about Martha. "Martha, Martha you are troubled by many things.... Mary has chosen the better part." (See Luke 10:41–42).

My first morning back at the cabin, the Lord woke me up with a word. "*Correct*". It felt like such a great word. Not critique, not criticize. It doesn't feel nice to have someone critique me. But "correct" feels like a hand on a small child learning to wobble along on a two-wheel bicycle. The child wants the parental hand of correction to guide the bike. I wanted Father to make those little adjustments in my life to alter and correct my position if I'm going off centre. Correction felt like a good word. After I stumbled out of bed and opened my Bible, I sensed the Lord wanted me to read Proverbs—all of Proverbs, in The Passion Translation.

Once done, I suddenly realized–JESUS with the meat. Offering me meat at that campfire. That's correction! I no longer was satisfied with just the milk of the Word. He was giving me meat. And so was the book of Proverbs.

"How then does a man gain the essence of wisdom? We cross the threshold of true knowledge when we live in complete awe and adoration of God." (Proverbs 1:7a TPT)

I once again allowed myself to step away from questions that cause a faltering, timid spirit. *Trauma and disappointment do not define me or my faith*. I choose to believe and trust God for what He says and who He is. I throw myself into His protection for safe keeping. He is able to guard my heart and direct my life and the lives of those I love.

Back Again!

Overjoyed! Excited! Thrilled! All understatements. My tenth time at this darling prayer cabin. Lots of people are praying for me, excited with me! Arrived at 10 a.m., Dan dropping me off.

Walked the canal then thought I'd have a wee nap. Two and a half hours of deep sleep. Needing the bathroom, I staggered then fell into the chair. Took a long time to arouse myself. Wondered if something had gone wrong physically. I'm that tired. It's been a hard year. Thrilled to realize it has not been hard from all that emotional pain and work of healing but hard because of how much I have expended myself for others. Caring for my three clients; Dan's Mom came to live with us and then passed away.

Hiking up the mountain. What a thrill! My fear of heights has greatly improved. The Lord was so kind in causing so much moss to grow on the rocks at the top. Soft to sit on, lie on. Realizing I could lie down and safely rest on the rock. Drop-off such a short distance away. Like resting in the palm of God's hand—ignoring and shutting out the world around me. The fears, the distractions.

I'm enjoying quiet. I'm learning to be quiet and not always stimulated by music. Reading back in my Journal for the prayer cabin, I see two answers to my prayers. Praise God! At the end of my time I wrote, "This time is different from any other. No struggle at all to press in and connect." Way less music played. I read all of Isaiah today and pulled out verses for our next Treasure Hunt. I slept a lot. I did not know I was so tired. It's good to find out how tired I was.

Martha did the things that were necessary. They had to eat. But Mary chose ... I need to choose to press in. I am both Martha and Mary, I can do both. Martha, in order to become Mary—pushed through the crowd (all my troubling thoughts) to touch the feet of JESUS. ...the stages I go through to get to where I want to be in knowing JESUS. I am a responsible woman (Martha) I push though the crowd—sort, organize my thoughts. Push them away ... all distractions. To become Mary, washing JESUS' feet.

I am an instrument. Lord says I'm "fine-tuned". God plays me as His instrument. My heart is His harp, and He plucks on the strings.

White Swan

I ran down to the canal, the sun shining so brightly, and came upon a group of ducks and one very large white swan. As I marvelled at the beautiful swan, the Lord said to me, "That is how I see you." I stood and pondered, taking in the wonderful sight, before realizing something. There was only one large, beautiful white swan. The small ducks paled in comparison, so brown that they could easily not even be noticed. I started to understand that God wants us all to feel the way I did just then; my heart just so full as Father poured out His love on me. God wants each one of us to feel singled out like that lone swan. He notices, He cares, and He wants us to feel valued as if we are His one and only. In God it is possible for us all to feel we are dearly, singularly treasured. I no longer wanted to accept being just a duck that blended in with everyone else. I was special, and what made me feel special was when I accepted God's unfathomable love for me.

Dawn

Three days and three nights at the prayer cabin was comparable to a child's heart anticipating Christmas morning and the gifts they get to open. Sheer pleasure. Yet never had I experienced being a part of the dawn. What a thrill!

I set out in the dark, choosing to rely on instinct rather than take a flashlight. Even though it was dark, the birds' happy chatter indicated they knew what was about to happen. I now wanted another daughter so I could name her Dawn. Breathtaking wonder—that is what it was like to participate in the dawn. The dark behind; a new day and the sun about to rise. That's where we are living, those of us who choose Hope. Scripture tells us in 1 Corinthians13:12, that now we see through a glass darkly but one day ... face to face with our risen Lord JESUS. It's coming, I feel it.

Beaver

I was awake by 4:30 a.m. on the third day and knew I was done sleeping. Those wee hours of the morning have developed into the most precious treasured moments with my Lord, as He so frequently speaks to me at that time. This morning He reminded me of a time long ago when He used a beaver to help me know how to pray for my growing children. "Lord! Make them industrious and strong like a beaver, teeth able to fell the largest of trees. Skill and ability to build a fortress of strength for safe habitation. A large tail to smack when warning of danger, ability to swim any canal." God bless my adult children!

Again, I excitedly rushed down the hill to walk the canal. I wanted to witness the sun come up, experience the dawn again. Navigating the darkness while trying not to imagine what evil might leap out of the bush to grab me, I asked God for ministering angels to walk with me. I quoted scripture and imagined what those angels looked like. Then I settled on a bench, ready to watch for light to break.

Suddenly I heard a large splash! As if something tried to make a run for it. Then I spotted it. A beaver!! Many loud, thumping splashes followed, and I wondered if he was warning the other beavers of danger, or if he was telling me how large his tail was so that I'd be the one to run away. I crept down to the water, hoping to hide in the darkness, and became as still as I could be. I waited and waited and finally sat on the ground. I saw beavers head out in the canal, going back and forth, back and forth. I tried hard to still myself and become a part of nature. I began to pray, "Lord, please help him to know he doesn't need to be afraid of me." I started to speak truth to the beaver, "You don't need to fear me." How foolish that seemed when instinct tells it to protect, run, survive. Was I asking the beaver to go contrary to how he was made? Is that not how I felt when God asks me to trust Him, trust others?

I sat a long time, waiting, desiring so much to see him. Finally, he disappeared altogether, but I felt prompted by the Spirit to wait. I could sense the beaver, even under the water. I waited. When I was tempted to give up, the Lord said to me, "It's teeming with life." I let my body agree as I became one with the beauty of nature and life all around me. Then I heard a sound coming from the opposite direction. I turned my head to look, and there was Beaver! Standing! Munching away on his food. About twelve feet from my foot. I froze and gazed in appreciation knowing full well I could not disrespect him by grabbing my camera. We watched each other as he lazily swam, showing me his huge tail while munching on things floating on the water. A friend had prayed for me that I would again encounter God through an animal! Thank you, friend!

Several hours later I returned. The gorgeous sun warmed my path. I was curious to see where the door might be on the large beaver dam. I wondered how the beavers had kept safe in their fort with so many dogs running around. Crawling on my hands and knees part of the way, I finally reached it. When I asked Mr. Beaver if he minded me taking a picture, I got no response. He and the others were tucked deep below the pile of sticks and dirt. There had to be a girl beaver; a pretty scarf was woven in between the sticks and mud! When I saw no door, I realized the lodge had to be accessed under the water. Smart beaver! Wisdom and discretion to hide their entry. Like the key to our heart. If only we would be as wise in purity and discretion, and not flaunt what should be a mystery. What a treat! What joy! Thank you, Mr. Beaver.

The Rainbow

This stay at the prayer cabin happened just as normal life was being shut down due to the coronavirus disease, Covid-19. Dan drove me and lingered to pray with me awhile before leaving.

I wrote:

> I have become accustomed to being left with no car. As I sit in this fabulous chair, the tears start

> to flow; I am enveloped in the Presence of God. I realize at once that I need to forgive myself. I have been so hard on me. Where I failed my children, being harsh, impatient, not there for them as I would like to have been. I ask for forgiveness. I forgive myself, asking God to make that vulnerable spot in them a place of strength. I feel rest coming through my body as I hike up the mountain. Lingering at the rushing stream. Lord! Let me live in your River! Replenish, Refresh, Restore me. I want to learn to live in your River. The horrible pain of the last few months, the stress in my stomach is gone. Praise God.

That same day I decided to go running down to the canal even though the rain had now turned to hail. I wrote:

> Feeling the weight of a crisis in our family. The good news is we are coming together in unity! Praise God. But nonetheless it still is heavy weight.
>
> As I walk, pray, intercede ... I see the sky graced with a beautiful arching rainbow. I am at the end of the rainbow! The story goes that there is a pot of gold at the end of the rainbow. I pray as I witness this reminder of God's wondrous promise to Noah, "Your kingdom come, Your will be done. As it is in heaven, bring it to my earth, here and now!" The pot of gold is sweet honey from the Rock.
>
> And I hear that old hymn from my childhood. "Sweet honey in the Rock, sweet honey in the Rock. O, taste and see that the Lord is good. Sweet honey in the Rock." God's provisions are sweet, and they are rich.

> But as I near the end of the rainbow, it moves away. Always ahead of my grasp. That is how I have felt at times in my Christian walk. At times God has felt elusive, like a mirage that slips through my fingers.
>
> I can post the picture I took of this special moment with my rainbow. Yes, the rainbow is just for me. You will not see it in my picture. It does not show up. You need to believe my words. I was an eyewitness to this wondrous PROMISE OF GOD for my heart. You will need to choose to trust that I did have this experience. And so has been my walk of faith. JESUS joined the devastated disciples on that road to Emmaus in Luke 24:13-35. Walked with them long enough to touch their broken hearts. Making them believing hearts. Then He slipped away.

Once I was back in the cabin three deer came right up close; one deer looked right in my window as if wondering why I was inside that cabin! I felt so touched by God. My time ended with the blessing of these Scriptures that catapulted me into a new level of forgiving myself and walking in victory. I can release *me* from being too hard on myself.

"For God sees everything you do and His eyes are wide open as He observes every single habit you have. Beware that your sins don't overtake you and the scars of your own conscience become the ropes that tie you up." (Proverbs 5:21–22 TPT)

PART FOUR

ONWARD

Chapter Sixteen

Ready to Move

On one of my trips driving home from the Prayer Cabin, I found a real change in my heart. As I neared our neighbourhood, I realized that I had wanted to stay at the Prayer Cabin and not come home. We dearly loved our home and had no desire to leave it, but I had a sudden awareness that my heart was being pulled away from the home we had loved for close to 30 years.

Dan and I chose to spend our 35th wedding anniversary at the Prayer Cabin. After a wonderful sleep we climbed to the top of the mountain where we prayed and prayed until there were no prayers left in us. It is a wonderful gift to pray as a couple. We thought of everything on our hearts that needed prayer. We prayed about our future and where we should live. Dan had taken early retirement from his job as Senior Network Engineer for the City of Vancouver, and we needed to hear God's direction for our lives. Little did we know that the very valley we were looking out over as we prayed was the valley we were about to move to! The Lord gave us a Scripture for our future:

"For you shall go out in joy and be led forth in peace;

the mountains and the hills before you shall break forth into singing,

and all the trees of the field shall clap their hands.

Instead of the thorn shall come up the cypress;

instead of the brier shall come up the myrtle;

and it shall make a name for the Lord,

an everlasting sign that shall not be cut off." (Isaiah 55:12–13)

Moving to Rosedale

The decision to move came so quickly, and our family will never be the same again. We sold high in Surrey, benefiting greatly from the crazy market that caused buyers to bid on properties, and purchased a house in Rosedale. A house with a red door, on a cul-de-sac, with huge trees—hoping our friends will still come to visit!

I love to write about the deep and wonderful healing the Lord continues to grant me on my journey. When we looked for our house, the Lord in His kindness enabled us to be able to buy without that same crazy competition we had experienced in Surrey. God gave us a very wise realtor.

As soon as I walked in the house, I loved it. Everything about it made me want to linger. The Scripture hanging over the hot tub. The peaceful presence. When it was time for us to leave, the homeowner showed up and "talked my ear off." I stood for a long time as she told me all about the neighbours and much of the history of the house. When she described sharing the sweet nook under the rose arbour, drinking tea with a neighbour who was dying of cancer, I understood part of why I loved the house. The homeowner was much like me! Our realtor did not wait to put in our offer at the expected time but acted right away. The homeowner remembered us and immediately accepted our offer to buy the house. It was only after all this had transpired that I realized the miracle the Lord had granted me once again.

A couple of months before, I had been with my counsellor. (Yes, even at my age I continue to find more and more healing and growth from my upbringing and past! I don't want to ever be too old to learn, grow and heal more. Besides, the more I get "on top of my own stuff" the more healing and growth I see in my kids!) As I sat in the counsellor's office, I noted that she was wearing red. I couldn't remember her ever wearing red before even though I had known her for several years. I shared with her that I really dislike red, to the point of having a reaction inside of me when I thought much about the colour. We talked about whether it is the norm to dislike a colour to that extent. As always, toward the end of our appointment, she prayed for me. To find a gifted prayer counsellor that is experienced and so attuned to hearing God's voice has been a sheer gift from heaven! As she moved closer to pray for me that day, it suddenly became a real issue to me that she was wearing red. I found it so objectionable I wanted her to move away. I knew in my mind that it was an emotional reaction but still wanted to engage in her leading me in prayer, so I continued to cooperate, even though something in me cried, *No*!

As we continued, I saw the Lord come to me ... in red! The blood of Christ became very apparent to me and I experienced the Lord bringing a fresh and new healing deep inside of me. He has healed me so many times from extreme traumas that I have not had to remember or re-experience. I just have to get close enough to JESUS to give Him my fears, and He replaces them with His love and confidence. After that appointment I no longer had a reaction inside of me to the colour red. It was as though whatever was inside of me had been "diffused." Praise God! I love healing!

When we met the realtor at what eventually became our new home, the first thing I had noticed was that the large garage door was painted red. The back patio and back door were also painted red. We bought their red outdoor furniture as well. And I don't want to change the colour! In fact, I was delighted to pick a red barbecue to match the other things. Did you know God is into colour and loves to heal all of us?! JESUS gave me a new healing so that when this house that He picked for us came along, I would be able to take it all in stride and love it! Isn't that cool? Oh! And the house was built the same year our daughter Amber was born. It was 24 years old when we bought it.

Once settled, I had a desire to reach out to my siblings. For many years, I had hopes of restored relationships with them. I decided to ask my siblings to come and see our new home. The visit felt very strained, as it had been so many years since we were all together, but it went well. I followed up with meeting them individually. I was shocked to find out, during one of those visits, that my parents had already distributed their will among my siblings. Although this was hard to hear, I had expected it, as I had not been part of their lives. However, I was sad as I did not expect to find out this way. This helped me to understand more fully why my siblings appeared so awkward around me.

Back to Work

When we had moved, I had to give up my work and the ministries I was involved in. I had *believed* my identity was not found in all the ministry opportunities I participated in, but I didn't *know* for sure until I faced having none. My life altered so drastically. I had walked away from community where I felt so loved and appreciated. Making new friends is no easy task. I felt like we had moved into an area where everyone was already established and had no need for new friends. I was very grateful to find I did not need outward affirmation to be alright with my life, and that I could change; I was not stuck in a rut of always doing the same things.

The time came when I wanted to go back to work. I applied to work with a woman who had severe cerebral palsy. This was such a change for me, I had never done anything like that before. A friend with autism, yes, as he grew up with our kids and became like family, but nothing like this. I had never had any desire to be a nurse. In fact, I fared badly when my kids would cut themselves and need help. Suddenly I found myself doing all kinds of things I never imagined I would do. And I fell in love with the people I worked with.

I was trained as a Community Support Worker, without any formal schooling in that line of work. It was a very daunting prospect and I studied to pass the required exam to take a second job; a man fed only through a tube in his stomach. The first time I walked into his room, I had to turn away as I could not handle what I was seeing. As soon as I got to know my clients all my apprehension melted away and my focus became how I could help these dear ones. It was amazing to discover how much I could change who I thought I was, and learn new abilities I previously had no desire for. Healing is wonderful!

Another surprise for me was how well my clients were cared for by the staff in the home I worked in. I felt ashamed as I realized how narrow-minded I had been. Witnessing how lovingly, patiently and kindly the staff cared for these dear ones brought tears to my eyes. Without realizing it I had believed that only Christians would act in such a caring manner. What I witnessed would put many to shame. There are good people in this world. People made in the image of God.

Because I was working two jobs, I was not able to maintain the times of devotion and worship of God that I was accustomed to. I was forced to learn how to read the Bible and get my fulfillment from God like most normal people do. It was so satisfying to see I could also learn and be adaptable in my study and pursuit of God.

Since I now had three people I was lifting in and out of bed with the aid of a lift and harness, I put in much effort to strengthen my body. I began swimming 40 lengths once a week and enjoying many walks with my beloved Dan. I reasoned that if I looked after myself well enough, I would not get hurt. I also took great pride in learning more about eating healthily and even growing some of our own food in the garden. I really enjoyed my work, and it helped a lot with letting our kids go, allowing them to become independent.

One day Dan's mother had a fall. Having just come from work, I joined Dan as we visited her in Emergency. She had the same sling under her that I had just used at my job, the same pads laying beside her bed. A most bizarre thought entered my head, and I dared not say anything until I had some time to process my shocking idea. After going for a swim I gathered my courage, and asked Dan what he thought of us bringing his mother home to our house and me looking after her!

So, we did. I marvelled at how God had thought far ahead of us as I had been trained, with pay, to know how to look after my mother-in-law! Our home was already equipped for wheelchair access. It was with great joy we took Mom out of the care home she was in, although it was a good one. Bringing her home meant she would be surrounded by all my flowers, have visits from her grandchildren, and enjoy my cats taking turns sitting on her lap and keeping her company. She had been surrounded by people dying; now she was surrounded by family. At 97 years of age, she still baked her cookies and helped clean the grapes and blackcurrants from my garden so I could make jam.

My Mother-in-Law

Dan has always valued his family, and throughout the years enjoyed a strong bond with his mother. He, too, grew up in a pastor's home and experienced high expectations placed on his conduct and behaviour. Even though his mother was a stern disciplinarian, once he became an adult this attitude changed. In his mother's eyes, her son could do no wrong. Surely, she seemed to believe; he deserved to have everything handed to him. She was a wonderful, dynamic pastor's wife that loved to give. She would give us many vegetables and an abundance of flowers out of her garden. She loved to talk and had many friends. She was a smart, strong woman and so very kind. It took me several years to understand why there were things that bothered me, since she was such a kind generous woman.

It took me a long time to figure out that control can look good on the surface. I felt that my purpose in her life was to make sure she saw and heard everything about Dan's life. I felt I did not have any value of my own, in her eyes, outside of looking after Dan. I know there are many people like this, and I learned to adjust. As our children grew, I loved her through my children's eyes, and she was the best Grandma a kid could ever want. We often left our kids with her while we went on little holidays.

For many years I allowed my heart to grow cold toward her, until one day, soon after the miracle with my dead dahlia plant and me discovering my own love of gardening. We were hurrying to get in the car to go visit her. At the last minute, I heard a prompting from the Lord to cut some of my beautiful flowers for my mother-in-law. My heart cried, *No*! I didn't feel I could share with her anything that was important or meaningful to me. Also, flowers were her thing and I felt humbled to admit to her that I had learned to love them. But I would never want to disobey God, so I ran back to cut a bouquet of flowers to take with us. To my surprise, that act of obedience brought about a big healing in my own heart. From that day on, all the friction and agitation in my spirit toward my mother-in-law was gone. We moved forward into a pleasant relationship. She accepted what I had to offer, and I enjoyed her in our lives.

Dan is a lot like his mother, and I have been the beneficiary of that tendency to be viewed in someone's eyes as perfect, no flaws or weaknesses. Hardly a day goes by that my man doesn't want to say or do something to let me know how wonderful I am. He has been a solid, faithful rock in my life no matter what storm we have gone through. Everyone should have someone in their lives that believes in them like he has believed in me.

A few weeks before my 97-year-old mother-in-law came to live with us, I found myself flooded with excitement, like preparing for the birth of a baby. I realized I loved her as if she was my own body. A miracle of LOVE had taken place in my heart. She would get to soon go home to be with JESUS and I would get to be part of assisting her until then!

Will You Dance with Me?

Over the last number of years, when I really wanted or needed to connect with the Lord, I would see myself at His feet. I would kiss them, rub my cheek against His skin, wonder if His legs are hairy, enjoy the reality that I get to serve Him, be energized by Him.

Recently this all changed. I had a vision of JESUS. JESUS, the gentleman that He is, asked me to dance. He was huge! He took my arms with His hands and we danced like ballroom dancers. Even though His body was so large, my body seemed to sink perfectly into Him as we moved together. I was aware of scary things going on around us, almost like a cavern I could fall into, but I buried my face into His Body. It felt so wonderful, restful. I became aware that if I buried my face into Him, He would sweep me where I needed to go. There still are scary places I need to go that feel way beyond my ability. JESUS' invitation to me to dance with Him assured me that He will keep me safe if I keep my eyes on Him. I don't need to look over the cavern; I only need to lean into Him and let Him hide my eyes. He carries me.

The next day when I got up, my body felt extremely taxed and spent. I was aware that lifting Mom in bed to drink had taken more than I was able to sustain. I was not physically strong enough. As I sat in my special spot to have my early morning time with the Lord, I heard His invitation once again, a gentlemanly, "Will you dance with Me?" As I leaned my body into His, my eyes and face buried into the warmth and comfort of who JESUS is, I found He wanted to rub my shoulders and neck. It felt a bit unreal and I thought, *"Is this right that God should rub my back?"* As I cooperated, my special cat (who has previously demonstrated an ability to be used by God), came rushing to sit next to me, staring and purring loudly. She followed me closely for about ten minutes as if she wanted to be part of what was happening.

This experience was only a very few minutes. When it ended my brain seemed much clearer and my shoulders, arms and neck felt restored. I have ongoing issues with pain in my bones and usually have some constant pain. But all the added extra strain that I had been experiencing from lifting Mom was gone! I then went swimming and my body felt so much better! I LOVE JESUS so much. I can't wait to be with Him constantly, but I also don't want to miss anything on this earth that He still wants me to be a part of. Life is exciting and wonderful, whether it's giving birth or assisting with end of life care. The end is also exciting.

My prayer for you, my dear reader, is that you, too, can be swept off your feet in love for JESUS.

A Mother's Love

I went to help my mother-in-law as she lay in bed. She was not getting up much anymore, and as I reached over her to adjust her blankets, sun streaming through her window, she commented on my hair. She had seemed overwhelmed with my kindness in caring for her every need, and told people her daughter-in-law was really an angel. This particular day, she expressed a burst of love like I had not heard before. She appeared mesmerized with the beauty of my hair and the kindness I had shown her, and she said such sweet things. I allowed the words of a mother to sink in. I had not felt a mother's love for so long, and now I was receiving it. I opened my heart and allowed the healing to flood deep into my being. It felt so wonderful to be loved for who I was. Here I had thought I was doing all the caring and loving, yet I was receiving a miracle of love that I had longed for and given up hope looking for—love from my own mother. I became a more whole person that day, and knew I would be able to love my children in a deeper way because of this experience. Just over three months later she went home to be with her Lord, and joined the wonderful husband she had lost so many years before.

Goodbyes

The day we were having her celebration of life, my father, at almost 101, died also. (He lived 9 years beyond my mother's death). The phone call came early in the morning; our kids had slept over so they were right there with me. Again a miracle from God transpired in my life as we walked through this service for a woman dearly loved by her church and friends. The room was full of love, and in that setting I was able to say to all the kind people that offered me sympathy, "My Dad died today, too." I did not have a relationship with any of my siblings at that time, but was flooded with support from loving people anyway. It felt so kind of the Lord to walk with me in this way.

All my visits with him never brought about honest, open, real conversations. I was never to get his view of why our relationship was so broken. When I offered my forgiveness, he responded with, "That's so nice to forgive; the only way a Christian is to be," yet never putting himself in that role with me. I was so grateful to have my husband and my grown children to support me during that difficult funeral. It was extremely hard for me to process my feelings and thoughts towards my father as people praised his work and his fathering skills, describing a godly man that had excelled and raised his children so well. My parents were always held up on a pedestal in their church denomination, held in esteem where there was no place for me. No place to be real and have feelings, desires, and needs. No place for hurts and failures.

Even though this was sad, I was not subject to someone else's opinions of me. Much of my Christian walk has been filled with people telling me God always answers prayer and there will always be a good outcome, but very little is taught on when babies die, divorce happens, jobs are lost, forgiveness is never granted.

The reality of life is that there is not always a happy ending even when you are all Christians and believe in the same God. I had believed Christianity was all about building bridges. But how do you move forward in life when important relationships are never restored? I was so grateful that God had previously helped me have my own heart be whole, healed and restored even without the important relationships that I so desired. I did not have to be subject to someone else's lack of ability to have a healthy relationship. I could be whole before God and true to myself. I could still choose joy.

Soon after, I unexpectedly heard my father had left me a small amount of money. I was thrilled, especially when it arrived on my birthday, which is also his birthday. I excitedly shared my tithe money with the church, and joyfully gave some to our children. As the week unfolded, I found terrible and debilitating oppression coming over me. It was hard to keep working and functioning. It was so drastic I went to my pastors, asking for prayer. I wondered if maybe I had to give the money away, as it somehow seemed to affect me so deeply. As I wrestled it out before God, He finally opened my eyes to see what I had not been seeing. Even though I had done all I knew to do regarding forgiveness and having the right attitude in my heart, I had to acknowledge a truth God now wanted me to see. My attitude had been a harsh bitter root of judgment against my parents. Somehow accepting their money with my judgemental attitude was causing a compromise in my life. I had opened my life to a harassment that was robbing my peace. I needed to get on my knees before God and do some soul-searching, offer more forgiveness, and receive a new cleansing of my heart. After some more prayer and sharing with our kids, my peace was restored. I blessed my parents and moved forward, learning to not be so hasty in my choice of words. Praise God for a hard lesson learned.

Our Place of Refuge

Along with special traditions in our family like Sunday chocolate, sleeping on the floor Christmas Eve, and tuna salad after church, we also like to name things. "The Place of Refuge" became the name of our new home, and our wi-fi network name is The Refuge. Labeling our home as a Place of Refuge came with a cost. I've learned more about what peace means and the price we pay for it. Many arguments, battles, have been fought and won in our home. As we've communicated and come to a place of resolve and healing in our relationships, it has created an atmosphere of peace for others to know how to be humble, open and honest. Humility goes a long way in bringing peace!

When we moved here, we truly did carve out a different life for ourselves. We settled into a routine that we love. Dan has been able to pursue his love of classic cars to his heart's content, while making many friends and developing his own business of wiring old cars. The mountains, always changing, are amazing; and we love the farms. It's not far to find water: lakes, streams and waterfalls abound. A bear walked by our house the other day. We enjoy taking motorcycle rides, exploring all the sights. We also love to walk. It does wonders for a marriage to walk and to pray together.

The first year in our new home I dedicated my time to setting up our "nest" and doing all I could to put our children first. The move was sudden and altered their lives so drastically. Even though they no were longer living with us, I tried to make them the most important thing in my life, praying for them and always being available to them. I have been so grateful that a strength in our marriage has been to cultivate an attitude of gratitude and to be content with all things. A gift we want to leave our children is to know how to be content in all things, how to live satisfied with where you are, who you are at any given time, and how to appreciate the beauty in each moment.

I had already cultivated a time of devotion and worship for myself, but Dan and I started to schedule praying together every morning. So many things to pray about! When I would feel incapable of helping our children, now out on their own, I found great strength in realizing we could do more for them by praying for them. We could still "mess with their lives," but in prayer! I found it so different to pray with my husband than how I typically pray alone. It is a hallowed, holy place. This has done wonders for our marriage and catapulted us into a place we had not enjoyed before. I have fallen in love with my husband all over again. The atmosphere in our house, I believe, has become one of peace. Many people who visit comment on feeling Christ's presence in our home. We have enjoyed leading many groups of Bible study and prayer, and entertaining guests. We are so grateful for our Place of Refuge.

Chapter Seventeen

Treasure Hunts

I found courses online that piqued my interest, and have taken many courses on developing the ability to clearly hear God's voice. Something wonderful was birthed in me those days of leading *Praying the Scriptures*, and I attempted to do the same here in Rosedale in our Place of Refuge. My passion clearly lies in hosting an atmosphere for other people to also recognize God in their lives.

"The unfolding of your words gives light; it imparts understanding to the simple." (Psalm 119:130).

My courses made a clear distinction between the Old Testament prophets, and life for the church after JESUS came and walked this earth. I believe prophecy is as simple as taking a relevant scripture for that day and encouraging a friend's heart with it. The prophetic word is alive and brings us life, helping us to understand how to apply scripture to our day-to-day lives. Revelation 19:10 tells us that the testimony of JESUS is the spirit of prophecy. He brings *life* to our lives. Helping people take scripture and let it open their understanding for everyday life brings so much joy, and is a great foundation to build upon.

One day the Lord inspired me with an idea to invite various friends, with a common passion for God, to gather at my house. I called it a Treasure Hunt; a safe group where women could discover what treasured word God had for their hearts. The goal was to have a fun environment where we could collectively listen to the Voice of God. Kimber, home at that time, excitedly helped me prepare for the first one. I invited my old friends on the prayer team, as well as my new friends that I thought would have a desire for something like this. As had been our custom with the prayer team, we started out with worship. After a time of worship, I gave a little teaching on how to hear from God, while explaining guidelines of what is acceptable in the prophetic word and including some "do's and don'ts" to make it a safe place. My dear friend who led us in worship would help me tremendously by immediately following my instructions, showing the group what I wanted. She always seemed to understand my expectations of the women during our time together.

Before everyone had arrived for the Treasure Hunt, I sent a request for each woman to bring an item that made her think of God. This prompted the women to begin thinking about how God is real to them before they even showed up. There was great laughter and sometimes tears around the room as each one shared their item. Some things were as simple as a feather, picture, teddy or a cross necklace. Meaningful conversation began to happen. The hardest thing for me to do in these Treasure Hunts is to get women to stop talking and cooperate as a group. To open the door for people to share, and then make sure each person gets equal time, can be a major undertaking. I needed to apologize several times, as it was very hard to lead without possibly hurting someone's feelings. I tried to keep us on task to speak words of life and hope over each other.

Listening is a skill our culture has not developed well. We pray and pray but when do we stop to listen to what God has to say? I've had many people throughout my life speak wonderful God-words to me. But the words I remember the most are the ones that Father has spoken directly to my heart. That is where lasting change has come from.

Next in our Treasure Hunt we went around the circle reading scripture, just like I had done with the other women years before. Once the women were comfortable, I opened up the floor for them to speak into each other's lives. I have never done this without lots of tears and heartfelt God-moments. It's a surprising and humbling thing to feel God speaking to your heart in a tender and meaningful way. One of the most important things in my life is to LISTEN to God and I dearly love to assist other people in doing the same.

When preparing for the Treasure Hunt, I had printed out small papers with a scripture and an application for each woman. After we had a break for food, I had each woman pick one of those papers. Even though they picked randomly, I had prayed lots over those papers for each woman to get the one that was right for her own heart. There were more bursts of joy or tears as God again spoke personally to so many of the women. The allotted four hours didn't seem to be adequate time for all of this!

The second Treasure Hunt was different. I set up several places around my garden where, after the usual worship and instructions, I released the women to go be alone and totally silent in order to hear God for themselves. No talking or interacting was allowed. I found it helped if I gave them a question to ask such as, "Lord, what do You think of me?"

Then we gathered again as a group to share what we felt God had said to us. One dear gal shared how she saw my bird cage in the garden, open. She felt that God had impressed on her heart that she had been feeling like a bird trapped in a cage, but now the door was open. She was free to fly. It was thrilling to hear what the women would share.

Each Treasure Hunt took on a different form and was bathed first in prayer. Sometimes I would go to the prayer cabin first and prepare. Lately the Treasure Hunt takes the form of a Virtual Treasure Hunt as we grapple with Covid-19 restrictions. Following are some examples of the notes printed out for women to choose from and take home:

"And I will be to her a wall of fire all around, declares the LORD, and I will be the glory in her midst." (Zechariah 2:5)

> I want to be your everything, your "one and only." I jealously guard you. I'm involved in your every move. I have great plans for us. You can trust me. I continue to be that barrier wall that keeps you safe within, and the evil outside your heart. I am your jealous lover.

"Be strong and courageous. Do not be frightened, and do not be dismayed, for the LORD your God is with you wherever you go." (Joshua 1:9)

> I am not only with you; I am intimately partnering every step of the way. Courage is valiant and carries you on top of the waves. You are "my courageous one." My heart bursts in pride as I enjoy relationship with you. You are stronger than you think and feel. Your life matters to me and has impacted many people.

"You've kept track of my every toss and turn through the sleepless nights, Each tear entered in your ledger, each ache written in your book." (Psalm 56:8)

> You already are seeing great meaning and purpose in your struggle. You have glimpses of joy and that's not to tease or disappoint you. You can trust me. I am your Healer and you will heal others through your touch, your voice, your words. The more you feel and experience me as the great HEALER, the more you can impact others.

Have No Opinion

I've learned many valuable things from my on-line courses, but one of the most useful things was this: Have *no opinion*. JESUS did only what He heard the Father telling Him to do. He went away regularly to listen and pray, and did not act independently or outside of the Father's will. My homework one week was to go the entire week having no opinion, and journaling my experience to submit to the class. Do you have any idea how hard that is?! Our whole culture highly values and is built around opinions. Turn on the news and in no time, someone has a microphone in front of their face and is asked, "What do you think about that?"

As I attempted what felt like an impossible task, I started to see how opinionated I really was. I found that I was now very quiet and listened so much more. Most relationships are built around shared opinions, as we tend to gravitate towards others who have opinions similar to our own. I discovered that the more I worked to shut down my own voice, the more I was empty enough to hear God clearly in my own spirit. I learned that opinions can be like white noise, blocking our ability to hear God. When reading scripture, if I cancelled my own opinion of what I was reading, I found new understanding and life. Even when reading familiar verses, I discovered so much I had not noticed before. It was a very liberating exercise!

As I did in previous years, at the beginning of 2020, I asked the Lord for a word that described what He wanted to be my focus for that year. He gave me the word UNOFFENDED. He wanted me try to live as an unoffended woman. Wow, what a challenge! As I have pondered and studied it, I realized our world thrives on offense. We are offended at everything! We are even encouraged to stand up for our rights with an angry, offended stance. But that is not God's way.

"Great peace have they which love thy law: and nothing shall offend them." (Psalms 119:165 KJV)

What is it That You Believe?

Earlier this year I penned these words as I attempted to organize myself to lead a group:

> TRAUMA pierces our soul, stamps us, moulds us into its image. All week long those words hung in the air as I realized that something in my spirit no longer agreed with that statement. For so many

years I found a multitude of ways to express my heartache, my struggle in living this life. Feeling like I was missing an arm or a leg. Living in a world that required all limbs in order to be accepted, functional, valued. It has been an intense struggle with lots of pain, growing in this life I've been gifted with. The cocoon striving to become the butterfly. The odd one out that tries so hard to be relevant, accepted.

Those of you who know me know how I value connectedness, community, coming under authority and being held accountable. Two amazing prayer counsellors gifted me with their incredible skill and ability to pray with me, guide me on my healing journey. It was with great joy and much pain and struggle that I discovered I didn't have to be whole first in order to live a full, whole life. I could give all of me even when I felt deformed. I could already be effective, real, and warm towards others.

This was how I used to describe myself: "If I were to think of myself as a tree and the trauma of life happened, and my tree grew deformed and in different ways than my parents or God intended me to be, what do I do? Do I chop the tree down and discard the whole plan or do I grow into all I can be, growing towards the light?" Again, I repeat this statement that troubled me. "TRAUMA pierces our soul, stamps us, moulds us into its image."

And I now understand why it bothers me. I am made in God's Image! With His likeness. He gets the final word as He's the one that loved me and formed me in my mother's womb. I was a thought in His loving heart even before I was conceived.

> Father gets to say who I am and what I can be. I am like Him. God says there is nothing too hard for Him. He makes all things new. His forgiveness and love are unfathomable! He casts my sins as far as the east is from the west. I will accept how God says I am. Not succumb to other people's restrictions placed upon me. Trauma does not define me. God does!
>
> I can and have chosen "better not bitter". A life choice that pays many dividends. I do not have to live as a woman who has been a victim of trauma! I can walk free from that and not accept that as a defining moment for the rest of my life! Yippee!

A few months later the Lord brought me back to this piece that I had written, and He ever so kindly showed me this picture, and helped me to see healing as much more than this. God does not want me to feel like some obstruction is going through my body as this photo would depict. I have accepted this picture so many times through the years only to find God has so much more healing for me! It is possible to live without feeling altered by trauma. Healing can be complete; I can feel whole again. I no longer need to respond to life in a certain way because of trauma. Praise God!

No Longer Afraid of the Dark

Once as I entered into an extended time of worship and prayer, I found myself in a place I could vividly picture, where I could shut out all distractions and quiet all voices in my head. Not very big; peaceful, dark, cool, quiet; with large stones over my head, all dripping with moisture. I was to listen, listen to the drip, drip of water, as my awareness of God greatly increased. I was surprised that it was dark. My understanding had been that God is light and I could find Him in light.

In time, as I prepared myself to pray for people in the course I was taking, I learned to listen for God's words to come to me. I found myself challenged on a very deep level to read/pray the Psalms. As I daily prayed them out loud, I discovered I was thrust into a whole new dimension of life-giving words pouring out of my mouth, bringing life and new understanding to my soul.

One time as I was again vocally praying the Psalms, I had a vision. The darkness of the huge black sky captivated all my attention, and a multitude of brilliant stars took my breath away! It felt like I could step right into this vastness, this grandeur of God's creativity. The stars continued farther than my eyes could see.

This wasn't just a picture in my head as I was praying. It was different. It was an experience that the Lord took me into. I have since then been struck to the core of my being with new understanding that is still unfolding. The stars would not be seen without the backdrop of the dark sky. The Lord wanted me to become comfortable with the darkness. In the quietness, JESUS told me, "Don't be afraid of the dark. Darkness and light are the same to Me."

"There is no such thing as darkness with you. The night, to you, is as bright as the day; there's no difference between the two." (Psalm 139:12 TPT)

This troubled me at first as I had always thought to fear the dark. Then I pondered, "There was dark before satan fell. Maybe we are not to let him take ownership of the dark!"

"...God separated the light from the darkness." (from Genesis 1:4).

I wrote in my journal:

> Then my understanding started to unfold as I realized running away from the dark, can equal running away from quiet. It gets dark at night to

signal change, change of pace, time to rest and sleep. It's not God's plan for us to be in "full-on" mode, working, light 24 hours a day. There is rhythm, shifting gears, rest. Like He rested on the 7th day. Darkness signals a change, time to shift and do different.

So, I walk into the dark. I'm not to fear the dark but accept that it's a time for rest. Rhythm, seasons. Hebrews tells us to fear lest we fail to enter promised REST. There is rest in accepting darkness. I want to be at peace in the dark. When I accept this rhythm, I can put to rest my thoughts inside my head. When at rest in myself, I find my spirit fully alive with God, my own internal voices silenced. Besides, JESUS already conquered sin and death, putting the enemy as defeated under my feet because they are under His! I can trust Him in this.

This morning as I go back into prayer, I see JESUS coming to me out of the dark the same way I saw the brilliant stars seen only with the backdrop of black sky. He says, "Look for Me in the dark. No longer run from/shun the dark. Look for Me coming to you from the dark." I look up at the morning sky, knowing that even though I can no longer see the stars I don't doubt at all that they are there. Of course the stars are there. I won't get to see them again until it's dark. I enter the rhythm of timing, faith and sheer thrill of expectancy in talking with JESUS.

"I am standing in absolute stillness, silent before the One I love, waiting as long as it takes for him to rescue me. Only God is my Savior, and he will not fail me. For he alone is my Safe Place. His wrap-around presence always protects me as my Champion Defender." (Psalm 62:5–6 TPT)

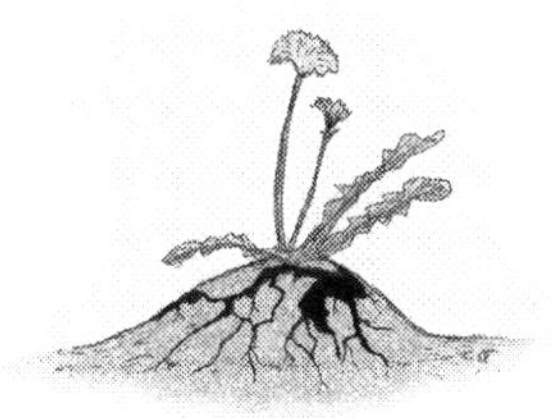

Chapter Eighteen

I Am God's Quill

In church earlier this year, as I entered worship deep in my spirit, I found I was taken into a vision. I was a pen, and my writing had taken all my ink. I have written my pain and suffering, detailing it throughout the years. Loss, betrayal, rejection, and misunderstandings have taken their toll. I've written and written and written some more. I've finally exhausted my pen. There is no more ink; I've run out of my need to express my pain. As I worshipped and entered into what the Lord had for me, He removed my empty pen from my hand, placing His pen in my hands. A large quill-like pen that needs to be dipped in ink—like I remember from my childhood when I kept an ink-well on my school desk.

JESUS says He is the Author. Look to Me (Hebrews 12:2). I am the Author and the finisher of your faith. He is the Author and finisher of my life. I was the author of my life, but now I let God be my Author.

"No record of wrongs," is what I heard over and over as the worship service continued. "[LOVE] does not dishonour others, it is not self-seeking, it is not easily angered, it *keeps no record of wrongs."* (1 Corinthians 13:5 NIV emphasis added). I have done my homework, done the self-care and hours of soul-search-

ing and deep healing. I no longer want to keep records of wrongs done to me.

I release my pen and put it down, I take up God's pen, His quill. I write with healing and with grace. The inkwell, His Holy Spirit. Flow River, flow! I want the river that flows from the Throne of God to flow through me. I want to be God's scribe. No longer any need to prove, defend, or justify. I accept Peace, I offer Peace. I am living out of PEACE. I am NOT the captain of my ship, the charge of my destiny. God is! I want Him to Author me, write and rewrite me in the purity of His Spirit. May Father deliver me from the need to pick up that old pen once again, emptied of ink, and thoroughly used up. I release the old, embrace the new, and enter His PEACE that surpasses all my understanding.

Oh the grace, the mercy, the joy that is set before me! I embrace, I love, I laugh, and I dance. The depth of suffering has enlarged my capacity for Joy—my ability to enjoy life to its fullest.

Making Sense out of Suffering

To this day, as I sit here writing this in my 65th year of my life, I still cringe when I read Psalm 27. It is a Psalm that I have grown to love, yet I also know it was what my mother clung to on that frightening ship voyage during the war, newly married to a man she hardly knew. She trusted God with all her heart as she gave her life in complete surrender to whatever God had in store for her as a missionary to Africa. She trusted Him with each of her five children, and had dedicated me to God as an infant, before witnesses, in a solemn commitment to raise me well. Yet look how I have suffered under her watchful care. How do I make sense of a God like that, a faith like that? To trust, to act, to live your life and yet find so much heartache. How do I come to terms with my own personal struggle *and* a loving God?

A wonderful story in the Bible helped me to understand suffering in relation to my own broken heart. The book of 2nd Samuel begins with David being told that both King Saul and his son Jonathan were killed in a horrible battle. As much as King Saul was determined to kill David, Jonathan was bound to David in close friendship. At the news of the deaths, the nurse of Jonathan's 5-year-old little boy knew his life had to be protected, since it was customary to kill all family members of the conquered ruler so as to remove any lineage to reclaim the throne. She picked up Mephibosheth and ran, but in their hurry to get away, he fell and became crippled in both his feet.

Years later, King David wanted to extend God's kindness to any surviving members of Saul's family in honour of his best friend, Jonathan. When told about one surviving member, Jonathan's son Mephibosheth, David called him to come and take an honoured spot at David's own table. Mephibosheth was given Saul's inheritance, and invited to be part of King David's family. The crippled boy, now a disabled man, sat at the king's table for the rest of his life.

Young Mephibosheth would not have understood why, from no fault of his own, his family was gone, and he had to live in hiding. He had a choice when summoned by King David. He could continue to run and hide, or he could accept David's invitation.

As he accepted the King's kind offer, so I have needed to accept Father God's offer that invites me to sit at His table for the rest of my life. If I stayed stuck in the "Why?" and "I don't understand!" I would have never accepted the offer to be included, to come and sit and learn a new life. I have chosen to believe what God says to me rather than insist I get an explanation before I move forward. I chose a new identity, even to be called by a new name.

Overcomer

Revelation 12:11 tells us we overcome by believing in God and the word of our testimony. The word of my testimony is that God has been so very good to me.

It seems apparent to me now that from a young child I was "groomed" for a purpose. I believe when I left Africa as a 13 year old, people with bad intentions for my life expected my family to be back as they had done for many years. Five years in Kenya, one year in Canada.

But I was turfed out of my home and onto the streets. It seems so harsh. Sometimes I think of Joseph's life in Genesis 37. Through the murderous jealousy of his brothers, he was thrown into a pit and left to die. Then he was falsely accused and thrown in prison. Yet circumstances in his life eventually landed Joseph as ruler over the country. A person with no guile. No need for revenge. Offering the kindness to others that he had experienced from God. The famous saying comes from this story in Genesis 50:20, when the very same brothers stood asking for food in famine days: What the enemy meant for evil, God meant for good.

If my life had not so drastically changed as a young teenager, I would have gone back to Kenya. Only God knows what would have happened to me. I believe my abusers wanted to use me to make babies for human sacrifice. That is what I was possibly spared from. I have a testimony and my words say God is kind and He has plans for my life and they are good.

Looking in the Rear-View Mirror

In retrospect, as I poured through my journals from those years of my written agony, I see it now with fresh insight. Dan and I had so much pain wrapped up in one church. We were very involved and gave so much of ourselves. I am very grateful the church gave me so much opportunity to serve, but when we left

I felt like we were no more valuable to them than a church pew. They would do no more than miss the pew they were accustomed to using. I felt another layer of hurt from suffering so deeply amongst people that did not seem to care to know.

Through my new eyes (literally!), now more mature and with much healing having transpired in my heart, I can also see how my coping strategy played a big role in causing me to feel this way. In the worst of my suffering I learned how to "put on a face" and function when necessary. When the pain was extreme, I'd lay on the floor in our living room so the boys could climb over me as they watched their programs, just waiting for daddy to come home. I learned how to keep functioning, looking normal, even while deeply suffering.

When Dan would get home and ask me how I was, I'd reply, "Fine." That was what I wanted to be—fine. I thought that if I convinced him I was okay, maybe I would be okay. And he'd often believe me as I attempted to portray myself as alright. I seemed to have the ability to do this so well that most people had no idea of my suffering. Even my husband would be shocked when I'd put my pain into words; he'd really thought I *was* okay. I'd present myself at church as "all put together". I was Department Head for the Sunday School class and believe I did a good job. The kids and their parents loved me. For our new pastor I put on a spread that said WELCOME all written out in large letters with only vegetables. It took so much out of me to do these things, yet it gave me purpose and the ability to try to prove that I *was* alright. Then at home I'd seethe in anger and pain, wondering why nobody cared, why no one wanted to help me. Those I did tell were often stumped, not knowing how to help me and then acting like I'd never said anything the next time we'd meet.

Dan was so relieved in the beginning when the psychiatrist said she had a diagnosis for me and could see evidence of severe childhood trauma. "PTSD," she said. Dan eagerly asked in relief, "So what do we do about it?" To which the doctor replied that she didn't know. Most people had no idea how to help me. I recognize that is not a reason for me be resentful or angry; I no longer harbour negative feelings towards people I thought had failed me.

As far as our "Christian culture" goes, I find we tend to be babes in immaturity with expecting all things to go well all the time. We put out a prayer request that we get the job, that our puppy won't die, or that all will be well. Then the person posts on social media, "Got the job!" and people respond, "Praise the Lord, God is good!" And I cringe. What is said when divorce happens, the husband dies, or you lose everything? We are silent in those times as our faith does not hold us the same. Most of us have not been taught how to build our spiritual muscles so that we are strong. When winds of adversity come, we need to lean into them and grow, not retreat and pout. The caterpillar never reaches the stage of a beautiful butterfly without the struggle. The beautiful smelling aroma is not released from the rose to make perfume without the crushing. Yet we demand that of God. We have faith that is more of a presumption than a real belief in God and knowing His ways. We presume upon God and try to force our own will by quoting what we think are the right Scriptures, thinking we can force God to do what we say.

Moses said that he knew God and he knew His ways (Deuteronomy 29:29; 30:11-16; Psalm 103:7). But what are God's ways? What is He really like? Does He feel pain the way we do? There were many babies slaughtered in the time of baby Moses, yet what we read about is the miracle of Moses rescued from the river. What about the mothers whose hearts were broken in the death of their child?

What about Mary, the mother of JESUS? If she had cried out in faith, quoted all the right scriptures in begging God to spare her son, would He have been spared from death? Did she even ask for that? When JESUS was born, His birth resulted in the death of all male children under two years of age in that area. What about those mothers and their faith? How do we believe in a

God that doesn't make sense to us? JESUS walked this earth and I know He loved His disciples. Yet every one of them died a horrible death because of having faith in Him.

I want to give Him my lack of understanding when things don't go the way I expect. Asking "why" when tragedy strikes is a natural human response. If we never asked why, never did any self-examination or reflection, we would never move forward—we would not grow. I have found the secret is to partner with God, to agree with *His* Words while I'm in that place of desperation, that place of "Why!!!?" Catching myself in that pain, and then allowing God's Grace to fall on my heart like fresh spring rains on parched ground. I can make myself accept His kind love language for my wounded heart. God says it will be worth it all. One day when I am in heaven and I have the full picture, I will see it all. The end from the beginning. I will agree with God that it all makes sense, and He did the right things for me through my whole life. I can make a decision to bring heaven to earth now by accepting God's great love for me and agreeing with Him.

We are taught to pray from the Lord's Prayer, "Thy kingdom come, Thy will be done." I look ahead to see what it's like in heaven and I bring it down to my part of the earth today. Rather than allow myself to be "caught", taken captive by despair and lack of understanding, I make a choice to agree with God. He loves me deeply and has good plans for my life. I don't let the despair win. In time, the fruits, the results in my life show that I am the winner! I actually can change me, and the hard things in my life become different. I am triumphant in my life now! This life is only boot camp (says my husband). We have all of eternity to enjoy. Our choices now make a difference as to the rest of our lives and for eternity. We don't have to wait until heaven to enjoy what He has for us. I pray daily, "Thy kingdom come to me now. I need it now ... and later!"

I can reason that Amber's heart defect may have been because we were poisoning ourselves with pollution, greed, pesticides, and many other things. But how can I turn around and blame God for us being selfish, self-centered people at heart? So, I arrive at wanting to know who to blame. Is God cruel, distant, cold or uncaring? Hmm… that's kind of how I felt about my Dad. Interesting. Maybe I project onto God the harshness of people around me. Is satan, my enemy, to blame? Is he the scapegoat for all the reasons we suffer? One of the hardest things for me to ever process was why I felt God left me when I needed Him the most. I was taught to not ask questions when it comes to our spirituality. Just trust, don't ask God why. I have found that to be faulty thinking. I ask God lots of questions and I open my heart to hear His answer, even if the answer feels hard. I say, "How do you, Lord, want me to respond to this? What am I to learn as I walk through this challenge?"

My life verse has been so real to me over and over.

"Trust in the Lord with all your heart and LEAN NOT on your own UNDERSTANDING" (Proverbs 3:5 NIV, emphasis added).

Frequently I have needed to remind myself not to lean on my own understanding. God never does what I expect Him to do. In fact, He usually seems to do the complete opposite to what I think. I don't understand God and I choose to not draw conclusions about God while I'm in the hard place. Waiting it out has brought me great dividends.

We read in Genesis that God set people up as caretakers of the land. We are to care for our earth as caretakers. How is that working for us? Many times, we can't connect consequences to our behaviour. Then when things go wrong, we tend either to blame God or blame the enemy for trying to mess up our lives. Not that I think I did something wrong and suffered my own consequences with Amber's death, but it very well could be consequences of communal mismanagement of this earth. Wholeness and healing have come to my life as I've learned to grow in taking responsibility for myself. The blame-game only causes us to go around in circles. If I were to go stand out in the middle of the freeway, quote scripture, and think positive thoughts, I'd still get run over by a truck. Gravity still happens. God has set an order about this world. We are a part of that created order and when we don't fit into it, when we resist and carelessly use and abuse, we suffer the consequences. Furthermore, we sometimes suffer other people's consequences.

"For the eyes of the Lord run to and fro throughout the whole earth, to give strong support to those whose heart is blameless toward him." (2 Chronicles 16:9)

This tells me God's kind eye is looking every single day to help me, show me support. He is looking for people who are not full of blame. I must choose to have a heart that is not full of blame either towards Him or towards other people. Blaming God is shooting myself in the foot. Looking for how to respond with God, rather than react, is the way to grow in our purpose.

In Jeremiah 1:5 God says, "Before I formed you in the womb I knew you, and before you were born I consecrated you." Before conception we were a thought in God's heart. Wow!

If I was a thought in God's mind before I was even born—and the Bible tells us we were born with a purpose, on purpose—then I was okay at birth. Generational issues passed down the family line have taken effect over time; environmental mismanagement can change the course of one's life. I ended up with results other than what God had planned for my life. It's our human condition and I, too, have chosen to sin against God's will for me.

I am so grateful that at the Cross of JESUS, for those of us that believe, we can be freed from all chains. Believing that fact is not enough, though. We also need to change our brain and heart—to think it, too, and change how we react and respond.

I believe that God is not fair; He is just. Fairness is a man-made concept through which we try to perceive God. We won't really understand His justice until we see life from God's perspective. I can trust that He is just.

So, where does our faith fit into all of this? Our worldview? Our thoughts about who God is and who we are? How I fit into this world plays a role in how I feel. How I feel causes me to sink into depression or despair … or I can choose joy. I tell myself what to believe and my emotions will follow.

I love word pictures. That is the most common way I hear and understand God. He shows me a picture in my imagination and then I look for words in the Bible that make the picture clearer. In writing out this final chapter, I see a picture. In this picture I see God as a tap, a faucet that water pours out of. We read in the Bible that we are washed through the reading and understanding of Scripture. His Spirit cleanses, revives and refreshes us. In my illustration, if I am a cup, I need to go over to the tap and put myself under the running water or it would not benefit me in any way. I could be off in a corner, quoting scripture, begging God and doing all kinds of things to meet my needs but if I don't act on putting myself where my need can be met, I don't get what I need.

For a long time, I was not emotionally or mentally capable of placing myself under that faucet. I needed help. We are all designed to need each other. The depression and pain in my past, the immensity of my struggle, was so great I could not rely on my own thoughts to give me a clear perspective. I needed professional help, and I needed friends that loved me unconditionally. At times I needed medication. I needed someone to bring me water when I could not walk to get it myself. I needed enough help so that I could one day, on my own, walk to that tap to get the water. God hadn't left me, but my lack of understanding how to heal was separating me from Him. I needed people to help me fight through the pain of my past and present struggles. (See Galatians 6:2, 5)

Understanding Has Come

Understanding has come to me in this way. Psalm 119:130 says, "The unfolding of your words gives light." As I have needed to get to know what God is like, I can understand His Word. When my concept of Scripture was twisted, I interpreted the Bible incorrectly. As I grew to know my Father as loving, kind and patient, as I studied how God sent JESUS to this earth, I came to know more of what He is like. JESUS coming here = God's Word unfolding before our eyes. Now I am to unfold my life, in understanding and walking it out like Christ showed us. As I've accepted the facts of Christ's kindness, patience, endless love, creativity, restorative power—as I've allowed His words to come alive inside of me as my belief system—as I've rejected the voice that tells me, "You're not worthy, not good enough, not valued or wanted." I have become strong as a lion with courage to show for it. I have fallen in love with The Voice of Love. God's words are:

"The rarest treasures of life are found in his truth. That's why I prize God's word like others prize the finest gold. Nothing brings the soul such sweetness as seeking his living words." (Psalm 19:10 TPT).

It isn't enough for me to see on a page the words (acts) of what God says. It had to come alive inside of my heart, like a baby chick pecking its way out of a hard and resistant shell until finally new life is born. Then I remind myself, "Your word is a lamp to my feet and a light to my path." (Psalm 119:105) It is the Light for me to see my way, the Lion, the Teacher, coming behind with God's Voice saying, "This is the way; walk in it," just as I had experienced at the prayer cabin. I've thought of this verse indicating the Lamp is God's Word, His responsibility. He has given it for me to open. The light is my flashlight, my responsibility, to shine it when and where I need it.

There are many more people who have faced various types of captivity, have been prisoners, including prisoners of war. But whether we have been tied up, tortured, drugged, beaten, or abused, we always have one thing: our will. We still get to choose our attitude and what we believe, no matter how big the oppressor. Our will is God's gift to us. It's the precious gift we have to give back to Him. I use my will to choose living for God, all the days of my life. Even when nothing makes logical sense to me, I choose to let my heart believe and trust.

God's Finishing School

The purpose of our passing years with all their joys and sorrows is to wean us from self-worship, to mature us in love. Getting older is not about us getting better. Growing older is intended to make us more gentle, more thoughtful and considerate, more gracious and sympathetic, less childish and demanding. This is the reason for the trials and tribulations, the conflicts with pain, the struggles with disease, the financial reverses, the ingratitude of loved ones, the disappointments of false friendships, wrongful suffering, and the grief of bereavement.

All life's varied experiences, even down to old age, are working together to mature and ripen our character and develop pure, godly love. All sunshine would not make us into good fruit, nor would all gladness and joy produce the richest character. Darkness as well as light, rough cold weather as well as gentle warm summer, are needed to mature and enrich us in God's love.

Our trials, therefore, are not just something to be endured as an unfortunate but unavoidable evil. It is part of God's plan. When properly accepted they may constitute "God's Finishing School for Character Education and Enrichment" before we enter eternity (adapted from *Don't Waste Your Sorrows*, Paul E. Billheimer page 125).

At Peace With My Scars

As I was deciding to write this book, I said to a friend, "I am not going to include any scripture in my book; I don't want to appear as though I'm preaching at people." Ha! My goodness! Sharing scriptures is part of who I am; I can't share myself without the Words that have become the fabric of my life.

I do have a real enemy. This enemy, satan, doesn't want me to know God or heal and grow. One of the hardest "pills to swallow" in my life is this: I made every attempt to keep our children away from the confusion and hurt that I felt from my family of origin and my upbringing. Dan and I raised our children in a loving, consistent home that was full of faith. I believed I was sparing them the pain and suffering I had endured. I am proud of my achievements and all the ways God helped me. But I did not realize that I would give birth to the very thing I tried to keep them safe from. I thought I had kept it out of my home. My kids still suffer, fall and get hurt the same as everybody else. So goes the plight of each and every one born into this world. We need to individually have our own deep wrestle of faith and trust and learn how to live in a world that wants to take from us and mould us into an image we are not created to be. Our struggle is real, and it includes us all.

I encourage my heart with these words—that God is faithful, to every generation (see Psalm 119:90). I can trust that the things in the Bible are for me, and will be for my children and my grandchildren as well. Romans 8:32 tells us that God did not spare even His own Son but gave Him up for us all. How can He not do the same for my children as well?

Lots of joy and healing has come through me loving my own children and being loved by them. Most of all, the largest healing in my life has come through me learning to awaken to the Voice of my Lord that speaks so tenderly to my once-broken heart, breathing life and hope into all the dark corners that were sealed off. Allowing myself to be known by God, loved by God. Learning to love myself and letting others love me. Forgiving others, forgiving God, and forgiving myself. If I had not pushed through and endured the suffering, I would have never found this deep well of JOY that bubbles up from within me, overflowing into other people's lives as well.

Most mornings as I start to stir and awaken, I envision myself as a baby lathered in kisses – my Father God's kisses. And I pray, "Lord I receive Your Love. I allow Your Love to sink inside of me. I allow myself to love me. I choose to see other people through Your eyes of Love."

"Then he [JESUS] showed them the wounds of his hands and his side—they were overjoyed to see the Lord with their own eyes!" (John 20:20 TPT)

JESUS showed His scars. When He was raised from the dead, He easily could have had His visible scars healed, too. But He didn't. He chose to keep the scars and allowed us to touch them. My scars are my testimony. They remind me of God's great grace and power to redeem, heal, and set free. I am at peace.

Although I had felt like my life was a fairy tale gone bad, I've learned to throw myself into the loving arms of my Heavenly Father who adores me. He is able to ease every suffering, touch those deep parts that hurt so badly that I did not know how to live. Even better than a fairy tale, the truth of my life has been that—even though I am someone who felt unwanted, even unlovable for so long—I have been redeemed. Fully alive unto my loving Father God, and able to give out to others from the abundance in my life. God is so amazing, kind, tender and able to heal all brokenness, no matter how deep.

Some Things I Have Learned

How much I dislike religion. JESUS had some very harsh things to say to the religious people whose main focus was about keeping rules and restrictions. These things stifle the compassion of Christ and interfere with God's healing.

At the end of my very last hospital admission, the Lord impressed on me these verses that profoundly helped me start to live a new life. So simple, so practical and doable. Great direction! My second favourite life verse:

"So here's what I want you to do, God helping you: Take your everyday, ordinary life—your sleeping, eating, going-to-work, and walking-around life—and place it before God as an offering. Embracing what God does for you is the best thing you can do for him. Don't become so well-adjusted to your culture that you fit into it without even thinking. Instead, fix your attention on God. You'll be changed from the inside out. Readily recognize what he wants from you, and quickly respond to it. Unlike the culture around you, always dragging you down to its level of immaturity, God brings the best out of you, develops well-formed maturity in you." (Romans 12:1-2 MSG)

It is a wonderful thing to have a heavenly visitation. Whether angelic, the Voice of God or a heavenly impartation. Astounding! Yet it's a whole other dimension to learn how to be a willing, open vessel that the Light shines through. 2 Corinthians 4:7–10 tells us,

"But we have this treasure in jars of clay, to show that the surpassing power belongs to God and not to us. We are afflicted … perplexed … persecuted … so that the life of JESUS may also be manifested in our bodies."

Other translations call us "earthen vessels." I am a cracked pot, a vessel with scars and holes. It is my choice if I hide in shame, depression, discouragement, or confusion; or if I come to a place of healing, acceptance and peace where LIGHT can shine through those cracked places of my willing vessel. Becoming whole is not making the cracks disappear but letting light shine through them in an even grandeur way. I am a vessel; He is the Light.

JESUS in me causes me to act like Him, and I am to represent Him to the world. That is where it is crucial to live a life without opinion and without offense. Both are like poisoned water that affects the ability to hear with purity of heart. We are broken, earthen vessels. I want to speak not out of my earthly-ness but from the wisdom of God.

This Christian life isn't all about getting what we want. In John 6:26, JESUS told the crowd that they wanted to be with Him because He fed them, that they hadn't understood the miracles. They wanted to know what they could get from Him, sometimes turning away from Him when He said things that were hard to hear. Sometimes when we fail to get what we want, we either turn away and live a defeated Christian life in discouragement and depression, or we present a god that is not real; a man-made god. Faith isn't believing you will get what you want. Faith in God is knowing Him.

I cannot be like JESUS until I know who He is. I cannot know who He is until I am willing to cancel out the impurities in my heart and spirit. Trying to make God like me is the wrong way around. Making Him understandable is diminishing His Greatness. JESUS wants our hearts. He wants a relationship with us. He wants us to get to know Him so well that we act like Him. He is so good. I love Him so much!

I Am a Book

My child, the one I own,

I've been a part of every single page of your book, your life.

I've loved writing on your pages, watching you write.

I've cried with you when you've wanted to rip a page out. Felt them darken and curl with pain.

I've been with you as the wind of my Spirit has blown dry the wet page. Releasing dirt and grime.

I've rejoiced as you've shared your pages with my others. My heart bursts with pride when you've allowed others to write on your page, when you've included the thoughts of others.

You are my book, my darling child. The one who makes me laugh as I enjoy you!

You will be known, and you will be read by many. Your book counts.

You won't be placed in a library collecting dust.

Open your cover, fan out your pages.

My light is about to shift through and once again expose and open every page of your life.

I have cemented you, daughter. The sifting, the fire, the grinding heat has not been for no gain.

All has counted for great growth. Take heart, be of good courage. You well know the power of My Name.

I am the One who has made you promises that I keep. I have contained your pain. It has not spilled out onto others. I have blotted out all transgressions and have made you new. Whiter than snow. Go ahead and walk on my snow. Go AHEAD! Then look back at your footprints. Do you see black oil—grime? Or do you see I've made you whiter than snow?

~January 2020

Postlude

I am a Voice

I have a Voice

I have heard the Voice

The Voice of Love

I've heard it through the wind in the trees

The fresh dawn of the morning

The bleating of the newborn lamb

The silence of a newly hatched bird

The ferocity in a clap of thunder

The strike of a lighting bolt

The last beat of a dying heart that leaps to life in my memory

The Voice of LOVE has awakened my soul

October 2020

Thank You

Thank you, my dear reader, for journeying with me in these pages of my opened heart. What an honour and gift you have given to me in your precious time! I cherish your interest.

I need you to know as you read these God stories, that I did not feel at the time that God was providing enough help for me. I have felt like a leper that nobody wanted to come near. So many years have felt wasted and lost. You must choose, dear reader, to believe and hope, even when your life feels lost. I never anticipated that my life could benefit others in any way.

To my surprise, going back and connecting with all that old pain, in order to write this book, I found lots of laughter, smiles and joy in the past memories with my children. They had been forgotten due to the imbalance of pain in my life. But writing this book has enabled me to regain the good times once again!

This book is written in hopes of releasing my joy and healing to the world.

The desire of my heart is for you, too, to be captured by the Lover of your soul—for you, too, to hear the Voice of Love bubbling up, quickening what your heart longs to hear. We are sojourners in this land we call home, eagerly waiting for our new home in heaven. Life is so much easier as we travel together. I would love to hear from you. sandyisabeliever@gmail.com.

Resources

Freedom in Christ Canada

"Identity in Christ" Card
The Steps to Freedom In Christ by Neil T. Anderson
www.ficm.ca

Nightshift Street Ministries

nightshiftministries.org.

The Prayer Cabin at Lifeteams

a ministry training school located in Abbotsford, BC
www.lifeteams.ca/facilities

Laurel Hildebrandt MTSC CCC

Wellspring Christian Counselling,
Counsellor, Speaker, Author of Treasure the Moments: Spiritual Insights for Motherhood and The Shadow People
Coming soon: Levelling Prayer Technique
www.Laurelhildebrandt.com

Paul Billheimer

Quotes from *Don't Waste Your Sorrows* (Fort Washington, PA: CLC Publications, 1977). Used with permission.

About the Author

Sandy Phillipps radiates hope and joy from a life of intimate pursuit and passion to know and be known by God. Through her leadership, ministry roles, and living out her God-given purpose, she has proven that trauma does not have to define anyone for the rest of their life.

As she has experienced the joy of having God hold her heart, she cherishes each and every heart that comes into her life, and loves to help people in their own healing journeys.

Sandy treasures her husband of 40 years, her cats, and her many walks through the farming community in Rosedale, British Columbia. She is a mother to three adult children and is eagerly awaiting her first grandchild.

Manufactured by Amazon.ca
Bolton, ON

18322775R00164